Challenging Strategic Planning Assumptions

Challenging Strategic Planning Assumptions

Theory, Cases, and Techniques

Richard O. Mason
and
Ian I. Mitroff

School of Business Administration
University of Southern California
Los Angeles, California

A Wiley-Interscience Publication

John Wiley & Sons   New York · Chichester · Brisbane · Toronto

This publication is designed to provide accurate and
authoritative information in regard to the subject
matter covered. It is sold with the understanding that
the publisher is not engaged in rendering legal, accounting,
or other professional service. If legal advice or other
expert assistance is required, the services of a competent
professional person should be sought. *From a Declaration
of Principles jointly adopted by a Committee of the
American Bar Association and a Committee of Publishers.*

Library of Congress Cataloging in Publication Data:

Mason, Richard O
   Challenging strategic planning assumptions.

   "A Wiley-Interscience publication."
   Bibliography: p.
   Includes index.

   1. Policy sciences. 2. Planning. 3. Hypothesis.
I. Mitroff, Ian I., joint author. II. Title.
H61.M4256   361.6'1   80-29657
ISBN 0-471-08219-8

Printed in the United States of America

10 9 8 7 6 5 4 3 2 1

To West, Vince, Jack
And to Terry and Donna

Preface

This book is about the complex problems we all face in our professional and personal lives and the methods for coping with them. It is based on a simple premise: We all live our lives according to the *assumptions* we make about ourselves and our world. To cope better, we need to surface those assumptions and to challenge them. New assumptions then become springboards to effective change.

We have chosen strategic planning as the arena for exploring this idea because we are dedicated to helping the public and private organizations, which so influence our lives, to devise better strategies. Many, we believe, need to break through the assumptions that bind them. We hope our book will help them in this important task.

This book is not written in a traditional mode. It is not solely a textbook, a philosophical treatise, a research monograph, a series of case analyses, or a "how to" book. Rather, true to our commitment to philosophical pragmatism, it is all of these. To the extent possible, each concept is carried from a theoretical abstraction through an experiential test to techniques for applying it.

RICHARD O. MASON
IAN I. MITROFF

Pacific Palisades, California
Manhattan Beach, California
February 1981

Acknowledgments

The dedication speaks to the intellectual and personal history of this book. We first met in Berkeley in the early 1960s and were privileged to share the creative mentorship of C. West Churchman, whose ideas permeate this book and whose friendship has enriched our lives. We had each faced in our own ways a world of complexity and eagerly sought better methods for coping with it. Churchman's Space Science Seminar was a marvelous forum in which to explore our ideas. His philosophy and the philosophies of others that we enthusiastically read, discussed, and debated served as the grounding for our individual inquiry Throughout, we were interested in practical things: how to solve real problems, how to manage organizations, how to create strategy, how to design cities, how to run social programs. West gave us ideas for dealing with these practical problems.

Vincent P. Barabba showed us how an effective leader can take these ideas, extend them, apply them, and infuse them with action. First at the U.S. Census Bureau, then at the Xerox Corporation, then again at the Census Bureau, Vince paved the way for us to work on essential public and private policy issues and to refine our methods. In the process he has become a collaborator and a friend. We owe much to him and to the members of those organizations for the development of the work reported in this book.

Jack D. Steele has expressed confidence in us and in the approach to management policy and strategy this book represents. He has also given us an opportunity to work together at the School of Business Administration, University of Southern California. He plays a key role in the future of these ideas.

We also wish to express our appreciation to all our other close friends and colleagues who have made this book possible. In particular, we wish to thank James Emsoff and Ralph Kilmann, with whom we collaborated on several of the projects reported in the book.

Throughout our more than 15 years of friendship and collaboration we have each had to renegotiate parts of our personal and professional lives. The new love of Terry and the sustaining love of Donna have made these changes possible and joyful. Our work owes much to them.

R.O.M.
I.I.M.

Contents

Part One

Background

Chapter One

Complexity: The Nature of Real World Problems

COMPLEXITY

A Little Experiment

Try a little experiment. Make a short list of the major problems or issues facing policymakers in the world today. Now take your list and arrange it as a matrix like the one in Figure 1-1. For each element in the matrix ask yourself the following question: Is the solution to one problem (the row problem) in any way related to the solution of the other problem (the column problem)? If the answer is yes, place a check mark at the point where the row and column intersect; otherwise leave it blank. When you have completed the process, review the matrix and count the number of blanks. Are there any?

"No fair!" you may say. "There were a lot of check marks in my matrix because many of these world problems are linked together." World problems involve all nations. One would not expect to get the same result if the focus was, say, on one's company, city, family, or personal life. Really? Try it and see.

Recently, several managers at a major corporation tried this little experiment as part of a strategic planning effort. Among the issues and problem areas they identified were the following:

1 Satisfy stockholder dividend and risk requirements.
2 Acquire adequate funds for expansion from the capital markets.
3 Insure a stable supply of energy at reasonable prices.
4 Train a corps of middle managers to assume more responsibility.
5 Develop a marketing force capable of handling new product lines.

3

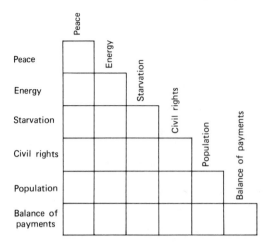

Figure 1-1 Problem interaction matrix.

6   Cope with government regulation.
7   Acquire, through merger or acquisition, new technologies for producing new product lines.

The managers found that all of these problems and issues were related to each other. Some were only related weakly, but most were related quite strongly. Repeated attempts in other contexts give the same result: *basically, every real world policy problem is related to every other real world problem.*

This is an important finding. It means that every time a policymaker attempts to solve a particular policy problem he or she must consider its potential relationship with all other problems. To do this one must have both a comprehensive set of concepts for dealing with any policy and a rich set of tools for acquiring the holistic information needed to guide policy making. This is the subject of this book.

Characteristics of Complexity

There are several characteristics of policy making that the foregoing little experiment is intended to illustrate:

1   Any policy-making situation is comprised of many problems and issues.
2   These problems and issues tend to be highly interrelated. Consequently, the solution to one problem requires a solution to all the other problems. At the same time, each solution creates additional dimensions to be incorporated in the solutions to other problems.

3 Few, if any, problems can be isolated effectively for separate treatment.

These are the characteristics of complexity. Complexity literally means the condition of being tightly woven or twined together. Most policymakers find that the problems they face today are complex in this sense. Moreover, almost all of today's problems seem to be getting more plentiful and complex.

Charles Darwin once observed that there was a tendency for all living things to advance in complexity of organization. His prophecy seems to be especially true of social systems. Our nations, our cities, our corporations, our school systems, our health systems, and our governments all seem to be growing larger and in the process becoming more complex. As a consequence, policymakers are placed in a virtual race against Parkinson's third law: Expansion leads to complexity. Complexity leads to decay. Thus the more complex, the sooner dead.

There is an especially vexing aspect of complexity as it presents itself to policymakers. It is organized. As we have seen in the little experiment, there tends to be an illusive structure underlying problems that gives pattern and organization to the whole. Organization is usually considered the route to the solution of a complex problem. In reality, however, organization in complexity can become an insurmountable barrier to the solution of a problem. As Warren Weaver (1948) has observed, this is the major challenge to real world problem solving because we have very few intellectual tools for coping with "organized complexity."

The tools we have available seem to work best on simple problems, those that can be separated and reduced to relatively few variables and relationships. These problems of simplicity usually have a one-dimensional value system or goal structure that guides the solution. Three factors—separability, reducibility, and one-dimensional goal structure—mean that simple problems can be bounded, managed, and, as Horst Rittle (1972) puts it, "tamed."

Ironically, problems of the utmost complexity can also be tamed as long as the complexity is "disorganized." That is, whenever the number of variables is very large and the variables are relatively disconnected, the problem can be tamed with the elegant simplicity of statistical mechanics. For example, there is no known way of predicting how a given individual will vote on a political candidate. However, using polling procedures and statistical techniques it is possible to predict with a fair degree of confidence how an entire population of voters will vote. Similarly, it is difficult to predict whether a given customer will purchase a new product or not. However, using market research methods, a fairly good estimate can be made of a new product's potential market share.

Perhaps one of the greatest insights of the twentieth century is the discovery that when a problem situation meets the condition for random sampling—many individual elements exhibiting independent, probabilistic behavior—there is a potential statistical solution to the problem. In short, disorganized complexity can generally be tamed by statistical means.

Unfortunately many things that once were disorganized have become organized in their complexity. For example, some of our largest industries, such as the electrical power, telephone, and insurance industries, formerly operated on the assumption of disorganized complexity. At one time power companies could predict such factors as the frequency of demand, peak load conditions, and transient stability after power surges reasonably well and could design facilities to meet these requirements. However, with the expansion of the system and the installation of a more intricate set of tie-lines, much of this predictability has been lost. As a result, blackouts and other aberrations have occurred in the system. This is the price we pay for organizing complexity into these systems. Something similar has occurred in the telephone industry, where laudable efforts to develop world-wide networks have presented many new and difficult problems in predicting the frequency of calls, the probability of a large number of calls competing simultaneously for the same line, and the probability of overlapping calls to the same number.

One place where the assumption of disorganized complexity has proven invaluable in the past is in the actuarial sciences. Today, however, the insurance industry is discovering that many of the risks once assumed to be reasonably independent and hence analyzable according to standard actuarial methods are no longer so. People, organizations, and facilities have become more tightly woven together over wider geographical areas. Consequently, the probabilities of death, accident, fire, or disaster on which the risks and premiums are based are no longer as straightforward as they once were. The result is that the statistical methods that applied under conditions of disorganized complexity have become less reliable as the system has become more organized.

The great difficulty with connected systems of organized complexity is that deviations in one element can be transmitted to other elements. In turn, these deviations can be magnified, modified, and reverberated so that the system takes on a kind of unpredictable life of its own. Emery and Trist (1965) refer to this condition as "environmental connectedness" and have labeled this type of environment the "turbulent" environment.

Emery and Trist cite an interesting case to illustrate the nature of environmental connectedness and the great difficulties it presents to policy makers. In Great Britain after World War II, a large food canning company began to expand. Its main product was a canned vegetable—a staple in the English diet. As part of the expansion plan, the company decided to build a new, automated factory, requiring an investment of several million pounds sterling. For over a decade the company had enjoyed a 65% market share for their product line and saw no reason for this strong market position to deteriorate. Given this large volume, the new plant offered the "experience curve" advantages of economies to scale and made possible the long production runs required to meet the demand from the traditional market.

After ground was broken, but well before the factory was completed, a series of seemingly detached and isolated socioeconomic events occurred. These relatively insignificant events were to change the destiny of the company. Taken collectively, they rendered the factory economically obsolete and threw the corporate board of directors into a state of turmoil. The scenario of events went something like this. Due to the release of wartime controls on steel strip and tin, a number of new small firms that could economically can imported fruit sprang up. Initially, they in no way competed directly with the large vegetable canner. However, since their business was seasonal, they began to look for ways to keep their machinery and labor employed during the winter. Their answer came from a surprising source—the U.S. quick-frozen food industry. The quick-freezing process requires a substantial degree of consistency in the crop. This consistency is very difficult to achieve. However, it turned out that large crops of the vegetable were grown in the United States and a substantial portion of U.S. crops was unsuitable for quick freezing (a big industry in the United States) but quite suitable for canning. Furthermore, American farmers had been selling this surplus crop at a very low price for animal feed and were only too happy to make it available at an attractive price to the small canners in the United Kingdom. The canners jumped at the opportunity and imported the crop. Using off-season production capacity they began to offer a low-cost product in the large canner's market. The small canners' position was further strengthened as underdeveloped countries began to vie with the United States in an effort to become the cheapest source of supply for the crop.

These untimely events in the large canner's supply market were compounded by events in its product market. Prior to the introduction of quick-freezing, the company featured a high quality, higher price premier brand that dominated the market. This market advantage, however, was diminished by the cascading effect of several more unpredictable events. As the scenario unfolded the quick-frozen product captured the high quality strata of the market, a growing dimension due to increased affluence. The smaller canners stripped off the lower price layers of the market, aided in part by another seemingly unrelated development in retailing—the advent of supermarkets. As supermarkets and large grocery chains developed, they sought to improve their position by establishing their own in-house brand names and by buying in bulk. The small canner filled this need for the supermarket chains. Small canners could undercut the price of the manufacturer's brand product because they had low production costs and almost no marketing expenses. Soon supermarket house brands (which had accounted for less than 1% of the market prior to the war) became the source of 50% of the market sales. The smaller canners were the benefactors of almost all of this growth.

As a result, the company's fancy new automated factory was totally inappropriate for the current market situation. The company's management had failed to appreciate that a number of outside events were becoming connected with each other in a way that was leading up to an inevitable general change. They tried desperately to defend their traditional product lines, but, in the end, this was to no avail. After a series of financial setbacks, the company had to change its mission. It reemerged several years later with a new product mix and a new identity. Management had learned the hard way that their strategy problems were neither problems of simplicity nor problems of disorganized complexity. They were problems of organized complexity.

Many corporate policy planning and strategy issues exhibit this property of organized complexity. The vegetable canning company's automated plant decision clearly was made under conditions of organized complexity. Pricing problems also frequently display this characteristic. Recently, a large pharmaceutical firm addressed the seemingly simple problem of setting a price for its primary drug line. The company's management soon learned, however, that there was an intricate web of corporate relationships woven around this one decision. Below the surface there was a structure of complex relationships between the firm's drug pricing policy and physicians, pharmacists, patients, competitors, suppliers, the FDA, and other parties. These relationships organized the complexity of the firm's pricing decision problem. Purely analytical or statistical methods were rendered inappropriate. How the company dealt with this pricing problem of organized complexity is reported in Chapters 3 and 4.

In today's world, public policy presents some especially vexing problems of organized complexity. Policies formulated to solve one problem create others and many unintended consequences ensue as the underlying structure plays itself out. Several examples illustrate the point.

For some years now the United States has been following a policy of farm price-support programs with the intention of helping disadvantaged farmers. The programs serve to reduce some of the uncertainty inherent in agriculture production and thereby permit farmers to streamline their decision making. One of the side effects of this change, however, was that large farmers were encouraged to mechanize, while small farmers suffered a reduction in their competitive position. Many small farmers liquidated their farms, resulting in massive layoffs of farm workers. Millions of farm workers, unemployed, fled to the inner cities where they became part of the urban crisis. Farm policy, economic policy, and urban policy, it turns out, were all part of a single, large, but highly interrelated system of organized complexity.

The selective service system policy in recent years is another example of a system that has proven to be much more complex than was originally envisioned. It was conceived as a means of raising military manpower. However, in the context of the Vietnam War it also became an unintended national youth policy. As anyone who was actively involved in higher education at that time knows only too well, the Vietnam War draft made educational policy as well. The attitudes, hopes, and fears of many of our young men and women were changed, and their view of their society, its institutions, and its future was shaped in part by this selective service policy. The selective service system was a youth policy and an education policy as well. Its complexity was organized.

Even the once relatively straightforward process of conducting a census of the U.S. population has become much more complex. Census data is not only used as general information for policymakers but is also used for apportioning seats in the House of Representatives and for allocating billions of dollars of public funds. These allocative uses of the data have led many affected groups to take on new interest in census methods. Current methods result in an undercount of the population. For example, omissions in previous censuses are estimated at more than 5 million persons. These unenumerated people tend to be black, Spanish speaking, or members of other ethnic groups. These groups are putting pressure on the U.S. Census Bureau to change its methods. As a result, the policy decision as to what methods to use in taking the census has become a very complex matter. An approach to aid the U.S. Census Bureau in making this decision is described in Chapter 4.

"Wicked" Problems

Today, few of the pressing problems policymakers face are truly problems of simplicity or of disorganized complexity. They are more like the problems described in the illustrative cases above and the ones we uncovered in our little experiment—problems of organized complexity. These problems simply cannot be tamed in the same way that other problems can. For this reason Rittle refers to these problems of organized complexity as "wicked" problems.

Wicked problems are not necessarily wicked in the perverse sense of being evil. Rather, they are wicked like the head of a hydra. They are an ensnarled web of tentacles. The more you attempt to tame them, the more complicated they become.

Rittle (1972) has identified several characteristic properties of wicked problems that distinguish them from tame problems. These properties are:

1   Ability to formulate the problem.

    a.   Tame problems can be exhaustively formulated and written down on a piece of paper.

    b.   Wicked problems have no definitive formulation.

2   Relationship between problem and solution.

    a.   Tame problems can be formulated separately from any notion of what their solution might be.

    b.   Every formulation of a wicked problem corresponds to a statement of solution and vice versa. Understanding the problem is synonymous with solving it.

3   Testability.

    a.   The solution to a tame problem can be tested. Either it is correct or it is false. Mistakes and errors can be pinpointed.

    b.   There is no single criteria system or rule that determines whether the solution to a wicked problem is correct or false. Solutions can only be good or bad relative to one another.

4   Finality.

    a.   Tame problems have closure—a clear solution and ending point. The end can be determined by means of a test.

    b.   There is no stopping rule for wicked problems. Like a Faustian bargain, they require eternal vigilance. There is always room for improvement. Moreover, since there is neither an immediate or ultimate test for the solution to the problem, one never knows when one's work is done. As a result, the potential consequences of the problem are played out indefinitely.

5 Tractability.

   a. There is an exhaustive list of permissible operations that can be
       used to solve a tame problem.
   b. There is no exhaustive, enumerable list of permissible operations
       to be used for solving a wicked problem.

6 Explanatory characteristics.

   a. A tame problem may be stated as a "gap" between what "is"
       and what "ought" to be and there is a clear explanation for every
       gap.
   b. Wicked problems have many possible explanations for the same
       discrepancy. Depending on which explanation one chooses, the
       solution takes on a different form.

7 Level of analysis.

   a. Every tame problem has an identifiable, certain, natural form;
       there is no need to argue about the level of the problem. The
       proper level of generality can be found for bounding the problem
       and identifying its root cause.
   b. Every wicked problem can be considered as a symptom of
       another problem. It has no identifiable root cause; since curing
       symptoms does not cure problems, one is never sure the problem
       is being attacked at the proper level.

8 Reproducibility.

   a. A tame problem can be abstracted from the real world, and at-
       tempts can be made to solve it over and over again until the
       correct solution is found.
   b. Each wicked problem is a one-shot operation. Once a solution is
       attempted, you can never undo what you have already done.
       There is no trial and error.

9 Replicability.

   a. The same tame problem may repeat itself many times.
   b. Every wicked problem is essentially unique.

10 Responsibility.

    a. No one can be blamed for failing to solve a tame problem, although solving a tame problem may bring someone acclaim.

    b. The wicked problem solver has "no right to be wrong." He is morally responsible for what he is doing and must share the blame when things go wrong. However, since there is no way of knowing when a wicked problem is solved, very few people are praised for grappling with them.

Characteristics of Wicked Problems

Most policy planning and strategy problems are wicked problems of organized complexity. These complex wicked problems also exhibit the following characteristics*:

1 Interconnectedness Strong connections link each problem to other problems. As a result, these connections sometimes circle back to form feedback loops. "Solutions" aimed at the problem seem inevitably to have important opportunity costs and side effects. How they work out depends on events beyond the scope of any one problem.

2 Complicatedness Wicked problems have numerous important elements with relationships among them, including important "feedback loops" through which a change tends to multiply itself or perhaps even cancel itself out. Generally, there are various leverage points where analysis and ideas for intervention might focus, as well as many possible approaches and plausible programs of action. There is also a likelihood that different programs should be combined to deal with a given problem.

3 Uncertainty Wicked problems exist in a dynamic and largely uncertain environment, which creates a need to accept risk, perhaps incalculable risk. Contingency planning and also the flexibility to respond to unimagined and perhaps unimaginable contingencies are both necessary.

4 Ambiguity The problem can be seen in quite different ways, depending on the viewer's personal characteristics, loyalties, past experiences, and even on accidental circumstances of involvement. There is no single "correct view" of the problem.

*This list of characteristics of complex problems is due, in part, to Professor James Jackson and was prepared for a course—called the Nucleus—taken by all master's degree students in the UCLA Graduate School of Management.

5 **Conflict** Because of competing claims, there is often a need to trade off "goods" against "bads" within the same value system. Conflicts of interest among persons or organizations with different or even antagonistic value systems are to be expected. How things will work out may depend on interaction among powerful interests that are unlikely to enter into fully cooperative arrangements.

6 **Societal Constraints** Social, organizational, and political constraints and capabilities, as well as technological ones, are central both to the feasibility and the desirability of solutions.

These characteristics spell difficulty for the policymaker who seeks to serve a social system by changing it for the better. Policymakers must choose the means for securing improvement for the people they serve. They must design, steer, and maintain a stable social system in the context of a complex environment. To do this, they require new methods of real world problem solving to guide their policy-making activities. Otherwise, they run the risk of setting their social systems adrift.

Implications for Policy Making

The wicked problems of organized complexity that policymakers face today have two major implications for designing processes for making policy:

1 There must be a broader participation of affected parties, directly and indirectly, in the policy-making process.
2 Policy making must be based on a wider spectrum of information gathered from a larger number of diverse sources.

Let us consider each of these implications in turn. The first implication indicates that policy making is increasingly becoming a political process, political in the sense that it involves individuals forming into groups to pursue common interests. Turn again to the results of the little experiment conducted at the outset of this chapter. You will find that in almost every case there are a variety of individual interests at stake in each problem area cited. Furthermore, one of the major factors creating the linkages between problem areas—organizing their complexity—is the number of diverse individual interests that cut across problem areas. Individuals are part of the problem and hence must be part of the solution.

This means that the raw material for forging solutions to wicked problems is not concentrated in a single head, but rather is widely dispersed among the various parties at stake. For any given wicked problem there is a variety of classes of expertise. Every affected party is an expert on some aspect of the problem and its solution. Furthermore, the disparate parties are bound together in a common venture. Thus some form of collective risk sharing is needed in order to deal effectively with the consequences of wicked problems. This suggests the need for a substantial degree of involvement in the policy-making process by those potentially affected by a policy in its formulation process. Effective policy is made *with*, or if adequate representation is present, *for*, but *not at* people. At least those involved should be able to voice their opinion on the relative goodness or badness of proposed solutions. True to this principle, the methods for real world problem solving described in this book involve group processes and serve to extend the level of participation in the problem-solving process.

The diversity of parties at stake is related to the second implication. Since much of the necessary information for coping with wicked problems resides in the heads of several individuals, methods are needed to obtain this information from them and to communicate it to others. This means that as many of the different sources of information as possible must be identified. The relevant information must be obtained from each and stated in an explicit manner.

Contained in the minds of each participant in a wicked problem are powerful notions as to what is, what ought to be, why things are the way they are, how they can be changed, and how to think about their complexity. This represents a much broader class of information than is commonly used to solve problems of simplicity or of disorganized complexity. Also, this participant based information is less likely to have been stated and recorded in a communicable form. Consequently, as Rittle (1972) has suggested, this information must be "objectified"—explicitly, articulated—so that the basis for each party's judgments may be exchanged with others. Objectification has the advantages of being explicit, providing a memory, controlling the delegation of judgments, and raising pertinent issues that might have been ignored otherwise. It also stimulates *doubt*.

To be in doubt about a piece of information is to withhold assent to it. Given the range of diverse information that characterizes a wicked problem, participants in the policy-making process are well advised to develop a healthy respect for the method of doubt. In dealing with problems of organized complexity one should start with Descartes' rule: "The first precept was never to accept a thing as true until I knew it was such without a single doubt." This does not mean that one should be a "nay sayer" or a permanent skeptic. To do so would impede responsible action that must be taken. What it does imply is that one should withhold judgment on things until they have been tested. The methods presented in this book are means for eliciting the reasons, rationale, and assumptions underlying the information used in complex problems. They may be used to test this information as well.

All problem-solving methods presuppose some form of guarantor for the correctness of their solutions. Problems of simplicity can be tested and solutions guaranteed by means of repeated solving, just as a theorem is proven in mathematics. This is because simple problems can be stated in closed form. The solutions to problems of disorganized complexity can be guaranteed within some stated confidence interval or degree of risk because the problems are statistical in nature. However, since there are no clearly identifiable correct solutions to problems of organized complexity, neither analytic nor statistical proofs can guarantee results. For solutions to wicked problems, the method of doubt is the best guarantor available.

Dialectics and argumentation are methods of *systematizing* doubt. They entail the processes of (1) making information and its underlying assumptions explicit, (2) raising questions and issues toward which different positions can be taken, (3) gathering evidence and building arguments for and against each position, and (4) attempting to arrive at some final conclusion. Being fundamentally an argumentative process, these four processes are inherent to policy making. For every policy decision there are always at least two alternative choices that can be made. There is an argument for and against each alternative. It is by weighing the pros and cons of each argument that an informed decision can be reached. In policy making these processes of dialectics and argumentation are inescapable.

In addition to the need for participation by a variety of parties and the existence of diverse information sources, two other characteristics of wicked problems should be noted. One is that they must be dealt with in a holistic or synthetic way as well as in an analytic way. Two processes are necessary: to subdivide a complex problem into its elements and to determine the nature of the linkages that give organization to its complexity—the task of analysis—and to understand the problem as a *whole*—the task of synthesis. A critical dimension of wicked problems of organized complexity is that they must ultimately be dealt with in their totality. This calls for holistic thinking. Analysis is only an aid toward reaching a synthesis.

A second characteristic of these problems is that there is some form of latent structure within them. They are organized to some extent. Organization is not an all or nothing phenomenon. Consequently, systems thinking and methods can be used to gain better insight into the structural aspects of wicked problems. Satisfying this need also influenced the design of methods presented in this book.

Quest for New Methods

The nature and implications of organized complexity suggest some new criteria for the design of real world problem-solving methods. These criteria are:

1 **Participative** Since the relevant knowledge necessary to solve a complex problem and also the relevant resources necessary to implement the solution are distributed among many individuals, the methods must incorporate the active involvement of groups of people. For this reason, modern behavioral science approaches are an integral part of the methods covered in this book.

2 **Adversarial** We believe that the best judgment on the assumptions in a complex problem is rendered in the context of opposition. Doubt is the guarantor. For this reason the methods in this book are all dialectical in nature.

3 **Integrative** A unified set of assumptions and a coherent plan of action are needed to guide effective policy planning and strategy making. Participation and the adversarial process tend to differentiate and expand the knowledge base. Something else is needed to bring this diverse but relevant knowledge together in the form of a total picture. For this reason, the methods in this book are based on holistic systems theory and are designed as aids for achieving synthesis.

4 **Managerial Mind Supporting** Most problem-solving methods and computer aids focus on "decision support systems," that is, on systems that provide guidance for choosing a particular course of action to solve a particular decision problem. Problems of organized complexity, as we have seen, are ongoing, ill structured, and generally "wicked." The choice of individual courses of action is only a part of the manager's or policymaker's need. More important is the need to achieve insight into the nature of the complexity and to formulate concepts and world views for coping with it. It is the policymaker's thinking process and his or her mind that needs to be supported. For this reason, all the methods in this book involve intensive immersion of managers and staff in the process. The methods are geared to expand their insight into the problem.

Plan of the Book

"To be in hell is to drift, to be in heaven is to steer," George Bernard Shaw once wrote. *Challenging Strategic Planning Assumptions* is written for the steersman who stands at the policy helm attempting to guide his ship in a sea of wicked problems.

The book is divided into five parts.

Part 1 contains two chapters. This chapter has reviewed the ill-structured or messy environment in which policy, planning, and strategy decisions must be made. Chapter 2 presents an argument, rooted in the philosophical tradition of pragmatism, that describes the essential role assumptions play in real world action taking. This theory of practice underlies the methods which are presented in Parts 2 to 4.

Part 2 covers the Strategic Assumption Surfacing and Testing methodology (SAST). Parts 2 to 4 contain three chapters each, one developing concepts, one describing illustrative cases, and one detailing procedures. Chapter 3 contains an overview of the SAST approach. Chapter 4 summarizes the application of the method at a drug company and at the U.S. Bureau of the Census. Chapter 5 is an operating manual for applying the SAST concepts.

Part 3 covers a structured debate methodology in which two or more points of view concerning a strategic issue are presented. Chapter 6 develops the dialectical approach to the planning process. Chapter 7 summarizes the results of a field study at RMK Abrasives (a pseudonym for the real firm), a simulation on regulatory policy planning problem of airport congestion, and a land use policy debate. Chapter 8 is an operating manual for applying the concepts.

Both the assumption surfacing and dialectical debate methods produce statements of information that should be evaluated. The theory of argumentation has proven to be a useful framework for making these evaluations. Part 4 covers the application of argumentation and reasoning methods to complex policy, planning, and strategy problems. Chapter 9 integrates Toulmin's model of argument with a new theory of plausibility and shows how it can be useful in the policy arena. Chapter 10 contains several examples of the application of policy argumentation to real policy, planning, and strategy problems. Chapter 11 is an operating manual for carrying out the analysis of policy arguments.

Part 5 relates the methods in this book to other approaches to policy, planning, and strategy. Chapter 12 reviews a few current methods used to make business policies, plans, and strategies and compares them to the methods developed in this book.

Chapter Two ————————————

Toward a Theory of Practice

As we saw in Chapter 1, complex problems depend in countless ways on a host of critical assumptions. In short, complex problems depend on assumptions because it is not humanly possible to know everything of importance about a problem of organized complexity prior to the taking of action. If the policymaker deferred engaging in action before everything of critical importance was known with complete assurance, action would be postponed indefinitely. No action would ever be taken. Policymakers cannot afford this luxury. Of necessity, a policymaker must take some action and so he or she must make a host of major and minor assumptions about a problem situation.

The policymaker cannot insist on full "clarification" or "definition" of a problem before taking action on it. Often, it is only through taking action that a problem becomes clarified. If anything, the trick is to choose the appropriate set of actions that will add significantly to the clarification of a problem. Action and clarification, in other words, are not two separate things but rather two aspects of the same thing—successful problem management.

Most policymakers are unaware of the fact that much of their action rests on assumptions and, moreover, they are unaware of the particular set of assumptions they hold. Even worse, policymakers are generally unaware of any methods that can help them in examining and assessing the strength of their assumptions. Unfortunately, despite this need, few academicians have shown interest in developing methods to help policymakers examine their assumptions.

This lack of awareness is not a fault of the policymaker alone. The fault lies within our culture in general as well as with particular individuals. Our culture generally separates the development of theory from the development of practice and theoreticians from practitioners. We overemphasize the *solution* of *well*-structured problems to the detriment of the *formula-*

tion of *"wicked," messy,* or *ill*-structured problems. These cultural differences were discerned long ago by John Dewey (1925, 1929).

In Dewey's analysis, such difficulties are the result of Western culture's generally obsessive "quest for certainty." Since in Dewey's view perfect certainty or knowledge is impossible to mortals, such a quest is to be regarded as neurotic. It is the compulsive behavior of individuals striving to cope (survive) in an uncertain and precarious world. Instead of questing after perfect certainty, a human impossibility, one should seek for no more certainty than that which is minimally necessary to "get the job done." To insist on more is eventually self-defeating. As Dewey puts it:

This is where ordinary thinking and thinking that is scrupulous diverge from each other. The natural man is impatient with doubt and suspense: he impatiently hurries to be shut of it. A disciplined mind takes delight in the problematic, and cherishes it until a way out is found that approves itself upon examination. The questionable becomes an active questioning, a search; desire for the emotion of certitude gives place to quest for objects by which the obscure and unsettled may be developed into the stable and clear. The scientific attitude may almost be defined as that which is capable of enjoying the doubtful; scientific method is, in one aspect, a technique for making productive use of doubt by converting it into operations of definite inquiry (Dewey, 1929, p. 228)

In a word, the trick is to perceive the uncertain as an opportunity, not as a downfall.

This book attempts to lay the foundations for a *theory* of planning that is especially applicable to *real world* problems. We stress the words "theory" and "real world" for it has been all too common for the activities represented by the two to proceed in relative isolation from one another. That is, policymakers do not lack either abstract theories of planning or all-too-practical, ad hoc methods of problem solving. What policymakers lack are theories that are grounded in the best of practice, and practice that is guided by the kind of theory from which it can learn with benefit.

The theory of policy making, planning, and strategy formulation developed in this book draws on a philosophy of pragmatism. Pragmatism offers special criteria for evaluating a theory. What concrete differences will the theory make in people's lives if it is true? What experiences will be different from those that would follow if the theory were false? What is the theory's beneficial value to people in experiential terms?

In pursuit of theories that satisfy these criteria, pragmatist philosophers such as William James, John Dewey, C. S. Peirce, E. A. Singer, C. West Churchman, and Russell Ackoff, have emphasized four key ideals.

Drawing on their tradition, our theory of real world problem solving attempts to incorporate each of these ideals:

1 **Democracy** The ideal that all parties have a right and a capacity to participate in problem solving and to benefit from the results.
2 **Scientific Method** The ideal that the most appropriate scientific techniques should be used to produce knowledge for problem solving.
3 **Empiricism** The ideal that all problem solving should have a grounded experiential referent in the real world.
4 **Evolution** The ideal that all problems are couched in a dynamic context and that they change and evolve through time. Real world problem solving is eternally restless.

Further, we draw on a fifth ideal, holism—the ideal that all problems are linked to all others and must be dealt with as a whole. This does not mean that one must solve all problems simultaneously, clearly an impossible demand. Rather, it means that one must attempt to consider as large a problem set as possible in the formulation of any particular problem.

Holism places a special burden on the incorporation of the other four ideals. No one ideal can be emphasized to the exclusion of the others. For example, our theory is scientific but not exclusively so. It is also democratic, experiential, dynamic, and holistic, and these ideals place its scientific component into perspective. Accordingly, the theory is not classically academic as well.

A main thesis of this book is that real world problems are no less theoretical and no less interesting than the more restricted kinds of problems that have traditionally been of interest to academicians. The kinds of problems that have been of traditional interest can be termed "disciplinary puzzles" or perhaps "scientific puzzles." The term "puzzle" is appropriate, for it connotes a problem for which the "parts" are "given," available for review, and known beforehand. Puzzle solving requires assembling the given parts into a single, optimal, correct solution. With Dewey, however, our interest lies with problems for which there are very few *prior* "givens." We are interested in those issues for which different parties start from different premises or "takens" (Dewey, 1929, p. 178).

While we are deeply indebted to the so-called "pure disciplines" for much of the theory in this book, our primary interests lie with problems that do not fit neatly into any single discipline. In short, our basic sympathies lie with interdisciplinary and transdisciplinary thinking—what Churchman has termed the systems approach (1968, 1971, 1979).

The depth of our commitment to the furtherance of real world problem-solving theory is such that we have chosen deliberately to illustrate the theory in terms of three very specific and concrete methods for problem solving. In this way, we hope that this work will be of theoretical interest not only to the kind of researcher who wishes to broaden his or her concept of theory, but also to the practitioner who wishes to broaden his or her arsenal of practical methods. Ideally, we would hope that the theoretician would develop a more healthy respect for practice and the practitioner a more healthy respect for theory. Again, Dewey has put it well:

It is an easy and altogether too common a habit to confuse a *personal* division of labor with an isolation of function and meaning. Human beings as individuals tend to devote themselves either to the practice of knowing or to the practice of a professional, business, social, or esthetic art. *Each takes the other half of the circle for granted.* Theorists and practitioners, however, often indulge in unseemly wrangles as to the importance of their respective tasks. Then the personal difference of callings is hypostatized and made into an intrinsic difference knowledge and practice. (192⁰, pp. 37–38, italics added)

The only distinction worth drawing is not between practice and theory, but between those modes of practice that are not intelligent, not inherently and immediately enjoyable, and those which are full of enjoyed meanings. (1925, p. 290)

As we attempt to show, the three methods we present for real world problem solving have been chosen very carefully. All deal with the critical role that assumptions play in complex policy issues. Drawing on a democratic ideal, we show that it is natural for different observers to have different assumptions about the nature of problems. Whereas the first two methods deal primarily with a process for uncovering and assessing the assumptions of different decisionmakers, the third deals with a framework for analyzing the structure of policy arguments. The third method shows how assumptions logically fit together to result in the production of a policy plan or strategy. The end result is a set of both theoretically grounded and operationally applicable methods for locating the weak and the strong links in complex policy arguments.

THE INQUIRY/SOLVING PROCESS

Since the 1960s, there has been a growing number of attempts to construct whole systems models of the inquiry or problem-solving process.* The

*See, for example, Ackoff, 1978; Brightman, 1978; Gause and Weinberg, 1975; Gordon et al., 1974; Janis and Mann, 1977; Lee, 1968; Mintzberg et al., 1976; Mitroff, 1977; Mitroff et al., 1974; Newell et al., 1964; Pounds, 1969; Rittel and Webber, 1973; Sagasti and Mitroff, 1973; Schein, 1969.

basic purposes of these undertakings have been threefold: (1) to identify precisely and systematically the component parts, phases, and steps of the problem-solving process; (2) to understand more fully the relationship (interactions) between the component parts; and (3) to understand better the relationship between different styles of approaching problems and the parts of the problem-solving process on which these different styles prefer to work and are best suited.

A composite overview of the various models is presented in Figure 2-1. The boxes are meant to illustrate the major components or phases of the inquiry/problem-solving process that have been identified and found to be important. While the various phases are distinct from one another, it is important to emphasize that they are distinct only in the sense of representing identifiable activities. The various components are not meant to be taken as rigidly separable from one another. Not only is there often a considerable overlap between the different phases, but, depending on the particular problem, certain phases may be skipped, bypassed altogether, or performed simultaneously. The model in Figure 2-1 is thus meant to represent the various activities present in the process of inquiry and problem solving.

Figure 2-2 highlights the iterative nature of the model more clearly. That is, problem solving is a continuous ongoing activity rather than a static entity. Also, the model in Figure 2-2 is meant to be applicable to individuals as well as to groups. (Some group–problem-solving methods are discussed in Janis and Mann, 1977; Schein, 1969; Zander, 1977.) Figures 2-1 and 2-2 represent the processes that are important to consider if problem solving is to be effective. As we shall see, the more important a problem is, the more important it is to consider all the component parts of Figures 2-1 and 2-2 explicitly and systematically. Figures 2-1 and 2-2 derive not only from the literature on the inquiry/problem-solving structure of science but also from the literature on small group processes that occur in social problem solving.

Consider the extreme left-hand box in Figure 2-2, problem sensing. There is no absolute requirement that we start here or with any other box, for that matter. Indeed, one of the prime characteristics of the model is that one can start and end an inquiry at any point (box) in the model (Churchman, 1971). Where one starts and ends an inquiry is a function of one's problem, one's prior knowledge, the state of development of one's field, specialty, or discipline, the environment in which one works, the internal cognitive style of the particular problemsolver or decisionmaker, and the constraints of the problem situation (Ackoff and Emery, 1972). However, for purposes of discussion, problem solving is a good place to begin.

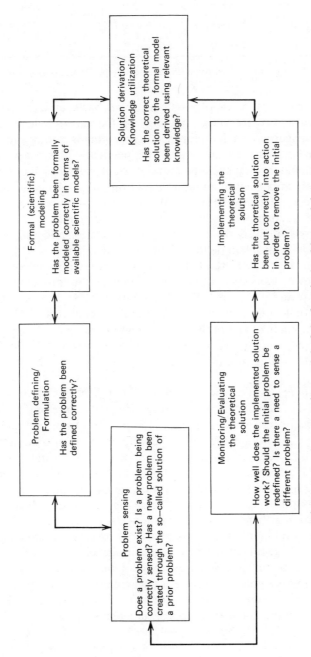

Figure 2-1 A composite model of the inquiry/problem-solving process.

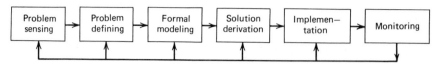

Figure 2-2   The iterative nature of the inquiry/problem-solving process.

The "relative" first phase of problem solving has been termed problem sensing because it refers to the "feeling" on the part of a decisionmaker (whether managerial or scientific) that "something is wrong and that action of some sort (as yet undetermined) is needed." This phase is essentially nonrational, arising from the moral spirit of the individuals involved. It is extremely important to emphasize that this step does not consist of a formal or precise definition of the problem. Rather it involves the "felt or even vague recognition" that "something is amiss." The formal specification of precisely what is wrong is the function and purpose of the next two phases: problem defining and formal modeling.

As Lee puts it, "Any method of inquiry starts off with a vague irritation of doubt. Dewey calls this initial stage of inquiry the 'problematic situation' " (Gause and Weinbert, 1975). The relative first stage thus consists of recognizing or feeling that there is a problematic situation. Notice that there are two kinds of errors that can be committed at this stage: (1) that of feeling or contending that there is a problem when in fact there is not and (2) that of feeling or contending there is not a problem when in fact there is.

Once a problem has been sensed (correctly or incorrectly), the next two phases consist of defining more precisely the exact nature of the problem. Problem defining consists of looking at the problem from several distinct and different *macro* points of view in an attempt to ensure that the problem is defined correctly. Formal modeling, on the other hand, consists of operationalizing and examining in detail a single *micro* view of the problem using the results from previous problem defining phase that appear to be "most fruitful," "promising," or "relevant" for the particular problematic situation at hand.

The problem defining/formulation phase constitutes the *semantic* phase of problem solving. It is concerned with such issues as: What is the basic *meaning* of a problem? and What universe of discourse is most appropriate for framing and conceptualizing a particular problem? As such, this phase is not very much concerned with a detailed statement of the problem but rather with choosing an appropriate *macro* view of the problem. By "macro" we mean taking a global, holistic view of the problem and not getting bogged down in the details of any single view. Often, this is done by considering several different views of the problem, each of which challenges the underlying assumptions of the other views. In other words, this phase is concerned with the choice of the appropriate worldview, discipline, field, or conceptual frame of reference to be used for expressing the problem.

People tend to have biases and "tunnel vision" when formulating problems. Engineers tend to look at technical things; psychologists, at behavioral things. Is the problem more appropriately conceived of as being a technical or a behavioral problem? Ackoff offers an example that is helpful in clarifying the role of differing frames of reference in the inquiry/problem-solving process:

The manager of a large office building received an increasing number of complaints about the elevator service in the building. He engaged a group of engineers to study the situation and to make recommendations for improvements if they were necessary. The engineers found that the tenants were indeed receiving poor service and considered three possible ways of decreasing the average waiting time. They considered adding elevators, replacing the existing ones by faster ones, and assigning elevators to specific floors. The latter turned out to be inadequate and the first two were prohibitively expensive to the manager. He called together his staff to consider the report by the engineers. Among those present was his personnel director, a psychologist. This young man was struck by the fact that people became impatient with a wait which seemed so short to him. On reflection he became convinced that their annoyance was due to the fact that they had to stand inactive in a crowded lobby for this period. This suggested a solution to him which he offered to the manager, and because it was so inexpensive the manager decided to try it. Complaints stopped immediately. The psychologist had suggested installing large mirrors in the walls of the lobbies where people waited for the elevators. (Ackoff, 1969, pp. 431–432)

The point should be clear. The choice of an inappropriate definition or conceptualization of a problem can be disastrous. The engineers conceptualized the problem in the preceding paragraph as an "engineering" problem, that is, as a problem *of the elevators*. The psychologist, on the other hand, conceptualized the problem as a "behavorial" problem, one *of people*. If we accept the engineers' conceptualization of the problem, then we are directed to find a solution that seeks to modify the elevators, such as putting in more elevators, speeding them up, improving their scheduling, and the like. If, on the other hand, we accept the psychologist's conceptualization of the problem, then we are directed to find a solution that seeks to modify the people involved. In this case, the solution seeks to sooth people's feelings of impatience by playing on their vanity through taking advantage of the fact that people like to look at themselves. Although both solutions represent a modification of the building, the difference between them (besides the tremendous difference in cost) is that one proceeds by locating the basic definition or root of the problem *within people;* the other, *within the building.*

This is *not* to say that engineers are always wrong and that psychologists are always right. Rather, the point is that "experts" from different disciplines tend to view problems in very different ways. Engineers are trained to look for and see technical problems. Consequently, they tend to propose technical solutions to them. Psychologists, on the other hand, are trained to view problems in human terms. They tend toward people-oriented solutions. The point of the discussion is that problems are not natural creations, but are instead human creations. Problems are cognitions and recognitions—products of our conceptual imagination. As a result, different analysts often can and do conceptualize problems in different ways.

A currently unresolved issue concerns defining an appropriate measure of performance for problem defining. Mitroff (1974, 1976, 1977) has suggested that the concept of the type three error proposed by Raiffa may be appropriate in this regard:

In my first operations research problem, I fell into the trap of working on a wrong problem.

One of the most popular paradigms in . . . mathematics describes the case in which a researcher has either to accept or reject a so-called null hypothesis. In a first course in statistics the student learns that he must constantly balance between making an error of the first kind (that is, rejecting the null hypothesis when it is true) and an error of the second kind (that is, accepting the null hypothesis when it is false). I believe it was John Tukey who suggested that practitioners all too often make errors of the third kind: solving the wrong problem. (Raiffa 1968, p. 264)

The error of the third kind of E_{III} is defined as the probability of solving the "wrong" (i.e., inappropriate) definition of a problem when one should have attempted instead to solve the "right" (appropriate) definition of a problem. Solving the "wrong problem" means accepting, without challenge, the less appropriate of two or more different formulations of a problem. Thus a type three error would be committed if a policymaker were to accept uncritically the engineers' definition of the elevator problem, to proceed to develop a formal model of the engineers' definition, and to extract a solution from it. Mitroff has shown how E_{III} can be operationalized so that estimates can be made of it.

The formal modeling phase consists of developing a detailed scientific model of the chosen macro definition of the problem. The formal model represents a more exact *micro* rendering of the problem. Whereas prob-

Exhibit 2-1   Psychologists's Model of the Elevator Problem

Potential Courses of Action	Potential Outcomes		
	O_1 Reduce Customer Complaints	O_2 Complaints Stay Same	O_3 Complaints Increase
A_1 = Install mirrors of dimensions d_1 in location l_1	E_{11}	E_{12}	E_{13}
A_2 = Install mirrors of d_2 in l_2	E_{21}	E_{22}	E_{23}
A_3 = Open a coffee shop in lobby	E_{31}	E_{32}	E_{33}
A_4 = Make reading material available	E_{41}	E_{42}	E_{43}

Conditions:
1. If the A_i are exclusive and exhaustive, then then $\Sigma_i P(A_i) = 1$ where $P(A_i) =$ the probability with which a decisionmaker chooses course of action A_i.
2. If the O_j are exclusive and exhaustive, then $\Sigma_j P(O_j) = 1$.
3. The E_{ij} are defined as follows: $E_{ij} = P(O_j/A_i)$, where E_{ij} is known as the efficiency of A_i for O_j.
4. Thus $P(O_j) = \Sigma_i P(A_i + O_j) = \Sigma_i P(A_i) P(O_j/A_i) = \Sigma_i P(A_i) E_{ij}$. Also, $\Sigma_j E_{ij} = 1$.

lem defining represents a "bounding" of the problem by determining the relevant problem variable, formal modeling refers to the constructing of a detailed, exact, scientific representation of the problem.

Exhibit 2-1 helps to clarify this. It is not enough to determine that the psychologist's conceptualization of the problem is more appropriate than the engineers'. One must also recast the problem in this new worldview. The formal modeling phase, to illustrate it in terms of the simple elevator problem, forces a specification as to which kinds of mirrors (e.g., size d_1 versus size d_2) placed in which location (decision alternative A_1 versus A_2) are more efficient for solving the problem (objective O_1). Thus for the elevator problem, one example of a scientific model would be:

$$H_0 : E_{11} = E_{21} = E_{31} = E_{41}$$
$$H_1 : E_{11} > E_{21} > E_{41} < E_{31}$$

where H_0 is the conventional null hypothesis and H_1 is the alternative. H_0 says that all four action alternatives are equally effective in solving the problem, whereas H_1 says A_1 is the most effective, A_2 next, A_4 third, and A_3 last. Ackoff and Emery (1972) treat this method of modeling extensively.

Because the concepts of the type one (E_I) and type two (E_{II}) errors of statistics are tied to a test of H_0 versus H_1, E_I, and E_{II} are examples of appropriate measures of performance for formal modeling. It should also be noted that the formal modeling phase corresponds to the *syntactic* level of scientific inquiry. It is "syntactic" because the scientist is concerned with the correct or valid manipulation of symbols within the formal language that is being used to express the problem.

The solution derivation/knowledge utilization phase is concerned with the appropriate utilization of the relevant existent knowledge so that a choice can be made between competing hypothesis such as H_0 and H_1. For example, we might sample people's preference for A_1 versus A_2. This requires not only the correct use of the appropriate evidence to decide between the two statistical hypotheses H_0 and H_1, but also a specification of the "appropriate evidence" to collect. This phase has been called, appropriately, the *empiric* level of scientific inquiry.

The implementation phase has been called the *pragmatic* level of problem solving. It is one thing to derive a theoretically or empirically sound solution to a formal model of a problem; it is quite another thing to ensure that the "correct" solution is actually implemented. Putting the solution into effect so that the projected results are indeed secured is the task of the implementation phase.

The monitoring phase is essentially an extension of the implementation phase. However, it raises somewhat different questions. The concern at implementation is: How can we effectively implement the theoretically correct solution? Given or assuming that the theoretical solution has been correctly implemented, the monitoring phase asks: Having completed the problem-solving cycle (Figure 2-1), is the original problem still present? Has the problem-solving process reduced or removed the problem? If not, is there a need to redefine the initial problem completely? Or, is the initial definition still correct? If not, what is needed is a refinement of the formal model? The theoretical solution? The implementation plan? Is there a need to reevaluate the evaluation criteria and one's expectations as to what is a realistically feasible solution to the particular problem? Are we still solving the wrong problem? Is our solution creating a new problem?

Depending on the answers to these questions, one will either consider the problem "managed" or one will reenter the problem-solving process (Figures 2-1 and 2-2) at the appropriate point. Thus for example, if the original definition of the problem is still judged to be appropriate, then one can improve on either the formal model, the theoretically derived solution, the implementation plan, or the evaluation procedure. Notice that this same line of reasoning applies no less to the initial entry into the cycle than it does to subsequent traverses. If the problemsolver feels that the definition of the problem from previous inquiries is still adequate, then there is no need to reinvent the definition. That is, one can enter the model in Figure 2-1 and exit it at any point, depending on the initial definition of the problem, one's state of knowledge, problem-solving style, and so on.

The importance of the preceding model of problem solving is essentially twofold. First, for problems of complexity, such as those discussed in Chapter 1, the problem-defining phase is critical. It may, in fact, be the most critical phase of all. Yet it is precisely this phase that has received the least systematic treatment in the scientific literature on the inquiry process. Compared to the rather extensive research concerning the kinds of information individuals seek and utilize to solve an already well-formulated problem, there have been virtually no studies of the kinds of information and methods that are most useful in helping individuals and groups to define problems and to minimize the type three error (E_{III}).*

Second, it has become clear that most complex social problems and indeed, as Mitroff (1974) discovered in his study of moon scientists, many physical science problems are "wicked" and ill-structured, as described in Chapter 1. Different individuals, groups and experts often have very different perceptions of the basic definition of a problem. (See, for example, Brightman, 1978; Mason, 1969; and Rittel and Webber, 1973.) This situation is not due to the incompetency or to an unwillingness on the part of different experts to agree. Rather, it is due to the fact that problems of organized complexity are by their very nature those that cannot be encompassed, bounded, or contained by the variables, methods, and frames of discourse of any single discipline.

As we discussed previously, complex problems are fundamentally those that require the interaction and sharing of perspectives and information from many different disciplines if E_{III} is to be minimized. Yet it is these problems for which we have, to date, lacked methods that enable different disciplines and problemsolvers to most effectively share their information and concepts.

The differences between "wicked," ill-structured problems and well-structured problems can now be further clarified. A problem may be ill- or well-structured depending on the circumstances. Reference to Exhibit 2-1

---

*See, for example, Chubin et al., 1978; Gordon et al., 1974; Rossini et al., 1978; Schein, 1969; Zagona, 1966; Zander, 1977.

is helpful in explaining the differences. The *minimal* conditions for the existence of a *well*-structured problem are: (1) the available courses of action A_i (decision alternatives) and the outcomes O_j must both be known and specifiable; (2) the sets A_i and O_j must tend to be invariant across different groups of decisionmakers; that is, there must be agreement between different experts regarding the basic definition of the problem (the available means A_i and the ends O_j); and (3) there must also be agreement between different experts regarding the values V_j of the outcomes O_j. In short, a well-structured problem is one for which it is relatively easy to obtain consensus concerning the basic definition of the problem. Finally, (4) the problem is solvable, if only in principle, by conventional problem-solving techniques.

The simplest type of well-structured problem is a decision-problem under certainty. This occurs when for each row one and only one of the E_{ij}'s equals one and all others equal zero. Thus the choice of a particular A_i guarantees the attainment of a particular O_j. For example, this occurs if $E_{11} = E_{22} = E_{33} = E_{42} = 1$ and the remaining $E_{ij} = 0$. Under this condition, a deterministic relationship holds between means A_i and ends O_j.

A well-structured decision-problem under risk occurs when $0 \leqslant E_{ij} \leqslant 1$ for at least one of the E_{ij}'s in at least one row. For example, this occurs if $E_{21} = 0.8$, $E_{22} = 0.15$, $E_{23} = 0.05$. In addition, all the E_{ij} values must be known or specifiable. If the E_{ij} values are unknown (but only the E_{ij}) then we have a minimally well-structured problem, or in decision-theory terms, a decision-problem under uncertainty (Raiffa, 1968).

An ill-structured problem is a problem for which *one or more* of the sets A_i (the decision alternatives), E_{ij} (the efficiencies), O_j (decision outcomes), and V_j (the weights of importance or value of the outcomes) are either not known or are not known with any great degree of certainty or confidence. This occurs for example when different experts have different A_i, E_{ij}, and so on. In short, an ill-structured problem is one for which it is *not* relatively easy to obtain consensus concerning the basic definition of the problem. Further, the problem may or may not be amenable to solution via conventional techniques.

CONCLUDING REMARKS

Because of the growing recognition that many of the problems in science, industry, and society are basically ill-structured with different reputable experts disagreeing as to the basic definition of the problem, and because of the need for developing new techniques, methods, and systems for handling such problems, ill-structured problems have been deliberately chosen for major emphasis in this book. This is not to say that ill-structured problems are *inherently* more important than well-structured problems. This would be akin to saying that the unstable and changing features of the world are somehow more important or fundamental than the stable and unchanging. Since each aspect of nature is only discernible in terms of the other, such a contention would be absurd.

Most critical at this time in our history is the need to develop new methods for coping with wicked problems of organized complexity. Most students of complex problem solving are in agreement as to the importance of assumptions in dealing with complex problems. However, no such agreement exists on how best to reveal and examine assumptions.

Thus once again we are reminded of the importance of developing methods for treating assumptions. In Chapter 3, we begin this critical undertaking. Before leaving on this journey, however, we wish to acknowledge once more our special debt to Churchman, Ackoff, Singer, and Dewey. Every aspect of the methods to be discussed builds on one or more of their ideas. The methods, covered in Parts 2–4 are grounded not only in contemporary practice, but in a long philosophical tradition as well. It is this tradition that (we hope) makes the methods noncapricious, nonarbitrary, and yet highly useful.

Part Two

Assumption Surfacing

Chapter Three

Strategic Assumption Surfacing and Testing Concepts

This chapter describes the essentials of the Strategic Assumption Surfacing and Testing (SAST) planning process. SAST has been found to be helpful in uncovering the critical assumptions that underlie policies, plans, and strategies. The process has been designed especially to uncover and challenge key assumptions on which every business plan of necessity rests. Further, it helps managers make better judgments with regard to the reasonableness of their assumptions.

The method is described with the aid of a specific case history. The case that follows is a composite, focusing chiefly on the experience of the executive corps of a large, primary metals company. However, the case also draws occasionally on experience at several other organizations, including a large equipment manufacturer, an insurance company, a pharmaceutical company and the U.S. Bureau of Census. (A more detailed discussion of these cases is presented in later chapters.) The situation has been disguised in order to preserve the confidential nature of the company's strategy and to honor our commitments not to disclose their plans. The company is referred to here as Majestic Metals.*

Much of this chapter was originally published under the title "Assumptions of Majestic Metals" © (1979) by the Regents of the University of California. Reprinted from *California Management Review* 22, No. 2, pp. 80–88.

*The composite form of presentation was chosen in order to describe in detail more aspects of the process than appear in any one case and to help maintain anonymity. The true name of Majestic Metals cannot be revealed. The name of the drug company and of the large manufacturer and the details of their costs and strategy must also remain confidential. Similar efforts at the U.S. Bureau of Census are reported in Mitroff, Ian I., Barabba, Vincent P., and Kilmann, Ralph "The Application of Behavioral and Philosophical Technologies to Strategic Planning:

AN ISSUE OF STRATEGY

As all serious questions of strategy do, the case begins with an issue facing the company's executive corps. In this instance Majestic's president has just received a document entitled "Majestic Metals: An Analysis of Corporate Strategy." It was the result of a year-long project undertaken by the corporate planning staff at his request.

At first, the report seemed to be exemplary in every detail. Easy to read. Well researched. Adequately supported by background analysis in the form of charts, graphs, and tables. Moreover, it reflected a "good sense" of the business.

The report's timing was appropriate too. The company was just completing the strategy development phase of its annual planning cycle. This would be followed by a brief evaluation and review period, and then within about 2 months the firm would be actively engaged in developing its annual 5–10 year long-range plan (chiefly a financial plan). This would be followed almost immediately by the preparation of the annual operating plan and the detailed budgets for each profit center and cost center. Consequently, there was some immediacy to the situation since, if the proposed strategy was to be acted on this year, a decision had to be made in time to guide the long-range operating plans.

Despite the excellent analysis contained in the project, Majestic's president was troubled. He applauded the fine work done by corporate planning. Yet in his gut he was unsure. This was a multibillion dollar decision. Other than the document, he had almost nothing on which to base his decision, except perhaps his own experience and intuition. Given the magnitude of the decision and his lingering uncertainty, the president felt the need for a critical examination of the proposed strategy as a whole. After this, he would be prepared to make a final judgment.

The essence of the new strategy proposed in the document can be summed up in one sentence: *Majestic Metals intends to change its basic direction towards a more market responsive, systems-oriented business in which the corporation's ability to innovate and to establish proprietary market positions will be the primary source of long-term growth.* This

---

A Case Study of a Large Federal Agency," *Management Science* **24,** No. 1 (September 1977), 44–58. Additional details on the process used at the drug company are published in Mitroff, Ian I., and Emshoff, James R., "On Strategic Assumption-Making: A Dialectical Approach to Policy and Planning," *Academy of Management Review* **4,** No. 1 (1979). We are indebted to Kilmann and to Emshoff for some of the data reported in this chapter; much more so for the concepts.

statement, so innocuous when taken out of context, virtually called for a corporate revolution. Majestic was traditionally a supply-oriented company. Its strategy was rooted implicitly in its rather substantial holdings of ore deposits. Majestic took pride in its long years of experience with a technology for transforming these ores into higher value metal products and in its efficient methods for moving these products to industrial markets. "Market responsive," "systems-oriented," "innovative," and "market dominator" were *not* typical of the adjectives one thought of when characterizing Majestic Metals.

As a result, the chief executive officer was on the horns of a dilemma. On the one hand, the proposed strategy of innovation was appealing to him. It was forward looking, and it identified lucrative markets that were sure to develop in the future. On the other hand, given its departure from more traditional business lines, he was unsure about the soundness of the new plan's underlying assumptions. Was this the "reality" of his company?

SAST

To answer this question, the company engaged in a program of strategic assumption surfacing and testing. SAST, which reveals the underlying assumptions of a policy or plan and helps create a map for exploring them, was designed expressly for coping with wicked problems of organized complexity. For this reason it incorporates the following principles:

1 **Adversarial** Based on the premise that the best judgment on the assumptions necessary to deal with a complex problem is rendered in the context of opposition.

2 **Participative** Based on the premise that the relevant knowledge necessary to solve a complex problem is distributed among a group of individuals and that the relevant resources necessary to implement the solution are also distributed among a group.

3 **Integrative** Based on the premise that a unified assumption set and action plan are needed to guide decision making and that the differentiation process of participation and adversarialness can be synthesized into a unified whole.

4 **Managerial Mind Supporting** Based on the premise that exposure to assumption deepens the manager's insight into an organization and its policy, planning, and strategic problems.

These principles are employed throughout five phases of SAST:

1 Group formation.
2 Assumption surfacing and rating.
3 Debate.
4 Information requirements analysis.
5 Final synthesis.

MODELS OF POLICY MAKING

Before describing Majestic's experience with the SAST, however, it is useful to place SAST in context by briefly reviewing the policy-making and planning process. Authors on policy and planning* have presented detailed models for carrying out the planning and policy-making process. As discussed in Chapter 2 most of these models contain the following stages or steps:

1 A felt need for change, for problem solving, whether this be in the form of a potential opportunity, an impending crisis, or a changing business environment.
2 Problem formulation. Structuring the issue as a planning or policy problem to be solved.
3 Premising. Choosing and communicating the particular set of goals, objectives, facts, assumptions, and hypotheses that will be taken as the presumptions or "givens" in deriving any policy.
4 Generating alternative courses of action.
5 Evaluating alternative courses of action.
6 Choosing a policy.
7 Implementing the chosen policy.
8 Monitoring, evaluating, and reviewing performance and redefining the initial problem.

It is at the second and third stages, *problem formulation* and *premising,* that SAST primarily comes into play although, as we shall see, it has

*Among the authors who present the models of planning and policy making are Steiner, George and Miner, John B. *Management Policy and Strategy* (New York: Macmillan, 1977) and Koontz, Harold and O'Donnell, Cyril, *Essentials of Management* (New York: McGraw-Hill, 1974). See also Hofer and Schendel (1978).

strong implications for all the steps in the planning process. The concern at these stages of policy making is essentially one of "organizational epistemology." It concerns management's *knowledge* about its company, how firm or well grounded this knowledge is, and how broadly this knowledge is held and understood by the people in the organization. SAST is designed to deal with all these dimensions of a firm's reality.

Majestic Metals had already been through stage 1 and a part of stage 2 when the SAST process began. They had also completed the initial phases of stages 3–5. A strategy had been proposed in the document; however, the president decided to review the process completed to date before making a final decision.

The SAST process at Majestic involved five steps:

1 Three separate groups were formed to take different perspectives on the strategy.
2 Each group used the "stakeholder method" (to be discussed later) in order to surface its assumptions.
3 The members of each group debated the assumptions among themselves and then ranked them according to their relative importance to the plan and the relative certainty of their validity.
4 The group debated the results between themselves and negotiated the statements of assumptions among themselves.
5 Finally, all the participants engaged in an effort to synthesize the results, to arrive at a consensus, and to establish data requirements and guidelines for the final decision.

Step 1: Group Formation

Due to the significance of the policy issue, Majestic's CEO recognized that he needed to draw on the knowledge of many people throughout the entire company—planning, sales, accounting, finance, R&D, and the like. He also knew that he needed to secure the involvement and understanding of as many of his management team as possible if the strategy was to be implemented effectively. As a result, he identified 20 key individuals to participate in the SAST process.

These 20 people were formed into three groups of six to eight people each. This group formation strategy was adopted because (1) there was a need for as large a distribution of knowledge and as many different perspectives on the problem as possible, (2) small groups tend to perform better on problem-solving tasks than very large ones, and (3) emerging principles of group behavior suggest that several homogeneous groups, *properly constituted,* outperform large heterogeneous groups in terms of their problem-solving effectiveness.* Briefly stated, the principles are:

1 *Minimize* the interpersonal conflict *within* a group by forming a group that has *maximum* interpersonal similarity and affinity. The point is that the members of the group need to get along well with one another.
2 *Maximize* the differences in knowledge and problem perspective *between* groups. The point is that each group as a whole will bring different information, habits of thought, and basic assumptions to bear on the problem.

In short, these two principles attempt to get the most out of a large group. Principle 1 breaks a large group down into small homogeneous groups, each of which tends to function well within itself because of the minimization of interpersonal differences. Principle 2 seeks to preserve the benefits of the differences, that is, of the fact that not everyone takes the same stand on the issues.

Principle 1 allows the group, as a whole, to take advantage of its similarities; principle 2, of its differences. Note that both of these principles are exceedingly important. The literature on group problem solving (see, e.g., Stumpf, Zand, and Freeman, 1979) stresses constantly that both good group *process* and good group problem solving *skills* (expertise) are needed for effective problem solving. Principle 1 is an operational way of producing effective group process. Principle 2 is an operational procedure by which a large group can take constructive advantage of its differences. Without principles such as one and two, a group can neither make the most of its similarities nor of its differences, both of which are essential to effective group problem solving.

Given these principles, what notions of similarity and affinity should guide the formation of the groups? At Majestic the 20 individuals were brought together in a workshop in which they generated a list of 35 issues

---

*These group formation principles derive in part from research conducted by Mitroff and Kilmann, "On Integrating Behavioral and Philosophical Systems: Towards a Unified Theory of Problem Solving," *Annual Series in Sociology,* Vol. 1 (1978, pp. 207–236); Kilmann, Ralph H., Lyles, M., and Mitroff, Ian I., "Designing an Effective Problem-Solving Organization with the MAPS Design Technology," *Journal of Management* 2 (1976), 1–10; and Kilmann, Ralph H., and Seltzer, Joseph, "An Experimental Test of Organization Design Theory and the MAPS Design Technology: Homogeneous versus Heterogeneous Composition of Organizational Subsystems," *Proceedings of the Eastern Academy of Management* (Eastern Academy of Management, 1976).

necessary to perform a thorough review of the proposed strategy. Using a version of a statistical clustering technique called MAPS,* each individual indicated (1) the particular tasks or issues he preferred to work on and (2) the other workshop members he preferred to work with.

The individuals were clustered into three groups based on their affinity for tasks and for co-workers. The MAPS technique has been also used with other organizations. Other methods for composing homogeneous groups have been used at other sites. For example, for an early study at the Bureau of Census, groups were formed on the basis of their personality types according to the theories of Carl Jung.† During a subsequent SAST project at the Bureau of Census groups were formed on the basis of policy options. This application is reported in Chapter 4. At a pharmaceutical firm, three policy factions already existed—one faction wanted to increase prices, another, to maintain prices and "wait and see," and the third, to reduce prices. This case is also summarized in Chapter 4. At an insurance firm, groups were formed on the basis of their basic beliefs about the business. One group was composed of supervisors, staff analysts, and journeymen involved in and committed to the provision of health care benefits to the employees of insured clients. A second group was composed of those involved in and committed to the provision of industrial safety and industrial hygiene services to insured clients.

In addition to being divided on some principle of similarity and affinity, each group is given a basic orientation. At Majestic, one group was assigned the task of defending the proposed strategy, another was asked to make the strongest case for maintaining the current strategy, and the third group was asked to explore a diversification conglomerate type strategy with heavy foreign investments. Each group started with the same strategic planning document as its primary data base and then proceeded to make the strongest case for its particular orientation.

It is important to emphasize the reasons for forming groups with different orientations. Organizations do not often reward members for challenging accepted ways of thinking or of behaving. As a consequence, the surfacing and challenging of assumptions can not be taken for granted or left to chance. We have found it necessary either to create artificial groups

---

*MAPS stands for Multivariate Analysis, Participation, and Structure. It is a method for designing social systems developed by Ralph Kilmann. See Kilmann, Ralph H., *Social Systems Design* (New York: North-Holland, 1977).

†Details are reported in Mitroff, Barabba, and Kilmann (1977). A similar framework for separating managers according to their problem-solving style is found in McKenney, James L., and Keen, Peter G. W., "How Managers' Minds Work," *Harvard Business Review*, May–June, 1974.

or to support already existing groups to insure that different points of view will be considered explicitly. A single isolated individual by himself or herself is rarely sufficient to challenge accepted habits of thought or behavior. It is much easier to challenge something if one is a member of a group that thinks the same way; hence the group offers support for challenging some other group. Unless a person is a member of a supporting group, an idea or a person will be generally labeled deviant, wacky, or flaky, no matter how creative the idea or person may be. Indeed, the more creative the idea, the more likely it will be labeled wild and wacky.

As will become more apparent as the process unfolds, SAST is inherently a behavioral process. We must never lose sight of the fact that we are fundamentally working with people. It is not organizations *per se* or impersonal groups that have ideas, but people. As a result, we place a strong emphasis on the conditions that help people to surface and to examine their assumptions in as supportive an environment as possible.

One of the techniques that we have found aids the working group's processes is to have them start by giving themselves a name. This activity tends to focus their attention and to release some creative juices. It also gives the members of the group a sense of identity, which proves to be very useful as the remainder of the SAST process unfolds. After the members of the group have chosen a name, each group is asked to summarize its primary point of view. These group focal points serve as an underlying world view, which aids in the generation of assumptions. Exhibit 3-1 shows the group names and focal points for four working groups at a large manufacturing firm. The planning problem this firm faced was the design of a top management decision support system.

Exhibit 3-1   Working Groups

Group Name	People People Inc.	Solar: Strategic Organization for the Linking of Analysis and Research	Super Scopers	Maverics Management Verification Integration Controls
Focal Points	Human engineering of system interface	User and management commitment to system	How data is used in making decisions	Organizational responsibilities of central support organization

Step 2: Assumption Surfacing

The three groups in the Majestic Metals case met separately, and began
the process of identifying the assumptions that might serve as premises
for deriving their assigned strategy. We have found that the surfacing of
assumptions is greatly facilitated by identifying the critical parties at stake
in the problem. Consequently, the first task was to identify as many of the
stakeholders in the policy issue as possible.* Stakeholders are all those
claimants inside and outside the firm who have a vested interest in the
problem and its solution. Prompted by such questions as Who is affected
by the strategy?, Who has an interest in the strategy?, Who is in a position
to effect its adoption or execution?, Who has expressed an opinion on the
matter?, and Who, because of their demographic or other characteristics,
ought to care about the outcome?, a list of stakeholders was generated by
each group. A simplified list patterned after those created by one of the
groups is shown in Exhibit 3-2.

There is a strong theoretical reason derived from the concept of teleological systems† for surfacing assumptions by means of a stakeholder
analysis. A business firm may be conceived of as the *embodiment of a
series of transactions among all of its constituent purposeful entities, that
is, its stakeholders.* The final outcome of an organization's plan will be the
collective result of the effects of the individual actions taken by its
stakeholders. *Thus a strategy may always be thought of as a set of assumptions about the current and future behavior of an organization's
stakeholders.*

The method used at Majestic to convert stakeholder distinctions into
policy assumptions was to pose the "inverse optimal question"‡: Given

*The "stakeholder" concept seems to have emerged initially in the systems
analysis work on organizations conducted by researchers at the Tavistock Institute in London. Rhieman, Eric, *Industrial Democracy and Industrial Man* (London: Tavistock Institute, 1968) and Fox, Alan, *A Sociology of Work in Industry*
(London: Coller-MacMillan Limited, 1971), pp. 57–68 contain good discussions of
the idea and its application to management. More recently Russell Ackoff has
linked the concept to planning in his book *Redesigning the Future* (New York:
Wiley, 1974). The notion has much in common with the role of the "client" in
systems analysis as developed by C. West Churchman in *The Systems Approach*
(New York: Dell, 1968), see also Churchman, C. West, *The Design of Inquiring
Systems* (New York: Basic Books, 1971), and Ackoff, Russell and Emery, Fred.
E., *On Purposeful Systems* (Chicago: Aldine-Atherton, 1972).
†Teleological systems are discussed in Churchman (1971) and Ackoff and Emery
(1972).
‡The "inverse optimal question" is the first stage in creating a dialectic as de-
scribed by Mason, Richard O., "A Dialectical Approach to Strategic Planning,"

your assigned strategy (e.g., defending or attacking a proposed policy) what must be *assumed* about each stakeholder so that these assumptions logically make your strategy *optimal*? Each group engaged in a modified form of the Nominal Group Technique in response to this question.†
Individual members first silently and independently generated their ideas and then shared them by means of a round-robin procedure. Ultimately each group generated a list of over 60 assumptions.

Initially, the assumptions flowed naturally and easily from the group. But soon the pace slowed and the surfacing process almost came to a halt. This was to be expected, in part, because the task required the managers to think in a manner opposite from their normal mode of thought. They were being asked to go from strategy back to assumptions rather than from assumptions to strategy. Once they got the hang of it, some of this type of blockage disappeared.

Each group generated its list of assumptions. A sample list, abstracted from the one produced by the group arguing in favor of the proposed innovation strategy, is shown in Exhibit 3-3. The groups were now prepared to test the assumptions by means of a debate.

Step 3: Within Group Dialectic

The advantage of group cohesion is that it enables a group to become ever more penetrating in unraveling the deep, underlying assumptions of a plan. At the same time, cohesion carries the disadvantage of funneling the group's attention into ever more narrow concerns. Thus any group's results need to be tested for the effects of this tendency. The first test is within the group itself.

Initially, the bias of irrelevancy was eliminated. To do this, each group took each assumption in turn and negated it. Then they simply asked themselves, if the opposite (i.e., the counterassumption) of any particular

Management Science **15**, No. 8 (April 1968), B403–B414. The article is reprinted in David Ewing, Ed., *Long-Range Planning for Management*, third revision. (New York: Harper & Row, 1971) and is the basis for Chapter 6 of this book.
†The nominal group process is a method by which a group of individuals independently and silently generate a list of assumptions and, then, share them one by one in a round-robin fashion. The assumptions are recorded on flip charts and later discussed and evaluated. The method is reported in Delbecq, Andre L., and Van de Ven, Andrew H. "A Group Process Model for Problem Identification and Program Planning," *Journal of Applied Behavioral Science* **7**, No. 4 (September 1971), and also in Van de Ven, Andrew H. and Delbecq, Andre L., "Nominal versus Interacting Group Process for Committee Decision-Making Effectiveness," *Academy of Management Journal*, **14**, No. 3 (1971), 203–211.

Exhibit 3-2   Sample Set of Stakeholders

Stockholders
Creditors
Current customers
  Large industrial (by industry)
  Small industrial
  Other
Materials brokers
Energy sources
Production employees (by skill classes)
Marketing force (by skills)
Labor unions
Local communities
  Plant locations
  Sites of ore deposits
  Possible new business location
Capital markets, investment bankers
Firms possessing new technologies
  High temperature
  Cryogenic
  Oceanographic
  Underground mining
  Composite materials
Federal government agencies
  Environmental Protection Agency
  Occupational Safety and Health Act
  Federal Trade Commission
  Bureau of Mines
Competitors
  Current in current businesses
  Current competitors also *likely to move* into proposed businesses
  Firms presently operating in proposed markets
  Others
Research: R&D firms, scientific labs, universities
Firms possessing marketing know-how in proposed businesses
  Electrical products
  Transportation
  Machine tools
  Agriculture
  Heavy equipment
  Packaging
Corporate management and staff

Exhibit 3-3   Sample Assumptions Pro-Innovation Strategy

---

1. Majestic's stockholders will not seek a higher dividend rate and will be satisfied if the 15% Earnings Per Share growth rate is maintained. (Stockholders)
2. Corporate management can make the transition from a raw materials transforming and industrial production orientation to a high technology business. (Management)
3. Energy sources will be available for expansion at reasonable costs. (Energy)
4. Funds for expansion can be acquired from the capital markets at reasonable rates. (Capital market)
5. The current marketing force will serve as a sound base for building the market responsive high technology product marketing force. (Marketing)
6. Environmental Protection Agency (EPA) and local pollution regulations will not substantially divert investment from the planned new technology expansion program. (EPA)
7. High temperature and cryogenic technologies can be acquired at reasonable costs through the acquisition of existing firms. (New technology)

---

assumption were true, does it have any significant bearing on the strategy chosen? A "no" answer indicates that the assumption is not very relevant for the problem. Several assumptions were discarded at this step.

The thus winnowed assumption set was now ready for its stiffest test within each group. Any assumption accepted as a strategic premise must meet two criteria:

1   It should have a significant bearing on the outcome of the strategy chosen and implemented.
2   It should be as "self-evident" and "certain to be true" as possible.

These two criteria are referred to, respectively, as *importance* and *certainty*. The criteria can be applied by having the group plot their assumption on an importance/certainty Assumption Plotting Graph. In its most general form, the Assumption Plotting Graph is simply a display of the relative importance and certainty of each assumption. The graph is a two-dimensional ordinal ranking of the comparisons made between the assumptions.

The group process involved in plotting the assumptions can be very revealing. The necessity of determining a position for each assumption focuses attention on it, demands a clarification of its meaning, and forces a comparison between it and other assumptions. The ensuing discussion improves the group's understanding of the assumptions and provides a

Exhibit 3-4   Typical Group Members' Rating of the Relative Certainty of Seven Assumptions[a]

Assumption i	Assumption j							Normalized Weighting for Graphic Display
	A_1	A_2	A_3	A_4	A_5	A_6	A_7	
A1. Stockholders	1	4	9	6	6	5	5	1.00
A2. Management	$\frac{1}{4}$	1	7	5	5	3	4	.51
A3. Energy	$\frac{1}{9}$	$\frac{1}{7}$	1	$\frac{1}{5}$	$\frac{1}{5}$	$\frac{1}{7}$	$\frac{1}{5}$	.00
A4. Capital markets	$\frac{1}{6}$	$\frac{1}{5}$	5	1	1	$\frac{1}{3}$	$\frac{1}{3}$	.08
A5. Marketing	$\frac{1}{6}$	$\frac{1}{5}$	5	1	1	$\frac{1}{3}$	$\frac{1}{3}$	.08
A6. EPA	$\frac{1}{5}$	$\frac{1}{3}$	7	3	3	1	2	.27
A7. New technology	$\frac{1}{5}$	$\frac{1}{4}$	5	3	3	$\frac{1}{2}$	1	.18

[a]Each entry in the matrix is the comparison of Assumption i to Assumption j. The rating scale employed is as follows: 1 = equal importance or certainty, 9 = Assumption i has absolute priority over assumption j, $\frac{1}{9}$ = Assumption j has absolute priority over assumption i.

deeper insight into this assumption's role in the organization's policy, plan, or strategy.

Sometimes a scaling more precise than the simple ordinal scale is required. This was the case at Majestic Metals. Referring to the list of remaining assumptions each member in the group compared each assumption with the other assumptions in a pair-wise fashion.* The result was a matrix of relative ratings such as the one illustrated in Exhibit 3-4. Matrices for importance and for certainty were prepared by each member. A computer was used to calculate normalized weightings.

At this point, each member shared his or her ratings and calculated weights with the other members of the group. In the event of major

*The method employed was one developed by Tom Saaty. Technically, the procedure was as follows: each member makes pairwise comparisons of the importance and certainty of each assumption using a scale from 1 to 0. The results are recorded in an $n \times n$ matrix A. The eigenvalue and eigenvector (characteristic root) problem $Aw = \lambda \max w$ (where λ is the dominant root) is solved yielding a vector of weights, w, which in turn are divided by the sum of the weights to produce a ratio scale of relative weights for each of the assumptions. We have implemented an algorithm for solving this on a minicomputer. In Figure 3-1, these weights were mapped onto a [1,0] scale for purposes of graphic display. See Saaty, Thomas L. and Rogers, Paul C., "Higher Education in the United States (1985–2000)," *Socio-Economic Planning Sciences*, **10** (1976), 251–263

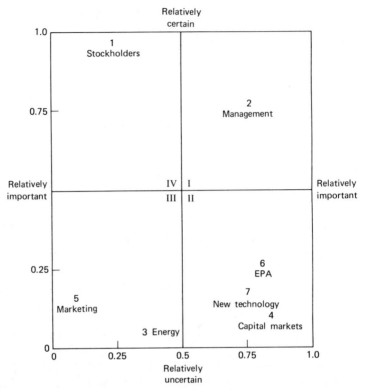

Figure 3-1   Graph of assumption weightings: importance and certainty.

discrepancies, the group discussion leader encouraged dialogue around the differences to see whether a deviant member had any special insight, knowledge, or compelling reason for arriving at a different rating. Notice that, instead of shutting off deviant ideas, this tends to encourage risk taking and innovation. After the ratings had been well debated, the group sought to arrive at a consensus weighting on both importance and certainty.

The results of the consensus weights are plotted on a graph such as the simplified one depicted in Figure 3-1. Now the group's attention is devoted to the four quadrants of the graph. Quadrant I contains assumptions that are rated as both relatively important and certain. These are candidates to become the pivotal or "bedrock" assumptions for the policy. Assumption 2—that Majestic's corporate management can make the transition from a raw materials to a high technology business—is shown in Figure 3-1. Quadrant II deserves special scrutiny. It contains assumptions that are considered important but about which management is uncertain as to truth, plausibility, reasonableness, or grounds for support. Note Assumption 4 in the illustration. The assumption asserts that funds for expansion can be required from capital markets at reasonable rates to finance the high technology strategy. It is, relatively, the most important assumption of all, but it rates very low on the certainty scale. Consequently, this assumption requires careful consideration. Because of this uncertainty, an extra effort was undertaken at Majestic to talk to investment bankers and to collect more data before the group finalized its specification of this assumption. The assumptions in quadrants III and IV are candidates for elimination, especially those in quadrant III. It appears, for example, that Assumption 5 concerning the abilities of the current marketing force adds very little to the strategy-making process. It might well be dropped. Using the graph as an aid, the group debated the candidacy of each assumption.

Finally, the group settled on its *pivotal assumptions* and prioritized them. *These were the basic assumptions that in the group's judgment should become the fundamental premises of the policy.* Each of the groups identified six to eight pivotal assumptions. Identifying pivotal assumptions is a critical part of the strategy-making process. Obviously, in a sense, all assumptions are important; similarly, none are known to be true with certainty. However, in the world of strategy, most assumptions are not truly mutually independent. Consequently, once a priority judgment is made that one assumption is more fundamental than another assumption, the second becomes constrained by limits imposed on it by the first. For example, if the assumption "high temperature and cryogenic technologies can be acquired" had been considered more important than the assumption "capital markets will provide adequate funds for expansion at favorable terms," the judgment on financing becomes conditioned by the prior technological assumption. In this case the ranking of the assumptions reflects the feeling that funds will be available specifically to acquire the new technologies. An opposite ranking would suggest that funds would be acquired first by whatever means and then used for several purposes, including the acquisition of new technologies. Thus a different ranking within the same set of assumptions can lead to subtly, or occasionally substantially, different statements of strategy. This is one of the reasons that ordering of assumptions and the identification of pivotal assumptions is such a central part of the strategic assumption-making or SAST process.

After each group had independently developed its strategy and identified its pivotal assumptions, it was time for the groups to compare their findings. Each group was instructed to work independently up to this

point in order to make the strongest case for its particular point of view
and to avoid wasting energy in arguments.

Step 4: Between Group Dialectic Debates

A *dialectic debate* occurs when a situation is examined systematically and
logically from two or more points of view. (Dialectic debates will be
covered more thoroughly in Part 3.) Its intent is to improve the final judgment on assumptions by subjecting them to the strongest possible critical
evaluation. In order to accomplish this, the three groups were brought
together and, along with the chief executive officer and a few other
Majestic executives, they all engaged in an intensive dialectical debate.
The purpose of the debate was to spell out the implications of each policy,
to reveal its underlying assumptions, and to challenge those assumptions
as effectively as possible.

The dialectic was conducted in the form of a structured debate.* In
turn, a spokesperson for each group was asked to present the group's
importance/certainty graph and to display, using a set of slides, the several assumptions the group had decided were pivotal. Then the spokesperson presented a case to demonstrate why these assumptions were
critical to the group's strategy and why these assumptions should be
chosen as the final strategic premises. Only *clarifying questions* were
permitted at the time of presentation because it was important that everybody first understood each of the assumptions in this newly generated
pool before debating and challenging them. *After* each group had presented its case, all three sets of assumptions were projected on a common
chart or slide, and the floor was opened for general discussion. Only then
were the assumptions and arguments permitted to be evaluated, debated,
and discussed.

It was noted earlier that the act of plotting assumptions on an
importance/certainty chart is a very powerful supporting device for
creating awareness and insight. It allows each member of the group to see
for himself or herself the points of agreement and disagreement among the
subgroups. The Assumption Plotting Chart allows the group to pause, to
reflect, and to take notice of the status of current thinking. This type of

---

*The theory of argument we employ at this stage is that found in Stephen E.
Toulmin's book *The Uses of Argument* (Cambridge, England: Cambridge University Press, 1958). Actually, Toulmin's theory requires that a claim (i.e., assumption) be analyzed as to its underlying data, warrants, backing (support for warrant), rebuttal (limitations on the warrant), and qualifiers. See Part 4.

feedback is missing in most group discussions. Instead, most groups are so involved in their own internal dynamics that they never stop to take stock of where they are and where they agree and disagree. Indeed, many groups seem to be powerless to do so. The Assumption Plotting Chart unblocks this barrier by serving as an "objectification" of the member's values and beliefs about the business. Thus some parts of their unconscious are permitted to surface and it becomes permissible to discuss these observations in the group. In the process, the discussion becomes more focused and open.

This surfacing and focusing occurred at Majestic Metals. As the groups revealed their Assumption Plotting Charts, one thing was immediately obvious. The groups had identified many of the same assumptions but they had rated them quite differently. For example, the group arguing for the conglomerate diversification strategy also assumed that corporate management could make the transition to a high technology business (Assumption 2 in Exhibit 3-3) but they rated it as much less important and very much less certain than the "status quo" group which took the opposing position. They were quite certain that management would *not* be able to make the transition. The collective pool of assumptions from the three sets of slides were then reviewed in an attempt to draw out the final assumptions.

Of course, there were some assumptions on which almost everybody concurred at the outset. They were extracted early as premises from which to proceed. There were also a few new assumptions that evolved through the discussion. For example, each small group had quite different perspectives on federal and local government activities with respect to pollution control and enforcement. These differences forced the plenary group to develop a much more refined series of distinctions and assumptions about government regulations.

Assumptions can be malleable in debate, and they may be pressed toward a synthetic agreement if the stage is properly set. Alternatively, assumptions can be prickly in debate, and they may steadfastly resist encroachment from the other side. Whenever such a stalemate was reached, an *assumption negotiation* process was used. Of the assumptions remaining in the pool, each group was asked to identify the key assumptions from each of the other two groups' lists that it found most untenable—the opposing assumption that most perturbed their point of view and was most damaging to their proposed strategy. Each group was then asked to reformulate their most threatening assumptions by modifying them to the point where they just barely supported their group's proposed strategy. The other groups were then asked to respond to the modified assumptions and to indicate whether or not they were acceptable in this new form. When agreement was struck, the assumption was drawn from the pool and placed in the final list.

This process was repeated successively, working back and forth among the groups in an effort to find a zone of compromise, until all that remained were assumptions that could not be changed in a manner that was satisfactory to the other groups. At Majestic, assumption negotiation reached its end with several candidate assumptions remaining disputed in the pool. How to proceed?

There is one other test that can be employed at this state in the process. We will merely sketch the test at this time since the use of this test or technique is the subject of Part 4. Each assumption can be treated as the product of some previous argument. Hence one can ask "What are the grounds for making this assumption?" We have found it useful to respond to this question by breaking the argument in favor of an assumption down into its component parts, basically its data and warrants (Toulmin, 1958). Data are the facts used as the grounds for a claim, the "hard" evidence so to speak. Warrants, on the other hand, are themselves assumptions that authorize the "mental leap" involved in moving from the data to the claim. Data answers the question "What have you got to go on?" Warrants answer the question "How do you get from here, the data, to there, the claim or a policy?"

For example, the innovation group at Majestic was asked to specify the evidential grounds for their claim that corporate management can make the transition from a raw materials transforming and industrial production orientation to a high technology business (Assumption 2). In response they cited many incidences where current executives had demonstrated knowledge of high technology in the past and other evidence of management's flexibility, intellectual capacity, and generalized management skills. This data, together with the warrant that these isolated incidences were *indicators* of management's future behavior, led them to conclude that corporate management could make the transition. The status quo group, on the other hand, cited incidences of rigidity and "feet-in-the-mud" behavior. By means of a similar warrant they concluded that management would not make the transition gracefully. The debate was concluded and the grounds were set for synthesis.

Step 5: Synthesis and Decision

The mood of conflict that had prevailed during the previous steps was deliberately shifted at this point to a mood of cooperation. In an attempt to achieve a synthesis all 20 participants were asked to propose assumptions that would resolve the controversies still at large. When a consensus was reached on an assumption, it became a premise or presumption for the plan. When no consensus was reached on an assumption it was identified as an issue for further investigation.

Follow-up and Planning Information Book

Each issue and key assumption was subjected to further analysis in order to adduce the data and warrants which underlie its claims. Where the available data was inadequate, business intelligence and management information systems activities were undertaken to acquire the specific data necessary to resolve the strategic issue.

Companies such as Majestic Metals and public agencies such as the U.S. Bureau of Census have used a variety of methods to obtain this follow-up information. Brainstorming is one of the most effective ways to identify possible information-producing activities for each issue. A free imagination helps to generate creative ways of obtaining information for critical issues. Whatever the methods used, most information activities tend to fall into the following three management inquiry styles:

1 **Research Approaches** Use of the scientific method to acquire additional issue or policy relevant information. Examples include:

    a. Market research.
    b. Operations research.
    c. Simulation models such as interactive financial planning models.
    d. Financial analysis.
    e. Competitive analysis.
    f. Econometric analysis.
    g. PIMS and other strategic planning data based analysis.

2 **Judgmental Approaches** Use of dialogue and reflection to assess the values, beliefs, and judgmental dimensions surrounding the issue. Examples include:

    a. White papers and position papers.
    b. Delphi panels.
    c. Focused discussion groups.
    d. Scenario writing.

3 **Monitoring Approaches**   Use of internal and external data sources to keep track of trends and events affecting the issue. Examples are:

   a. Key business indicators systems based on measurements of "critical success factors".
   b. Social indicators.
   c. Event monitoring, including sources such as:

       1. New York Times index.
       2. Predicasts.
       3. Yankelovitch, Kelly, and White monitor.
       4. G.E.'s Future Scan.
       5. Stanford Research Institute's Business Intelligence Program.
       6. University of Southern California's Center for Future Research Twenty Year Forecast.

Each of these approaches to acquiring issue relevant information has the characteristic that professional planning expertise is required to obtain and interpret the information. The cost of carrying out these planning activities and interpreting them can be quite high. As a result, this kind of knowledge production is often difficult to management. A planning book helps the management deal with this problem. A manager's planning book contains:

1 A prioritized list of most critical issues management faces as revealed by SAST.
2 An assessment of the current state of knowledge with respect to the solution to these issues.
3 A list of current and planned information producing activities designed to improve the state of knowledge relevant to the critical issues.

The planning book directs knowledge production towards the most critical issues facing the company. By reviewing the debate, stakeholders, assumptions and ratings, it is possible to come up with a rather precise definition of the information needed. Information requirements are thereby better specified and less vague. Usually as a result of the SAST process both the user of the information and the producer gain a better shared understanding of each issue and generally agree to the specific information activities that are being undertaken to resolve the issue. There are fewer surprises. Finally, the urgency of the issue will dictate the time frame and duration of the information producing activities.

   When the policy decision must be made, the results of the information producing activities are collected and related to the issues for which they were undertaken. Plugging the new data into the data component of an argumentation model such as is described in detail in Chapter 9 is often useful in this regard. A final debate is held to ferret out additional implications, insights, and understanding. A judgment is made on the best set of assumptions from which to proceed. Finally an appropriate policy is chosen based on the new information and the synthesis that emerged.

   The overall SAST process of which these five steps and the information follow-up are a part is summarized in Figure 3-2.

CONCLUSION

The strategic assumption surfacing and testing process and the subsequent data gathering activities aided Majestic's management arriving at a strategic decision; however, these activities did not make the final decision. Management still had to construct the reality on which the strategy or policy was to be based. Informed by the processes described previously, the president of Majestic Metals finally decided to embark on a plan that was a synthetic combination of the three prototype strategies; the plan was not as innovative as the high technology plan but it was more progressive than the plan simply to maintain the status quo. The emerging plan essentially involved a moderately paced sequence of vertical integration through acquisition. Each acquisition was selected to build on existing case technologies but to move toward (1) more consumer oriented markets and (2) higher level technologies.

   Efforts are currently under way to implement this chosen policy at Majestic Metals. Aspects of the new strategy have found their way into the long-range plan and the current operating plans. Majestic's president, however, has no absolute way of knowing that his choice is the very best possible. However, he is confident of four things:

1   The broadest possible knowledge within the firm was brought to bear on this strategic issue.
2   Various strategic options and their underlying assumptions were subjected to a thorough, systematic, and critical examination. Each point of view was considered as a whole and evaluated in the context of its competitors.
3   Each of the parties involved in the process understands, often for the first time, many of the premises that underlie the chosen strategy. They may not all fully agree to these premises, but they know the basis

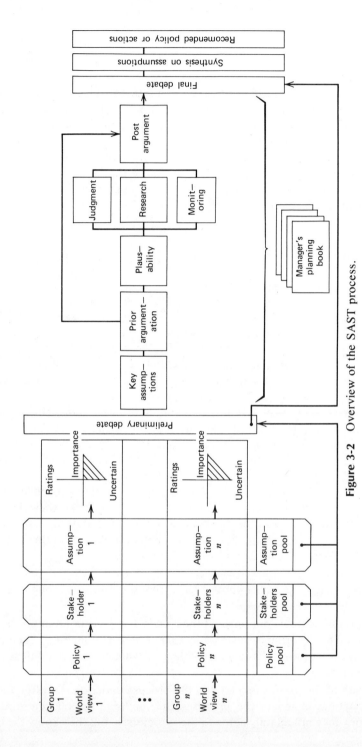

Figure 3-2 Overview of the SAST process.

on which the premises were chosen. This awareness and mutual understanding is probably the best guarantee the company has that its strategy has a chance to succeed.

4   A business intelligence and management information systems program has been undertaken in order to obtain data on the high priority issues affecting the strategic decisions.

Majestic's management team is well informed about the strategy they are following and the assumptions that support it. They believe that they have constructed an effective reality from which to proceed. For the chief executive officer, a little more uncertainty has been taken out of this inherently uncertain world of strategic assumption making. A decision with regard to a plan has been made. Key assumptions were not ignored but rather surfaced, challenged, and monitored over time. This is the purpose of the SAST process.

Chapter Four

Strategic Assumption Surfacing and Testing Cases

This chapter contains two cases that demonstrate the application of the SAST process to policy, planning, and strategic problems. The first case, "Census Undercount Adjustment Workshop," is a rather complete summary of the use of the SAST process to inform the decision on a major public policy issue. The case also contains illustrative results from each of the steps of the process. The second case, "Pharmaceutical Company Pricing Issue," is a short case that illustrates the application of SAST to typical business problems.

CENSUS UNDERCOUNT ADJUSTMENT WORKSHOP CASE*

Background

The January 14, 1980 issue of *Time* summarized the policy problem facing the U.S. Bureau of Census as follows:

Counting Americans every ten years would seem to be a noncontroversial enterprise, but the 1980 U.S. census has become immersed in politics up to its last decimal point. A growing number of people are worried about the accuracy of the tally because so much—political power as well as the distribution of billions of dollars in federal funds—is riding on the outcome. The nose count will not begin until April, but Census Director Vincent Barabba already predicts that it will be the toughest and most scrutinized ever. Everyone is going to be watching.

*The results of this workshop were published in an internal document of the Census Bureau, reprinted by permission.

Public interest groups were pressuring the Bureau of Census to adjust its direct headcount for the 1980 census. Why? Because estimates show that about 2.5% of the population was missed during the 1970 census. More important, the undercounting varies significantly according to the ethnicity of the area. Whites tend to be undercounted by only about 1.9%, whereas Blacks are undercounted by 7.7%. There are no reliable estimates of the undercount of Spanish-speaking people but it's sure to be higher than that for Blacks. Those favoring adjustment want the final census figures to reflect these missed people.

Why all this concern? The reasons are twofold. First, the U.S. Constitution requires that the census be used as the basis for reapportioning seats in the House of Representatives. Adjustment will probably shift the balance of political power among the states. New York will probably lose seats while California, Texas, and Florida will gain. Second, general revenue sharing funds are allocated to states and communities on the basis of census data. Every additional person added to a state or district means more money for them. Current estimates are that each individual is worth about $200 to the political entity that claims them.

To adjust or not to adjust and, if so, how? This was the complex policy issue the bureau faced.

In light of this growing concern, both inside and outside of the Census Bureau, about possible adjustment of 1980 census data to compensate for undercount, it was decided at the Bureau to take positive steps to assess the assumptions and issues involved in various suggested adjustment plans. To this end, the Bureau held a SAST workshop during the first week of September 1979. Workshop participants included management and professional personnel from the Bureau and the Department of Commerce and a few additional selected individuals.

The specific purpose of the undercount adjustment workshop was to test whether, in fact, the extensive discussion to date had identified comprehensively all the issues and assumptions. Assumptions identified in the workshop were examined in terms of their relationships with other assumptions and the importance and degree of certainty that should be attached to each.

Four working groups were formed at the start of the conference. These groups were assigned different undercount adjustment plans, which they were to support. On the first day, working independently, the groups identified stakeholders and surfaced assumptions in support of their position. The assumptions were ranked for their importance to a given plan and on the certainty or uncertainty with which an assumption should be viewed. On the second day, a review of assumptions involved in each plan was presented in a plenary session, and extensive debate on assumptions filled the rest of the day. Finally on the third day, information sources for further research on the most important issues were identified in a plenary session. The major phases of the workshop are described in the next section.

WORKING GROUP FORMATION

On the first evening, after listening to a presentation of the goals of the workshop and a description of the assumption-surfacing decision-making process, the participants split into four previously self-selected working groups to discuss the underlying issues involved in each plan. Prior to the workshop, the participants had been presented with four hypothetical plans for treating the undercount and each participant had selected the plan that he or she felt most capable of defending. Thus each working group constituted a relatively homogeneous membership as assignments to working groups were determined to conform as closely as possible to individual preferences.

The four hypothetical plans for adjustment of the 1980 census data that were used by the working groups in their discussions were:

Convention A The headcount itself without any adjustment other than imputation to a specific household based on knowledge gained from an independent source (e.g., neighbors and lists) or, in the case of administrative losses and equipment malfunctions, imputation based on supporting census records (e.g., address registers).

The issues felt to be particularly important were related to the credibility of the Census Bureau and the problem that an adjustment could set an unfortunate precedent for the future. Coverage improvement efforts already under way would preclude the need for synthetic adjustments to the final counts.

Convention B The headcount would be adjusted using all the imputation procedures used in 1970. This would involve imputations not only to a specific household based on knowledge gained from the census about that specific household, but would include adjustments to a particular class of households from information collected about that class from the census. For example, the proportion of housing units initially incorrectly reported as vacant in a sample applied to all housing units initially reported vacant.

This group felt that it was important that "state of the art" tools must be used to assure credibility of the Bureau and the census count. The 1970 census had used Convention B and it had been tested in the courts. The group felt that anything less would be indefensible. It felt that Conventions C and D could not produce valid estimates for small areas and thus would produce results equally indefensible.

Convention C Census data would be adjusted for undercount by age, race (Black/non-Black), and sex. Adjustments would be made utilizing a simple synthetic approach, and there would be corresponding adjustments to the microdata tape. This implies two complete count tabulations (one adjusted and one unadjusted) and one sample tabulation (adjusted).

This group felt that the disparity of the undercount was important and should be corrected for and that estimates of the relative undercount were available for age, race, and sex. Since no other characteristics have "known" amounts of undercount, adjustments should not be done on the basis of any other characteristics.

Convention D The headcount and other critical variables would be modified by experts in light of all pertinent information. These other critical variables include age, sex, ethnicity, relationships, income, race, and language. There is the assumption in this instance of the availability of evaluation results and reliable estimates of the uncounted population at the state level.

This group felt that if any adjustment was done to the actual counts, the adjustment should correct as completely as possible. The Bureau is best qualified to develop such an adjustment procedure and to perform this adjustment.

In order to enhance each participant's sense of role playing each group gave itself a name; the group supporting Convention A gave itself the name, "Headcounters from Missouri," Convention B, "Triple B Nonadjustment Company," Convention C, "Equalizers," and Convention D, "All or Nothing at All." This process was intended to surface effectively all assumptions and issues but not to set Census Bureau policy. Therefore, it was important for each participant to assume the role of a staunch protagonist for a particular position regardless of his/her own convictions.

ASSUMPTION SURFACING

The second day of the undercount workshop was devoted to discussion within each working group. Isolated from the other three working groups, each working group was to develop a comprehensive list of stakeholders, that is, persons, organizations, and institutions that the groups thought would have a stake in the decision of how to deal with the undercount and in the outcome of the census. The members of each group were also asked to think of other persons or groups who might have an interest in the decision on the undercount treatment but who had not made themselves heard or whose interest had not currently been recognized even by themselves, snaildarters.

During this stakeholder identification process, the assumptions that were necessary for each group's particular plan of action to be feasible gradually surfaced. Some of the assumptions were linked to a particular stakeholder, that is, the behavior of a stakeholder as a result of a certain decision on the undercount, while others were fundamentally necessary for the plan of action to take place. The stakeholders and the assumptions pertaining to them are contained in Exhibits 4-1 and 4-2 as an example.

Exhibit 4-1   Census Stakeholders

    I. Census Bureau

       A. Director
       B. Professional Staff
       C. Temporary Field Staff and Community Services Representatives

   II. Administration

       A. White House
       B. Secretary of Commerce
       C. Office of Management and Budget

  III. Congress

       A. General Accounting Office
       B. Oversight Committees
       C. Appropriations Committees
       D. Black Caucus
       E. Individual Members
       F. Specially Interested Members
       G. Congressional Research Service

  IV. Other Governmental Agencies

       A. Federal

           1. Statistical Agencies
           2. Program Agencies

Exhibit 4-1 *(Continued)*

3. Office of Federal Statistical Programs
4. Other Federal Data Users

B. State and Local

1. State Governments in Apportionment (i.e., Redistributing) Function
2. State Governments in Dispensary (Funding) Function
3. State Legislators
4. Recipient Agencies
5. Statistical and Planning Agencies
6. Local Review Boards

V. Vested Radical/Ethnic Groups

A. Black
B. Hispanic
C. APIA
D. American Indian
E. White Ethnics
F. Undocumented Workers
G. Minority Advisory Committees
H. Other

VI. Other Vested Interest Groups

A. Recipients of Government Programs

1. Aged
2. Disabled
3. Low Income
4. Unemployed

B. Employers
C. Labor Unions
D. Public Interest Groups
E. Churches
F. Political Parties
G. Ad Council
H. Regional Interests
I. Chambers of Commerce
J. Groups That Have "Gone on Record"

Exhibit 4-1 *(Continued)*

      1. National Academy of Sciences

      2. NCEUS (National Commissions on Employment and Unemployment Statistics)

      3. National Urban League

  K. Majority

VII. Legal Community

VIII. Media

  A. Minority

  B. Other

IX. Statistical Community

  A. American Statistical Association

  B. International Statistical Agencies

  C. Other Census Bureau Advisory Committees

X. Other Data Users

  A. Business Community

  B. Academic Community

  C. Genealogists

Exhibit 4-2   Convention A, B, C, and D Assumptions

Convention A Assumptions

I. Most Important, Most Certain

  A. Convention A will be supported by Census Bureau professional staff. (Damaging to Groups B, C)

  B. Census Bureau professional staff is concerned with setting a precedent for future politicalization of census. (Damaging to Group D)

  C. Census Bureau professional staff is not sufficiently satisfied with available measures below State level to perform an allocation. (Damaging to Groups C, D)

  D. Because importance of function of temporary field staff and community service representatives is diminished with allocation, data quality will be poorer.

Exhibit 4-2 *(Continued)*

E. Analysis of supporting data by Congress would lead to general support of Convention A (more losers than gainers under allocation). (Damaging to Group C)

F. If an allocation were made, employers would protest vigorously (in courts) that they should not be asked to hire people to comply with equal employment opportunity laws that even the Census Bureau could not find.

G. The majority of the population would feel that benefits should go to those who meet their responsibility of cooperating with the Census Bureau.

H. Other Federal statistical agencies fear data politicalization.

I. The courts would support Convention A as the least arbitrary and capricious procedure (due process was available to all U.S. inhabitants). (Damaging to Groups B, C, D)

II. Most Important, Least Certain

A. Diversity of congressional interests precludes passing a law related to allocation procedures.

B. Some racial/ethnic groups will take the position if there is no allocation for all, don't allocate.

C. If an allocation were made, labor unions would protest vigorously (in courts) that they should not be asked to hire people for EEO that even the Census Bureau could not find.

D. Other Federal statistical agencies would support Convention A because of numerator/denominator problems with two sets of numbers. (Damaging to Groups C, D)

E. Federal program agencies would want local area data that would be credible in court.

F. Given the facts, the media are more likely to support Convention A.

III. Least Important, Most Certain

A. The majority of the population would not perceive a benefit from allocation.

IV. Least Important, Least Certain

A. The White House and Secretary of Commerce will support Convention A to avoid the appearance of politicizing census results. (Damaging to Groups C, D)

B. The Administration will view support of Convention A to be consistent

Exhibit 4-2 *(Continued)*

with support of coverage improvement funds. (Damaging to Groups C, D)

C. Because of inability to organize around common benefits, recipients of government programs such as those for the aged, disabled, and low income are not likely to be organized as a major force to support allocation.

Convention B Assumptions

I. Most Important, Most Certain

A. Most stakeholders will assume that Conventions C and D imply adjustment at detailed (39,000 jurisdictions) levels.

B. Implementation of Convention D at detailed levels would not be complete until the end of 1983 at the earliest. (Damaging to Group D)

C. Reducing the overall undercount is of high priority.

D. Reducing the differential undercount is of *higher* priority and, unless the minority undercount is low, Convention B reduces the differential undercount more than Convention A. (Damaging to Group A)

E. Strict adherence to Convention A ignores gaps from administrative losses and equipment malfunctions, as well as vacant households, and will increase undercount by 2.5 percent. (Damaging to Group A)

F. Conventions C and D will be perceived as political adjustment to the enumeration. (Damaging to Groups C, D)

G. Undercount adjustments are estimates subject to substantial error and would cause inequity for most jurisdictions. (Damaging to Group C)

H. Conventions C and D deal only with population counts, not per capita income or other characteristics that may be important in fund allocation.

I. Conventions C and D imply two sets of population counts.

II. Most Important, Least Certain

A. Convention A will not be acceptable in the courts as it does not apply the "state of the art" to the enumerative process. (Damaging to Group A)

B. Conventions C and D will not be acceptable in the courts as they rely on "synthetic" means (as opposed to actual enumeration) to eliminate undercoverage. (Damaging to Groups C, D)

C. Conventions C and D imply no coverage improvement. (Damaging to Groups C, D)

Exhibit 4-2 *(Continued)*

III. Least Important, Most Certain

    A. Some stakeholders will feel that local government and groups that put forth efforts to improve coverage should not be penalized by an adjustment which gives others these benefits "free."

Convention C Assumptions

I. Most Important, Most Certain

    A. Timely adjusted counts are wanted by major stakeholders (not for apportionment). (Damaging to Group B)

    B. Major users of census data are capable of using multiple sets of data. (Damaging to Groups A, B)

    C. Convention C is easily explained. (Damaging to Group D)

    D. Convention C is timely. (Damaging to Group D)

    E. One standard adjustment is beneficial and cost effective.

    F. There will be adequate data available to estimate the undercount for use in adjustment (black/non-black, age, and sex) but *not* for Spanish/Hispanic and other minority groups.

    G. Convention C will receive broad support from various stakeholders (statistical profession, public interest groups, media, general public, public leaders).

II. Most Important, Least Certain

    A. Convention C is statistically defensible. (Damaging to Group A)

    B. Convention C leads to equity. (Damaging to Groups A, B)

    C. When the Hispanic (or other) community objects, Convention C will be supported by other stakeholders.

    D. The courts are more likely to uphold adjustments made by the Census Bureau than those made by other organizations.

    E. The Census Bureau cannot be held accountable for programmatic uses of adjusted data.

III. Least Important, Most Certain

    A. Convention C allows for prior announcement of adjustment procedure. (Damaging to Group D)

    B. From a privacy standpoint, Convention C is more acceptable than an adjustment that uses record checking.

Exhibit 4-2 *(Continued)*

Convention D Assumptions

I. Most Important, Most Certain

    A. Minorities will insist on complete adjustments at the lowest geographical levels, because this will bring them closer to the truth and equity for fund allocation. (Damaging to Group B)

    B. Special interest groups have enough power to influence Congress, the White House, and other public officials.

    C. Program agencies will require more than headcount adjustments (e.g., sex, age, race/ethnicity, income, and household composition, language) to improve program effectiveness.

    D. Only complete adjustments will be responsive to most needs. (Damaging to Group C)

    E. The White House will support the methodology that has the highest political acceptability and visibility. Convention D, in providing greater detail, will gain the broadest political support. (Damaging to Groups A, B, C)

    F. The Census Bureau can change operational procedures to improve timeliness, detail, and so on.

    G. The Census Bureau should take the initiative to insure quality and determine the method, not leaving the policy to be determined by legislative initiative.

    H. Convention D is the most flexible and least arbitrary approach and is most sensitive to most groups. (Damaging to Groups A, B, C)

II. Most Important, Least Certain

    A. The Director will provide unwavering support.

    B. Congress will enact legislation to force adjustments most similar to Convention D if the adjustments are not initiated by the Census Bureau. (Damaging to Groups A, B, C)

    C. The media can explain the validity of Convention D.

    D. States and localities that are adversely affected will not challenge the methodology. (Damaging to Group A)

    E. The Census Bureau has the best ability to develop a statistical and analytical methodology that will permit adjustment of critical variables in a timely fashion.

III. Least Important, Most Certain

    A. Litigation will be initiated to change allocation formulas to approximate Convention D.

Exhibit 4-2   (*Continued*)

IV.   Least Important, Least Certain

   A.   Convention D will forestall generation of multiple adjusted numbers for
         special interest groups. (Damaging to Groups B, C)

For instance, for a given plan to succeed, an assumption must be made
that a given stakeholder will not challenge the results of the adjustment, or
that the courts will uphold the adjustment, or that other stakeholders
desire adjustments to some detail. The final lists of assumptions were to
be limited to the most critical and ranked according to importance and
degree of certainty.

   In the process of surfacing assumptions and stakeholders, each group
brought out key points that were closely related to their choice of a
particular plan for handling the undercount.

Discussion Points for Group A

Group A felt that an adjustment of the actual census counts would
perhaps set an unfortunate precedent for the future. Linked to this was
the feeling that an adjustment could lead to future politicization of census
statistics. The Bureau, even if not actually politicized, might be perceived
as having been unduly influenced by political considerations and particular power groups.

   A second ongoing concern reflected in Group A's discussion was the
possible effect of adjusted counts in small jurisdictions. Programs such as
EEO and education programs (i.e., issues surrounding the Bakke decision) may be instituted based on adjusted census counts of minorities,
although, in fact, it is possible that the counts were overinflated by the
adjustment in some areas. For example, in the case of an EEO program, it
is hypothetically possible that an employer may be asked to hire a certain
number of minority employees who only existed because of the adjustment but did not really live in that area. It was felt that the courts might, in
an extreme case, throw out the adjusted counts.

Discussion Points for Group B

One of the first concerns expressed by the group was that of the political
aspect of a detailed adjustment procedure. For the sake of argument, it
was suggested that with a Plan B type of convention, which uses imputa-

tion procedures, the door would not necessarily be open for further adjustment. In support of their convention, the group concurred that administrative and mechanical failure (e.g., lost documents) brought about the imputation procedures used in 1970 and that the Bureau is obligated to employ at least such measures. Thus the question of whether a purely enumerative census is possible was raised.

The legality and constitutionality of an adjustment procedure was questioned, debated, and it was concluded that in this context, distinctions must be made between the apportionment, funding, and information functions of the census. It was also pointed out that if the final decision is not to adjust the counts, the Bureau could provide detailed estimates of undercount. If the final decision is to adjust the counts, such procedures would necessarily be simplistic; refinement would come years after the actual adjustment. Furthermore, no method of assigning confidence intervals is available.

Discussion Points for Group C

Initially, Group C's discussion focused on the strategy they wished to defend; the adjustment of actual census counts based on national estimates of undercount by age, sex, race (Black/non-Black) and Spanish origin. The final plan, however, represented refinements based on assumptions made about the lack of availability of accurate estimates of the undercount for the Spanish, the Asian and Pacific Island Americans, and other minorities. At first, the group toyed with the idea of adjusting based on estimates of undercount for Spanish and Asian and Pacific Island Americans as well as race (Black and non-Black), age, and sex. These items are all 100% subjects, which would enable a more timely (i.e., faster) release of adjustments. Timely release was seen as a key selling point for Plan C. The crux of this discussion was presented in two assumptions: (1) there was no adequate data available for adjustments on Spanish origin, Asian and Pacific Island Americans, and other minority groups; (2) these minority groups will attack the Bureau for failing to adjust for their groups. The implications of these two assumptions are that adjustment plans must be defensible, that plans based on inadequate data will be indefensible, and that it is unreasonable to believe that adequate data from some "new" procedure will be available in the time frame considered in the plan (i.e., the early 1980s). These considerations led the group to drop Hispanic and Asian and Pacific Island Americans as components in its adjustment scheme. Various technical solutions had been explored to end the dilemma of not including Spanish in the adjustment plan, but none were considered feasible.

The group decided that it would be best to issue a set of unadjusted counts for Congressional apportionment. Adjustments for undercount should be made only after that time. Thus there would be two sets of 100% census data (one unadjusted and one adjusted) and one set of adjusted sample data. This approach, while opening the possibility of court challenges over government funding based on census data, was considered constitutional and technically feasible. The final Plan C incorporated the adjustment of microdata records, which means that all characteristics data would be adjusted along with adjustments of counts.

Discussion Points for Group D

The group rapidly agreed that two issues were involved in the adjustment decision: first, whether or not any adjustment should be made to the actual counts and, second, if an adjustment were to take place, then the process of adjustment should use the best available methodology. In this light, several of the working group members revealed that their second choice for a plan for the undercount had been Convention A. The decision to adjust was linked to the issue of timeliness of the release of the counts. Related to this, it was felt that two sets of counts would be prepared: one unadjusted count for congressional apportionment to meet the January 1, 1981 deadline and a second adjusted count for fund allocation and other legislative purposes. One of the reasons that the issue of an adjustment to the census was felt to be very important was that the differential undercount was well publicized.

This working group felt that an adjustment of actual counts should consider variables other than national undercounts by age, sex, and race. Any adjustment procedure should take into account that there are regional differences and other interrelated characteristics in the amount of undercount as well as differences as a result of degrees of urbanization and so on. So, the factor for adjustment should not be applied across the board because it applied to the nation as a whole, but should vary by area, and it should take into account other characteristics, such as Spanish origin and income.

A final point of discussion for this group was that a multivariate synthetic adjustment to the census counts might not be technically feasible for 1980, but the techniques should be developed soon to be incorporated into planning for future censuses.

DEBATE AND INFORMATION SOURCES

During the second day each group's assumptions and their relative importance and certainty were presented at a plenary session. During the presentations, clarifying questions were allowed, but no discussion of the merits of the assumptions was permitted.

After the presentation of the assumptions, the groups met individually to determine which of the assumptions presented, if true, would be most damaging to their group's convention. In another plenary session, the damaging assumptions were identified (see Exhibit 4-2 as an example), and a debate on these assumptions took place.

Although the importance and certainty of the damaging assumptions were the basis of the debate, the discussion centered around the adjustment versus nonadjustment question and the extent to which an adjustment procedure, if adopted, could be carried out (what characteristics would be used, at what geographic level estimates of undercoverage would be made, etc.). As a result of the discussion, seven issues that continually surfaced during the debate were determined to be crucial to the choice of a convention.

After identifying these crucial issues on the third morning, the plenary group determined what types of information might be necessary to remove uncertainties associated with each issue or assumption. The participants were encouraged to exercise their creative thought and to make suggestions regardless of their feasibility. The result of this was a list of about 20 measures or information sources for each identified issue or assumption that might further clarify each issue.

The following are some of the main issues identified, key discussion points, and selected examples of suggested information requirements and/or measures that may be taken on each issue.

Politicization   An adjustment procedure may damage the credibility of the Census Bureau in that it may be perceived as an attempt to politicize the census in deference to key stakeholders or interest groups. In response to this, it was suggested that the Bureau must maintain its neutrality and analytical integrity by recommending a consistent adjustment methodology of which the public is informed prior to the census. It was pointed out that, ultimately, the perception of politicization depends on where the decision comes from; that is, if the President recommends adjustment, the adjustment is likely to be perceived as a political issue and more likely to be perceived as a technical issue, which in fact any adjustment procedure would be.

Possible measures to be taken to clarify this issue include content analysis of news items and congressional mail related to the 1980 census, discussions with political leaders and interest groups, and conducting public opinion polls on the issue.

Statistical Defensibility   Each of the four proposed conventions has its statistical drawbacks. A simple headcount (Convention A) theoretically does not account for persons that the Bureau "knows" should be present but has no direct evidence for (e.g., from a sample vacancy check). An imputation procedure employing data from an independent source as well as knowledge gained from the census (Convention B) may ignore, as in 1970, the *differential* undercount of certain minority groups. A simple adjustment that applies a nationally derived undercount factor (Convention C) may overstate or understate the counts, especially below the State level. A synthethic adjustment, which relies on several detailed characteristics at a more detailed level (Convention D), could possibly be theoretically the most defensible adjustment procedure, but the methodology has not been defined and could thus be considered subjective or even arbitrary. Furthermore, there are no means for estimating the confidence intervals for either of the adjustment methods. For all methods there is an inverse relationship between the size of an area and the accuracy of the undercount estimates.

Some of the methods suggested for investigation to reduce uncertainty included construction of mathematical models; study of other statistics, such as the GNP, which involve imputation procedures; study of under-registration of births, deaths, and so on; empirical analysis of undercount techniques used in 1970. One information source mentioned that will be realized early next spring is the planned conference of demographers, statisticians, and other experts.

Legal Defensibility   The assumption was that any of the conventions chosen may be subject to court litigation, although the degree of certainty on this issue varied with each of the conventions. Although the probability of court action under Convention A is low, such a procedure may find the Bureau accountable to the charge that the "state of the art" was not applied to the enumerative process. Convention B's claim to precedence, since such a procedure was used in 1970 and not challenged in the courts, gave some support to its legal defensibility. Only since 1970, however, has the census assumed a critical role in the allocation of funds, and it may now be more vulnerable to legal scrutiny. Conventions C and D, in employing synthetic adjustment methods, essentially "create" persons in certain geographic areas, and this point could be disputed in court because of the function of the census as source of data for apportionment of congressional seats and allocation of funds.

Although this issue was assumed to be of great importance, its uncertainty was emphasized by the consensus of opinion that, while legal counsel is valuable on this issue, the actual outcome of a court decision is always dependent on the presiding judge.

Many of the measures mentioned that might clarify this issue, however, included seeking legal counsel from a variety of sources: the Justice Department, Department of Commerce counsel, Federal Judicial Center, minority group legal counsels, state attorneys general, and constitutional scholars. Other more unconventional measures included setting up a moot court with law students, generating a test case, and establishing a scholarship for forensic statistics.

Does Accuracy Lead to Equity?   The issue of politicization and statistical and legal defensibility led to this fundamental question. Again, this issue was debated in terms of the increasing use of census data in funds allocation and the census as the constitutionally mandated means for apportionment. It was felt that equity is only an issue in the function of the census in funds allocation. As a means of obtaining equity, ensuring the accuracy of the data becomes a high priority. In pursuing accuracy by adjusting data to the 39,500 general purpose local governments, however, the Bureau may actually be moving farther away from this goal. To support this position, available empirical evidence was discussed. As has already been mentioned in the statistical defensibility issue, there are no means of estimating error on the adjustment procedures. Furthermore, in a detailed adjustment procedure, there will be many small jurisdictions that stand to lose minimally but only a few large jurisdictions that stand to gain substantially in terms of funds allocation. Also, there is no evidence that the undercount is confined to large cities; the undercount is also a regional phenomenon and is concentrated in the South. A detailed adjustment procedure would probably have the largest impact on improving population counts in the South. A final point was made that only Convention D proposes to include some sample characteristics, such as income, in the adjustment procedure.

To further clarify this issue, some suggested measures were to confer with legislatures about equity concerns, to perform simulations of the results of various adjustment procedures and analyze their impact on funding allocations, to conduct economic welfare analysis of the impact of adjustments on "winners" and "losers" in funds allocation, and to examine literature on the concept of equity in statistics.

Timeliness of Data Availability   The Census Bureau is required by law to release population counts by January 1, 1981 for use in apportionment of congressional districts. Other uses of census data for funds allocation, statistical analysis, and publications do not have such a pressing deadline. The issue of timeliness thus brought up the possibility of production of multiple data sets. Congress and the state legislatures might want to postpone reapportionment until adjusted counts under Convention D become available for this purpose; otherwise, they would have to use the actual counts. For other census data users, however, where timeliness may not be as important as the best possible count, there is pressure for adjusted counts. Timeliness is principally an issue for Convention D, which requires data analysis before adjustments are made.

Some information sources mentioned included consulting funds allocating agencies, congressional committees, and other countries that have experienced delays in releasing their census counts. Some possible measures to take were to analyze the impact of delayed data release on Federal, state, and local governments, as well as on the business community, and to exhaust all possibilities of expediting an adjustment procedure, if adopted.

Public Demand for Adjustment   The public demand for adjustment has primarily come from representatives of organized minority groups, such as the Blacks, who had a 7.7 undercoverage rate in 1970, and the Spanish origin population. The White population, which has the smaller relative undercount (1.9%), may not perceive such a need for adjustment, especially in view of the weight given to minority adjustment.

At a local level, persons residing in large cities where the undercount is acknowledged to be relatively high would demand some adjustment, and the situation is not clear for small places and rural areas. Given a fixed amount of dollars to be allocated by population distribution, small areas might stand to lose dollars as the population counts for governmental jurisdictions are adjusted.

Some suggestions for clarifying this issue included reviewing past public opinion polls on this subject, conducting new polls, discussing adjustment with minority groups, ethicists, political scientists, and religious leaders, and assessing the impact of adjustment (or nonadjustment) on EEO and affirmative action programs.

Congressional Demand for Adjustment   On a more definite and explicit level, Congress represents the same diversity of interests as the public on the question of adjustment. Since it is a legislative body, it is in the unique position of mandating an adjustment or even rejecting the census figures. In addition to having a personal interest in the figures used for apportionment, Members of Congress use census population figures as elements of fund allocation formulas. Moreover, some congressional members may feel that additional expenditures for adjustment nullify previously funded coverage improvement measures.

To clarify the importance of this issue, the Census Bureau may encourage congressional hearings on pending census and related legislation, review the legislative history of funds allocation based on census data, and review the events following the 1920 census, when Congress rejected the census counts. A final suggestion was made to review all the ideas proposed thus far in light of the visibility of the Census Bureau.

Conclusion

The Undercount Adjustment Workshop was successful in surfacing assumptions, many of which had been implicit prior to the conference. As a result of this process Bureau management personnel have a better understanding of the issues and assumptions involved in adjustment procedures. The relative importance of the various factors involved in adjustment have been explored, and a prioritized list is being prepared of information needs and sources that would be required for a final decision. Work also is under way to determine what information gathering techniques are feasible, given the resources available.

PHARMACEUTICAL COMPANY PRICING ISSUE

This case involves a drug company that was faced with a major pricing policy decision on an important product. The decision would have vast impact on the economic structure of the entire company. As a result, the decision required analyses of the entire internal financial structure of the company, as well as market considerations.

When the problem surfaced, there were already three existent and significant groups of managers within the drug company, each of which had a significantly different policy with respect to the pricing of the drug. Groups included: (1) the high-price group, (2) the low-price group, and (3) the mid-price group. Each group was making, unbeknownst to themselves and to the others, very different macroassumptions regarding important stakeholders and had very different detailed microassumptions about the problem. These three natural groups were formed into SAST groups. Stakeholder analysis was used to identify the assumptions of each group. The groups were asked to consider all the parties who might affect or be affected by an important decision. They listed as many parties or interest groups as they could who had a stake in the policy under con-

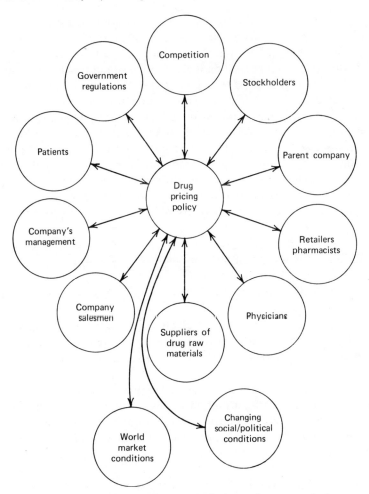

Figure 4-1   Functional stakeholder analysis for a pharmaceutical company.

sideration. For the most part, drug company categories are generic and, with little modification, apply to many business situations (see Figure 4-1). In the present case, the retailers are pharmacists, although it turned out it was important to differentiate between large-scale, chain retailers and small-scale, singly owned pharmaceutical outlets.

It can be seen from Figure 4-1 that the pricing policy is greatly affected by what is assumed about each of the stakeholder categories. For instance, it is difficult to support a policy of raising the price of the drug if it is assumed that the physician is price-sensitive to the needs of patients. In fact, the whole point of getting managers to identify important stakeholders is to help them confront the important question: What is it that you have been assuming about the stakeholders or that you have had to assume about them so that starting from these assumptions as premises you are able to derive your policy? In response to this question, the high-price group assumed that ''the physician prescribed the best quality drug for the patient.'' The low-price group assumed that ''the physician prescribes the lowest price drug that will serve the patient's needs.'' Finally the mid-price group assumed that, ''the physician was satisfied with the current price since it represented a good trade-off between price and quality.'' The controversy underlying these differences in assumptions among groups led to the stakeholder ''physician'' being rated as very important but also as very uncertain by each group. This became a major issue in the debate.

As a result of the SAST process two critical issues emerged that were significant for the choice of a pricing policy. These were:

1 How does the price of the drug affect the physicians' prescription behavior?
2 Will the parent company (of which the drug company was a subsidiary) provide the finances, advertising, and general administrative support necessary for the company to execute each strategy?

The second issue was resolved when the parent company indicated a preference for supporting a high-price lower volume business. The first was resolved through a careful analysis of the regret (see Chapter 5) involved in choosing each option. Here the final decision turned on a critical assumption concerning the physician's perception of price. The group finally coalesced on the assumption that if the price were raised and then subsequently lowered for market reasons the physician would still prescribe the drug. However, once the price of the drug was lowered the company could not raise the price and still expect the physician to prescribe it (see Chapter 5). As a result of this debate, the company decided to raise the price.

Chapter Five

Strategic Assumption Surfacing and Testing Procedures

This chapter describes in detail the typical operation of a SAST process. We do not attempt to describe all of the many variations that are possible with the process. Each application must be designed to meet the needs of the organization doing the planning. Potential users are also encouraged to experiment with the procedure outlined. When in doubt, users should examine their reasons for wanting to apply the procedure differently. One should ask such questions as: Would such a variation make sense to me if I were an *unwilling* participant in the process? A *willing* participant?

Exhibit 5-1 shows the schedule for a typical SAST workshop of $3\frac{1}{2}$ days duration. While some of the end steps, in particular the last half day, may be shortened or eliminated, the initial activities are critical and cannot be shortened or bypassed. In this chapter, we shall describe the conduct of the SAST method as though it follows the procedure outlined in Exhibit 5-1. We shall indicate at the appropriate points in the process some of the kinds of departures which can be made.

In general, although there is no fixed amount of time that must be rigidly adhered to for each activity, we do suggest that the sequencing of activities and the time allotted to them generally be followed as indicated. Careful thought based on our experience has been given to the amount of time required for each activity. Each step has specific purposes that must be achieved before a subsequent step can be undertaken effectively. As a rule, each step of the SAST process has been grounded in the best social science knowledge available. There is not only an intellectual rationale for each step, but a behavioral reason for doing it as well. These reasons are summarized as we proceed so that the reader can learn not only "what" is to be done "when," but also "why," and for what purpose as well.

Exhibit 5-1 A Typical Workshop Schedule for SAST

Time	Session*	Activity	Comment
Evening of Day 1: Introductory and Preparatory Activities			
5:00–6:00 P.M.	I	Refreshments	
6:00–7:30 P.M.	P	Dinner	
7:30–7:45 P.M.	P	Introduction	Chief Executive Officer
7:45–8:15 P.M.	P	Review of SAST method via a case study	Facilitator 1 Facilitator 2
8:15–9:15 P.M.	P	Group formation preliminaries 1. Nominal group technique: issue generation	Facilitator 1 Facilitator 2
9:15–10:00 P.M	P	2. Rating of issues: data for forming groups	Facilitator 1 Facilitator 2
Day 2: Group Formation, Assumption Surfacing, and Evaluation			
8:00–9:00 A.M.	I	Breakfast	
9:00–9:30 A.M.	P	Work groups formed	Feedback to participants of the result of the cluster analyses used to form groups
9:30–10:30 A.M.	G	Work in groups-tasks	Give your group a name. Identify the group's major themes. Evaluate the strengths, weaknesses, opportunities and threats (S.W.O.T.'s) resulting from the assumptions of the strategy from the point of view of your group's major themes. Propose extensions to the strategy from the point of view of your group's identified S.W.O.T.'s.
10:30–11:30 A.M.	I	Coffee break	
11:30–12:00 noon	P	Each group reports its results	
12:00–1:30 P.M.	P	Lunch	

Exhibit 5-1 (*Continued*)

Time	Session*	Activity	Comment
Day 2 (*Continued*)			
1:30–2:00 P.M.	P	Presentation of stakeholder and assumption surfacing methodology	Facilitator 1 Facilitator 2
2:00–6:00 P.M.	G	Assumption generation and plotting	Identify 7–10 stakeholders and at least one "low probability, high risk" stakeholder. Generate two or three assumptions for each stakeholder *and* specify counterassumptions. Evaluate and plot assumptions on importance-certainty graph. Prepare a 20 minute presentation for next day including charts of key stakeholders, assumptions, importance, and certainty.
6:30–7:15 P.M.	I	Refreshments	
7:15–8:30 P.M.	P	Dinner	

Day 3: Presentation of Analyses and Debate of Assumptions

Time	Session	Activity	Comment
8:00–9:00 A.M.	I	Breakfast	
9:00–11:00 A.M.	P	Each group presents its 20 minute report	Clarifying questions only (coffee break about 10:00)
11:00–12:00 noon	G	Identify damaging assumptions	Review the three other groups' assumptions. Identify the five to seven assumptions that conflict most with your assumptions or do the most damage to your group's concept of the strategy.
12:00–1:30 P.M.	P	Lunch	
1:30–2:30 P.M.	P	Each group reports on damaging assumptions	Solicit in round-robin manner, record on flip chart.

Exhibit 5-1 *(Continued)*

Time	Session*	Activity	Comment
Day 3 (*Continued*)			
2:30–3:00 P.M.	I	Coffee break	
3:00–6:00 P.M.	P	Debate on assumptions	Open discussion and debate on pivotal and damaging assumptions.
			Identify and list crucial issues that the strategy *must* resolve.
6:00–7:00 P.M.	I	Refreshments	
7:00–8:30 P.M.	P	Dinner	
Day 4: Integration of Assumptions and Identification of Carry-on Activities			
8:00–9:00 A.M.	I	Breakfast	
9:00–9:45 A.M.	P	Form "integration" groups, G-2	New groups are formed, each with at least one representative from previous groups.
		Brief presentation on synthesis, collaboration, and team-work	Facilitator
9:45–10:00 A.M.	I	Coffee break	
10:00–12:00 noon	G-2	Strategy improvement	Derive an integrative strategy that will resolve as many of the issues identified throughout these sessions as possible. Get the best of all possible worlds!!
12:00–1:30 P.M.	P	Lunch	
1:30–2:30 P.M.	P	Group presentations	
2:30–3:00 P.M.	I	Coffee break	
3:00–5:00 P.M.	P	Action steps	Identify carry-on activities
			Identify information requirements for tracking and monitoring assumptions.
			Assign task forces as needed.

*Session code: I = individual; P = plenary; G = groups.

As Exhibit 5-1 shows, the SAST process may be conceived of as proceeding in five broad phases:

0   Pre-Meeting Activities.
I   Introductory and Preparatory Activities.
II Group Formation, Assumption Surfacing, and Evaluation.
III Presentation of Analyses and Debate of Assumptions.
IV Integration of Assumptions and Identification of Carry-on Activities.

Each of these phases is discussed in detail.

PHASE 0: PRE-MEETING ACTIVITIES

Preparations

At least 6 weeks before the SAST session is to take place, the facilitators should meet with the executives in charge and other key parties in the planning process. The parties should be given a full briefing on the SAST process. It is important at this stage that the facilities to be used for the SAST sessions are identified and reserved. It is necessary to have a meeting room large enough to hold the entire group for plenary sessions and enough breakout rooms to accommodate the working groups. Ideally, these rooms are rather close together.

Good logistics are essential to the effective running of a SAST session. Typically, a communications center must be set up to handle and screen incoming calls for the executives involved. Typing and reproducing facilities are needed. Easels, flip chart, pads, magic markers, masking tape, notebooks, pencils, and so on should be available in adequate supply. Breaks, meals, and refreshments should be well planned. If at all possible, the SAST sessions should be held "off-site" in order to free people from the confinements and distractions of their offices. This may mean that lodging accommodations are required as well.

Who and How Many?

The SAST process requires six people at a bare minimum. This makes two groups of three. Twelve is better with three groups of four. We have found that beyond about 35 participants the process becomes rather unwieldy. The optimal number appears to be 18 to 24. About five to seven people seem to make the best working groups.

In general the participants should be selected so that they represent all of the relevant perspectives on the problem and the different skills and know-how necessary to implement a solution. Obviously, the key executives and their principal staff members and advisers should be involved. Beyond that, people who have special insight into possible technical, financial, marketing, social-cultural, personnel, operational, competitive, legal, aesthetic, and other aspects of the problem should be included. Also, people who are known to be reflective, creative, or holistic in their thinking should be considered. In general, the participant list should encompass enough authoritative and political power within the organization to formulate and carry out policy, enough creativity to stimulate new thinking, and enough direct experience to infuse the process with reality.

Prior to the meeting, the highest ranking executive involved should formally invite the participants to attend and strongly encourage them to arrange their schedules so that they can be present for all sessions. We have generally done this with a letter and follow-up telephone call. Accompanying the letter is a packet of background materials on the SAST process, planning methods, and the substantive issue involved. The participants are asked to read and review this material prior to the session.

This is the proper place to comment on the critical role of the facilitator of a SAST exercise. If the size of a group is above six, we believe it is advisable to have at least two facilitators. It is a principle of group dynamics that it is very difficult, if not impossible at times, to work with a group and accurately gauge one's effect on the group at the same time. While one facilitator is explaining something to a group, the other can be assessing its effect on the group.

Another way to put this is to say that it is very difficult to process the *substantive content* of a group's output and the group's *interpersonal dynamics* at the same time. Two facilitators are a necessity in this regard.

PHASE I: INTRODUCTORY AND PREPARATORY ACTIVITIES

The purposes of Phase I are:

1 To explain to the participants in concrete yet general terms the overall nature of the SAST process and why it is especially applicable to strategic management questions.
2 To elicit the active cooperation, motivation, and involvement of the participants in the SAST process.
3 To explain the necessity for applying the SAST process to the participants' particular problem or business/policy situation and to provide a

justification for the participants' involvement in time and in cost to them and to their organization.

4 To outline in general terms what it is that the participants will be doing over the next several days and why.

5 To describe what it is that the SAST participants are expected to accomplish by describing the expected outcomes and benefits of the process.

6 To conduct a Nominal Group Technique (NGT) exercise to obtain information for forming different working groups, each of which should take explicitly different perspectives on the issues under debate.

It is critical to the success of the SAST process to have the support of the highest ranking executive who is concerned or charged with managing the set of issues under discussion. If the highest ranking executive is lukewarm or negative towards the process, for example, or if he or she views it as a waste of time or a nuisance, then this attitude will be inevitably conveyed to the participants. The most effective sessions occur when the chief executive officer (CEO) is supportive, communicates that support to others, and then follows up on the results. At a minimum, the CEO should state the objectives he or she has for the session and the fact that the results will be used later. The CEO should also be present for all the sessions. Most CEO's have found that their active participation in one of the groups has been a rewarding and educational experience. Conversely, although the support and understanding of the highest ranking executive is critical, it alone cannot make up for deficiencies that may be due to the organization's current make-up and functioning or for a poor execution of the process.

The SAST process has been primarily designed to help those organizations that are functioning at some acceptable level of peformance and internal member satisfaction. If the conflicts over issues and the disputes between policies are primarily due to poor communication patterns, poor staff relationships, a breakdown of interpersonal roles, and so on, then basic organizational development (OD) or team-building is called for. It must be stressed that the SAST process is not a cure-all, nor was it intended to be, for every organizational ill or problem. The best planning process in the world will not work miracles in a poorly functioning organization. Although the SAST process can be used to help an organization confront interpersonal issues, it should be stressed that this must be done under the close supervision of a trained interpersonal facilitator. Organizational development requires someone who has extensive training and experience in group and organizational dynamics. The exploration of feelings in group settings is not something to be performed by a novice.

The ideal background for a SAST process leader is someone who has had extensive training and experience in both OD and planning methodologies. At a minimum, a SAST process leader needs to be sensitive to and respect human feelings. He or she also needs to appreciate interpersonal conflict and to understand planning.

Executive's Introduction

It is generally necessary to meet with the highest ranking executive several times prior to the introductory session. The CEO should understand the process in as much detail as is required to secure his or her explicit cooperation. The necessity for the executive's making a few, brief, introductory remarks as to the importance of the effort is covered. Further, the executive is informed that he or she may be called on by the facilitator to make additional motivating remarks throughout the process if and when the need develops.

   Immediately after the highest ranking executive's remarks stressing the importance he or she attaches to participation in the process, one of the facilitators explains very briefly the reasons for participation in the kind of process represented by SAST. Most of these reasons are covered in Chapter 3. The main point to emphasize is the need for examining assumptions as the organization's managerial problems become more and more complex; in addition, managerial problems are not of the kind where everything can be known with certainty prior to taking action and therefore on a substantial base of assumptions. These assumptions must be uncovered, challenged, and tested via some appropriate means. It is further emphasized that SAST was purposefully developed for the purpose of treating assumptions.

Case Study Review

The second facilitator then takes about a half-hour to explain the general SAST process by means of the Majestic Metals case discussed in Chapter 3. This method of presentation is generally effective. We have found that a *concrete* case is the best way for presenting a *general* methodology to practicing managers. Furthermore, the Majestic Metals case is so general that it can be easily extended or modified to make it applicable to the particular situation of the participants. Alternative cases to be used for this purpose are contained in Chapter 4.

   It is important to stress that the process is only presented in general terms at this time. The participants are informed that they will be going through the same general series of steps that the participants in the

Majestic Metals case did. Exhibit 5-1 can be passed out at this time or even prior to the introductory session to give the participants a feel for the concrete program.

Although the program can always be modified to take into account the special needs of the participants, it is important to avoid bargaining over the program content. This can become a dangerous and never-ending trap. On the one hand, a facilitator must display sensitivity and openness to individual needs. On the other, a facilitator must not come across as spineless and easily pushed around.

We prefer to avoid program bargaining if it occurs. Our general response is to say gently but firmly, "We have tried this format many times in the past, and we know it works. Let's get into it and then evaluate how it is working for you. We can make changes later, but first let's give it a chance." More elaboration at this point will rarely help, but will merely come across as defensive.

Extreme resistance or hostility to trying the process may be a sign that other interventions such as OD are called for. If there is extreme hostility, the facilitators have reason to ask why they are the special object of it. They are, after all, merely proposing a technique that they hope will be helpful to the participants. A trained facilitator is one who knows how to respond to such hostility without taking it personally.

Most groups do not respond with overt hostility but rather with a mixture of curiosity and a "wait-and-see" attitude. At this point, the expected and desired outcomes of the process are explained. The typical outcomes of a SAST process are:

1   A deeper understanding of the current assumptions that have been driving the organization, the business, the interaction with the environment, and so on.

2   A deeper understanding of alternative sets of assumptions by means of which a business can also be run or in terms of which the organization can be conceived.

3   A deeper understanding and appreciation of the fact that not everyone in the organization conceives of the business in the same way and why it is important to seek out and to respect such differences as an important input to the planning process.

4   An explicit analysis of assumptions in terms of their relative importance and certainty as the assumptions affect a business plan.

5   A prioritized list of *commonly understood and shared* assumptions.

6   A new, and, hopefully, richer plan based on an expanded set of shared assumptions.

7 An action plan for gathering more information from the environment in order to revise both the importance and the certainty of the shared assumptions.

8 The ability to put forth a stronger case for one's business plan based on the fact that differences in assumptions have been explored and aired (this is especially important in companies with decentralized planning systems, which require divisions to present and defend their plans to headquarters).

9 A checkpoint at which the process will be repeated if it is decided that the assumptions newly agreed on are not working out.

In short, the SAST process is designed to define the objectives of a business plan, to expose the strengths and weaknesses in a plan, to define market research needs for testing out a proposed plan, to show the interactions between assumptions, data, and decisions, and to allow for the tracking of key, uncertain elements in a plan as effectively as possible. (See, for example, Schendel, 1979, for a discussion of the need for this kind of assumption review.)

Group Formation Preliminaries

The introductory session terminates with one of the most critical activities of all, the conduct of an abbreviated Nominal Group Technique exercise (Delbecq and Van de Ven, 1971; Van de Ven and Delbecq, 1971). The NGT exercise is important for a number of reasons:

1 It helps to set the tone for participation.
2 It allows the diversity of ideas within the larger group to be publicly expressed and seen.
3 It provides the necessary input for breaking the larger group down into smaller planning groups.

SAST is above all a *participative* planning process. The SAST process leaders are present mainly for the purpose of helping the participants to bring forth, explore, and challenge *their* assumptions. The facilitators cannot determine "the correct" assumptions for the organization, because there is no single set of "correct" assumptions. The determination of an "appropriate" set of assumptions is a decision that must be made by the participants themselves.

Participation is not a luxury or a nicety in the SAST process. It is required. Complex organizations facing complex problems in complex environments require equally complex, but understandable, plans in order to manage their problems. Diversity of input from a variety of differing perspectives within an organization is a valuable and necessary source in order to formulate complex plans and in order to implement such plans successfully. Complex problems require the input of more than one individual if they are to be formulated appropriately and if they are to be implemented without resistance throughout an organization. No single individual, no matter how powerful he or she is (or think they may be), can command strict allegiance, let alone deep internalization, of any plan. Without cooperation of some form, complex organizations are stymied. The social science literature is quite effective in pointing this out time and time again.

The NGT exercise is conducted by asking each individual to take 5 to 10 minutes to generate and write down on a piece of paper three to ten issues that he thinks are critical to the plan or problem under discussion. Participants are urged to write down what each of them individually thinks is important, whether it will be of concern to others or not. Also they are strongly encouraged to write down as many unconventional or creative ideas as possible.

From the very beginning, the facilitators should stress that one of the prime benefits of the process as a whole is the chance to explore novel assumptions and ideas. The purpose of SAST is not to restate and confirm the obvious but to probe the unexamined and the previously "taken for granted." Thus the facilitators must from the very beginning set up an atmosphere of creativity, of risk-taking, of exploration. The participants must continually be urged to stretch their ideas and to see the broader picture.

After 5 to 10 minutes, the facilitators go around the room and ask each individual in turn to submit one issue, idea, or question that is of concern to that person. No debate is encouraged on the issues. If something is an issue for one person, then it is an issue and is written on a public list. Questions of clarification are permitted so that others can understand a person's thinking.

Everyone has the opportunity to submit at least one issue. Furthermore, at the end of the final listing of ideas, everyone will have the opportunity to vote with regard to the top five to ten issues he finds most important to consider. Debate is prohibited at this point in the process since it usually has the effect of inhibiting the production of new and challenging ideas. If anything, the respondents are encouraged to formulate new ideas as a result of witnessing the shared list.

The NGT exercise usually terminates after each person has had the opportunity to contribute approximately three ideas. In an initial group of 20 people, this means that a list will contain 60 or more items.

If possible, it is advisable to reduce the list of 60 or so ideas to five to ten critical issues on which everyone can then vote. To accomplish this, it may be possible to state certain issues in the form of polar opposites so that everyone can agree with importance of the issue as a whole but still take different stands on how to treat the issue specifically. For instance, everyone might agree that "marketing" is an important ingredient of any plan, but some people might prefer to market a product directly through their corporation, implying the creation of their own distribution channels, whereas others might prefer to use existing dealer networks. Thus the real issue is that of "dealers versus direct sales." The participants can indicate which end of the issue they consider most important to their outlook. In a similar fashion, people can state whether they wish to be a member of a group that will make the strongest or best case "in support of" an existing plan or to go into a group that will make the strongest case "against" a particular plan.

After the issues have been summarized, each person is asked to vote for the five to ten issues that are of most importance to him. Which of these issues should the plan treat explicitly? The votes of the individuals are tabulated later and used to form smaller working groups. The groups are constructed on the basis of similarity of profiles. All those individuals who tend to have the same perception of the importance of issues are placed in a similar group. This tends to ensure that those individuals who are motivated to make the strongest case for a particular position will be put together.

Putting like-minded individuals in the same group has the general effect of strengthening a particular outlook and hence of strengthening the underlying assumptions behind an outlook. If anything, we want the assumptions supporting an outlook to be strengthened as much as possible for then we have a better opportunity to observe them. Assumptions can always be softened later to make them "more reasonable," but it is hard to soften that which is invisible or never stated.

It is essential to create groups that will take different stands on issues. We want to ensure that issues are viewed from as many perspectives as possible and supported by as much clear and pertinent data as possible. Normally, such differences are not encouraged in organizations or used productively. This does not mean that differences between individuals do not exist. They do. Rather, most organizations do not know how to tap such differences and make effective use of them. The NGT is part of a technology—a *behavioral* technology for making use of the differences between people to create different working groups that will *explicitly* take different positions on issues. If the differences between individuals are not great to begin with, then this must be pointed out to the group as a whole; a broadening of the participants and perspectives is suggested. The creation or the existence of differences is critical to the SAST process. The motto behind the process is *When everyone thinks alike, no one is thinking!* Differences must be encouraged and supported in order to challenge assumptions.

It is important to note that careful consideration must be given to the scheduling of the first evening's activities. Enough time must be allotted to allow the participants to report *on time* so that the NGT exercise can be accomplished by the end of the first evening. Otherwise, the formation of the working groups will be delayed to the following day and the next day's activities delayed accordingly.

The NGT exercise may be streamlined under certain conditions. If there are already naturally existing groups that are taking different positions in an organization, this knowledge can be used to speed up the process. If, however, the groups are taking essentially the same position, then it is best to reconstitute them along the lines just discussed. The NGT exercise may be streamlined if extensive, previous groundwork has been done. That is, the organization may feel it has an idea of what the issues are, but not know how to resolve them. However, even in this case we have learned not to take the claims of an organization at face value. Most people have not been trained to probe beneath issues or to know how to encourage the surfacing of positions different from that of their own, let alone how to synthesize different positions. It is quite a different matter to bring forth issues in a collective group setting that has been especially constituted for that purpose. Most groups think, as a matter of course, that they know how to surface issues. This attitude has to be overcome as gently as possible. Most groups do not realize that they can benefit from assistance in learning how to get the most out of their own internal resources, that is, the group itself.

The introductory phase ends with the processing of the NGT data by the facilitators, that is, with the running of a computer program in order to constitute the working groups, which are formed the first thing the next day. Since the processing of the NGT data takes about a half-hour, it thus becomes critical to allow enough scheduling time for completing this task. Running the computer program normally takes place after the introductory phase has been terminated for the evening. Before departing, the participants are told that the NGT data will be used to put them into working groups that will, it is hoped, take very different perspectives on the issues. Thus it should be noted that the participants are given complete information on the steps of the SAST process and the reasons for them *at the appropriate time*. There is no reason to discuss everything at once, since this leads to information overload. On the other hand, disseminating the information inevitably creates a certain amount of anxiety because there is always natural curiosity about "what's going to happen next." Also, not being told everything at once can create the impression of secrecy. These feelings are also quite natural. The facilitators must realize that these feelings are present and are to be expected; however, they should not give in to the anxiety of the group. They must say, gently but firmly, "We will share with you what we will do and the reasons for it as we proceed through the process. We have to get into it before it becomes clear." The facilitators must steer a course between saying too much and too little. Above all, they must avoid being paternalistic; at the same time, however, they must make it clear they are not withholding information, merely saving it for the appropriate time of release. There are no firm rules in this area since in the first and last instance we are dealing with people with different needs. The facilitators must use their "clinical experience in dealing with groups," as it were, to gauge the needs, the abilities, and the readiness of a particular group to learn.

PHASE II: GROUP FORMATION, ASSUMPTION SURFACING, AND EVALUATION

The purposes of Phase II are as follows:

1 To form working groups that will develop different perspectives with regard to the set of issues under discussion.
2 To surface the assumptions underlying a particular group's perspective by means of the concept of stakeholders.
3 To show the relative importance and certainty of assumptions by means of a simple graphic plot.
4 To prepare a 20 to 30 minute presentation on each perspective in terms of the stakeholder concept and the plotting of assumptions.

Group Instructions

The results of the analysis of NGT are presented to the participants as a whole immediately after the convening of the second day's activities. The number of planning groups that emerge from the computer analysis is presented, and the names of the individuals assigned to each group are read off. Each working group is given a separate room, if possible, so they can begin work without interference and contamination from the other groups. Each working group needs a flip chart, pads, marking pencils, and a supply of forms. Ideally, each group will also have a reporter to take notes and summarize events. Usually, however, one or more of the participants records on the flip chart.

Before departing to their separate rooms, each group is told to give itself an identifying name, theme, or label that best expresses its distinctive character. The label should emphasize the group's particular approach or in some way set it off from the other groups. As trivial as this step may appear, it is crucial for producing a sense of unification and group spirit. Indeed, the low sense of spirit that characterizes so many organizations shows that this step is not frivolous.

The groups are also instructed before departing to identify the major themes that cut across their particular subsets of issues and to expand on them. That is, the groups are initially formed on the basis of a limited analysis of an NGT exercise (i.e., that subset of issues that different groups endorse as important to them). *The purpose of the NGT exercise is primarily to get the SAST process going.* The groups should not be misled into believing that there are *only* 60 or so important issues in a strategy. The contention of a fixed number of issues would be absurd and patently false. From the first evening when the NGT exercise is begun to the end of the group work, it should be stressed continually that the groups will be given a number of opportunities to add to their initial lists.

At this point the groups are told also to add issues to their lists that will further sharpen their particular group's perspective. Again, we wish to do everything in our power to widen the differences between the groups. Finally the groups are told to evaluate the strengths, weaknesses, opportunities, and threats resulting from their group's perspective and/or their organization's initial strategy if it has one.

This is a great deal to accomplish in an hour. If necessary, the group work can easily be extended into the morning coffee break (see Exhibit 5-1). However, it is best to cut this activity off after no more than 2 hours in order to allow the groups to reconvene. The purpose is to check whether the groups are really taking different perspectives and to reorient them if they are not. This can usually be done through some minor issue-trading between groups or by groups agreeing to take on or argue for a particular perspective.

In general, we have found that the orientations that different groups take can be described in terms of three simple dimensions. Figure 5-1 depicts the first two dimensions. The first dimension is a micro-macro one. This concerns whether a group's natural focus is on (1) the *individual*

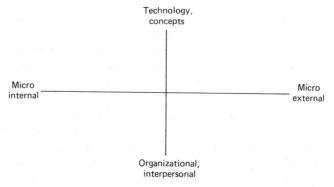

Figure 5-1 Strategy orientation.

components of an organization, process, or structure or (2) the organization, process, or structure taken as a *whole*. While the microperspective focuses on the specificity and concreteness of the parts and tends to treat the parts in isolation from one another, the macro is more concerned with capturing the spirit and sense of the whole than with making detailed statements about particular aspects of the organization, the environment, and the problems of both.

The second dimension is a "people" versus "technology" one. The difference is whether a group takes as its primary object of concern technical concepts and abstract ideas or organizational and interpersonal concerns. The technological focus tends to concern itself primarily with structures; the organizational, with people and interpersonal issues as they affect strategy.

Finally, groups differ in their postures of support with regard to existing plans. Some groups, we have found, tend to take a natural position of *arguing in support of* existing strategies; others adopt an attitude of *criticizing and challenging* them.

There are eight possible combinations for classifying participants according to these three binary dimensions. As an ideal, it would be desirable to have all eight extreme perspectives represented in a planning effort so that each perspective would be both represented and challenged. In practice, this will not always be possible, but it should be kept in mind. In fact, we have added three questions that tap these dimensions to the list of issues generated by the NGT in order to assess where people stand on them. For instance, it is a simple matter to briefly explain Figure 5-1 to people and ask them on which end of each dimension they tend to fall.

When explaining the typology of Figure 5-1, or any other typology, it is important to emphasize that no one quadrant is better than *any* of the others. They are merely different. This is often one of the strongest reasons for involving outside consultants or facilitators in the running of a SAST exercise. The facilitators are neutral. They have no stake in any one of the cells. They should ensure that the viewpoints of all cells are heard and appreciated.

After lunch, one of the facilitators takes roughly half an hour to go over the stakeholder concept once again in order to prepare the groups to use it in detail. If one has used the Majestic Metals case to introduce the SAST concept on the first evening, then one of the other cases described in Chapter 4 can be used at this point.

Stakeholder Generation

The generation of stakeholders is one of the key tasks in the application of the SAST approach. The reason is that *stakeholders are* the concrete entities that affect and in turn are affected by a policy. As such, they can be rather easily visualized by most people. While it can be difficult to "see" assumptions, most people can rather easily generate a set of stakeholders that bears on their perspective. From the stakeholders, it is but a short step to assumptions. *Assumptions are the characteristic properties of stakeholders that must be posited or hypothesized as premises in order to derive a strategy or a policy.*

There are several methods for generating a comprehensive list of stakeholders. In order to limit the discussion, we present seven that span the range of approaches. These are: (1) imperative, (2) positional, (3) reputational, (4) social participation, (5) opinion-leadership, (6) demographic, and (7) organizational.

The imperative approach is based on the notion of revealed interest. To use this method, one makes a list of as many as possible of the imperatives, slogans, and catchwords that have been uttered in the context of a policy issue. Also identified are any acts of defiance (e.g., strikes, sit-ins, and lying in front of trucks) or other actions that suggest dissatisfaction with the policy system. The *sources* of the imperatives and acts are identified and each is considered as a potential stakeholder. The deficiency of this method is that it misses silent stakeholders who may nevertheless have a strong opinion on the policy issue. Its advantage is that it identifies those who feel needs strongly and act on them.

The positional approach identifies those who occupy formal positions in the policy-making structure, whether internal or external to the organization, for example, government. Organization charts and legal documents are a good source for this method. The deficiency of this approach is that it ignores important information stakeholders, that is, those who are not formally a part of the organization and yet have an impact on it.

The reputational approach is a sociometric one. It entails asking various knowledgeable or important persons to nominate those whom they believe have a stake in the system. The deficiency here is that unorganized, nonelite, and disenfranchised groups may be ignored.

The social-participation approach identifies individuals or organizations as stakeholders to the extent that they participate in activities related to a policy issue. Membership in organizations or committees, attendance at meetings, voting, and other instances of observable behavior are taken as evidence of having a potential stake in an issue. The obvious deficiency of this approach is that many latent, currently nonparticipatory stakeholders (e.g., the "silent majority" or future generations) will be overlooked.

Since one of the reasons for identifying stakeholders is to assess their leverage and influence in the policy system, it is sometimes adequate to identify only those who tend to shape the opinions of other stakeholders. The opinion-leadership method does this. This approach has the advantage of identifying important stakeholders who are not part of the formal structure or do not have the same status as those selected by previous methods. Its disadvantage is that it is less precise and requires more judgment on the part of the analyst than some of the other methods do.

The demographic approach identifies stakeholders by such characteristics as age, sex, race, occupation, religion, place of birth, and level of education. For many policy, planning, and strategy issues, these distinctions are necessary, since it is to be expected that a policy will have a different impact on different demographic groups. The disadvantage of this approach is that it assumes homogeneity of interest within any particular group.

The last method selects a focal organization in the policy system and identifies the individuals and organization who have important relationships with the focal organization. Typical relationships are those of (1) supplier, (2) employee, (3) customer or client, (4) ally, (5), competitor or adversary, (6) regulator or controller (e.g., government), and (7) regulatee or controllee (e.g., subdivisions of a parent organization, legally controlled entities). The advantage of this approach is that it identifies potential parties or elements that other approaches can overlook. It has the disadvantage of not being comprehensive and of potentially missing some key stakeholders such as opinion-leaders.

Using these seven methods, we have found several techniques that facilitate the generation of stakeholders. Each group usually starts by making a list on the flip chart. When this process bogs down, we suggest

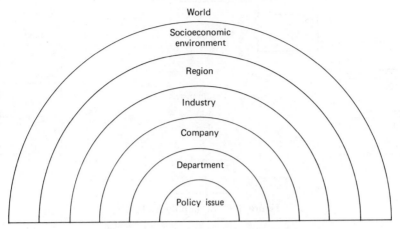

Figure 5-2   Hierarchy of stakeholders.

that the group begin to draw a systems flow chart of all of the activities and events that are a part of the issue under consideration. The flow chart frequently reveals many new stakeholders. Another diagrammatic technique that has proven useful is shown in Figure 5-2. The group's attention is focused first on stakeholders close to the policy issue. Then, by attending to increasingly broader environments of the problem, the group often discovers new affected parties. The form shown in Figure 5-3 is given to each group to help it get started in generating and recording stakeholders.

The following categories have been found to be sufficient to characterize the properties of stakeholders. That is, each relevant stakeholder will have *at least one* important property in *at least one* of the following categories. The categories are:

1   The purposes and motivations of a stakeholder.
2   Beliefs.
3   Resources:

    a.   Material.
    b.   Symbolic.
    c.   Physical.
    d.   Positional.
    e.   Informational.
    f.   Skill.

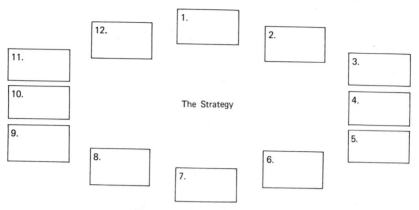

Figure 5-3   Stakeholder chart.

4 Special knowledge and opinions.

5 Commitments.

6 Relationships to the other stakeholders in the system:

  a. Power.

  b. Authority.

  c. Responsibility.

  d. Accountability.

Holders of different perspectives on a policy issue may disagree because they ascribe different properties to a particular stakeholder.

  Each group is asked to generate *at least 10* different stakeholders who are consistent with their perspective. If time permits, as many stakeholders as possible should be identified. However, there is no difficulty in getting a group to generate 10 or more within 30 minutes. Three or four of these should be "nonobvious", "wild card" stakeholders. If all the SAST approach accomplished was the generation of the obvious or easily uncovered set of stakeholders, then there would be little to justify its costs in time and resources of application.

  There is a story about a major water project that is helpful in generating nonobvious stakeholders. The story concerns the failure of planners for the Tennessee Valley Authority to take into account a seemingly insignificant stakeholder in the design and planning process of a major dam project. The seemingly insignificant stakeholder was a 3 inch fish called the snaildarter. Because the planners of the project had not explicitly considered the effect of the dam on the snaildarter, the construction of the dam was not only held up significantly, but was in danger of being canceled altogether. In effect, the argument of environmentalists—a group of stakeholders who took it as their task to speak on behalf of another group of stakeholders (fish) who could not speak for themselves—was that the dam would wipe out the snaildarters. Did the dam have the right to jeopardize the existence of a group of nature's stakeholders? Apparently not, according to environmentalists.

The merits of the case for or against the dam and the snaildarters are not at issue here. The point is that the failure to consider an important class of stakeholders can be disastrous. Because there are no rules for generating a "complete" list of "all relevant" stakeholders, one needs some guidelines. The psychological notion of "looking for the snaildarters in one's perspective" is helpful in this regard. Snaildarters are stakeholders that have a low probability of being involved, but they threaten the success of the policy, plan, or strategy if they are. The purpose of generating "snaildarters" is to force the proponents of a perspective to think of deeper assumptions they will need to overcome if their plan is to be successful. They need to explain how they will meet their snaildarters and conquer them.

Exhibit 5-2 contains a sample set of instructions to give to a working group to aid them in generating stakeholders.

Several additional points about the stakeholder generation process should be noted. First, it is not necessary to generate all possible stakeholders before going on to assumption surfacing. Discussion of assumptions often reveals new stakeholders. Second, stakeholder groups must be continuously redefined in terms of their comprehensiveness. For example, the stakeholder "customer" is generally too broad a category for effective planning. The market must be segmented into subgroups that have different interests, needs, or capacity to pay. As assumptions are discussed, the question of the appropriate segmentation of customers, suppliers, competitors, allies, and so on must be addressed. There is also a tendency to identify too small a stakeholder group. As long as the groups' basic interests in the problem are the same and the assumptions being made about them are the same, stakeholder groupings can be safely combined. Where possible, stakeholder groupings should be combined because this reduces the number of assumptions to be reviewed and evaluated. Furthermore, there is no reason that the stakeholder groupings all need to be at the same level of abstraction. Key individuals may be identified personally as well as by groups, departments, divisions, functions, companies, regions, countries, governments, and demographic or

Exhibit 5-2 Sample Group Instructions

Stakeholder Generation

Identify the key stakeholders in your plan. Stakeholders are parties on whom the company depends in some way for the full realization of the plan or who depend on the company for the realization of some of their own goals. Stakeholders have a vested interest in the plan.

Some prompting questions:

Who is affected by the plan?

Who has an interest in the plan and its outcomes?

Who can affect the plan's adoption, implementation, or execution?

Who has expressed an opinion on the issues involved?

Who, because of demographic or other characteristics, *ought* to care or *might* care about the plan?

Identify the "low probability, high risk" stakeholders. These are ones, like the Snaildarter, who are remote, easy to overlook, and, perhaps, unlikely to affect the plan, but should they become active, they may have an immense impact on the plan.

---

marketing segments. The only criterion for stakeholders is that they can affect the plan or be affected by it and that planning assumptions are being made about them.

After the groups feel they have generated a set of stakeholders appropriate for their perspective, they are asked to generate at least two or three assumptions for each stakeholder. Then they are asked to plot the assumptions on a large flip chart. If time is limited, we ask the group to plot only the 7 to 10 most important or interesting assumptions. Finally, the group is asked to prepare a 20 to 25 minute presentation for delivery on the morning of the third day. The presentation should cover (1) a clear statement of their strategy or policy perspective, (2) a list of their stakeholders and why the particular ones they selected are important for their perspective, and (3) a plot of at least 7 to 10 of their most important stakeholder assumptions with regard to their relative importance and

Exhibit 5-3   Sample Group Instructions

Assumption Surfacing

Generate a series of assumptions about each stakeholder by asking the question:

What must we be assuming about this stakeholder and its future behavior in order for the plan to be successful?

For every assumption, formulate a counterassumption—an assumption that is opposite from and a "deadly enemy" to the stated assumption. Where possible, counterassumptions should be stated in the affirmative. For example, for the assumption "The expected unit manufacturing costs $10,000," the counterassumption "The expected unit manufacturing cost is $20,000" (if it is supportable) is preferable to "The expected unit manufacturing cost is *not* $10,000."

Counterassumptions can be used to test the relevancy of the assumption. If the counterassumption's truth would have no significant impact on the plan, then the assumption is not very relevant and should be discarded.

---

certainty and a statement as to why the assumptions are critical for their policy perspective.

Exhibit 5-3 contains a sample set of instructions, which is given to working groups to aid them in surfacing assumptions. Exhibit 5-4 is a stakeholder assumption form that is useful for recording the results of the assumption surfacing.

After the assumptions are surfaced, the group is asked to plot them on an importance-certainty graph. Exhibit 5-5 contains sample instructions given to the group for this purpose. Figure 5-4 shows one of the forms that can be used for this purpose. With executive groups, we have found that a flip-chart size pad of graph paper is adequate.

The assumptions on the importance-certainty graph need only be plotted relative to one another. An ordinal scale is all that is usually required. It is not necessary to show, for instance, that assumption one lies at a point 2.368 units from the origin. What is important is the relative location of assumptions in a quadrant, not their detailed scaling.

Two or more assumptions relevant to a particular stakeholder or different stakeholders should be plotted even if they are contradictory. Contradictory assumptions should not be suppressed. If a plan entails the positing of assumptions that are in conflict, then this should not be ig-

Exhibit 5-4   Stakeholder Assumption Form

Date: Project:

Stakeholder Description:

Stakeholder Code:

---

1. Assumption	1. Counterassumption
2. Assumption	2. Counterassumption
3. Assumption	3. Counterassumption
4. Assumption	4. Counterassumption
5. Assumption	5. Counterassumption

---

nored. Indeed, this fact should be highlighted since it reveals something extremely crucial about a particular perspective: it depends on contradictory or conflicting states of the world. Since this is indeed often the case in the real world, we want to note it. For instance, many plans unconsciously assume that one's competitors are both "weak" and "strong" at the same time. Indeed, this can happen because, as Jung (1963) reminds us, in reality one's competitors do have weak and strong sides that coexist. If one emphasized one aspect and neglected the other, one's plan would be considerably weakened.

A difficulty that sometimes arises in interpreting the notion of uncertainty should be mentioned. By the uncertainty of an assumption we do

Exhibit 5-5   Sample Group Instructions

Assumption Rating

Rank each assumption according to importance and certainty and plot it on a graph. The most important assumptions are those that have the most significant bearing on the plan and its outcome. The most certain assumptions are those that are most likely to be true because they are self-evident or because there is substantial evidence to support their validity.

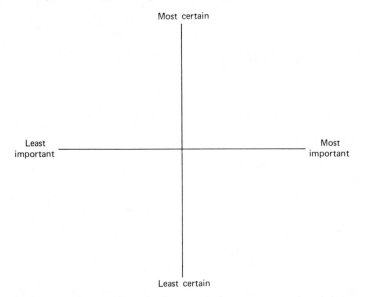

Figure 5-4 Assumption plotting graph: importance and certainty.

not mean that one is certain that the events described in the assumption will *not* occur or that the statement of events is false. Rather we mean that one is in an extreme state of doubt as to the likelihood of occurrence or the truth of the statement of events contained in the assumption. The statement is as likely to be true as it is to be false. If the statement is felt to be *definitely either false or true,* then the assumption is regarded as certain. Thus it is not whether an assumption is stated positively or negatively that makes it uncertain, but rather how confident we feel in our knowledge of it as an accurate or a true statement of the properties of the stakeholder to which it pertains.

Assumptions and facts, or so-called true statements, about the world of stakeholders bear a close relationship to one another. *A fact is an "assumption" concerning whose truth status we feel strongly confident. Conversely, an assumption is a "fact" whose certainty is doubtful.* Thus every assumption is potentially capable of being converted into a *judgment* of fact. Conversely, every fact is capable of being downgraded to the status of an assumption. In summary, a fact is an assumption in which our confidence is justified or warranted, whereas an assumption is a doubtful fact.

The SAST process is one of continual expansion and contraction. We are continually working back and forth between generating large lists of ideas, issues, and assumptions and boiling them down to more critical or important ones. The hope is that the ideas that emerge from the process will indeed be the most critical. Although there is no proof or guarantee that this is the case, a good argument can be made that this occurs due to the critical and challenging nature of the process.

PHASE III: THE PRESENTATION AND DEBATE OF ASSUMPTIONS

The presentation proceeds largely in accordance with the process described in Chapter 3. Subsequent chapters on dialectical debate will add more detail concerning the form the presentations and debate may take. It is, however, pertinent to emphasize here that each group presents the results of its analysis in a short, 20 to 25 minute presentation, during which questions of *clarification only* are allowed from the other groups. Unless these requirements are met, the presentation and debate aspects of the SAST process will be horribly confounded, just as they are in everyday life.

Each group deserves a continuous period of time in which to make its strongest case, undisturbed by confrontation with its antitheses. The antitheses are always there. In fact, they have been explicitly built in as a result of the process. They reside in the opposite groups. Because each group gets an opportunity to present its point of view, some of the antitheses will be forthcoming.

One of the prime benefits of the SAST process is that each group has the opportunity to witness the assumptions that underlie a position. Such assumptions are rarely discussed in the day-to-day activities of organizations. In everyday life, one is required to make all kinds of complex decisions based on the most superficial of analyses and incomplete data. The uncertainties of a position are rarely seen; indeed, people often go to great lengths to hide uncertainties. The SAST process reverses this. It assumes that a perspective has not done a good job in putting forth its case unless it displays a significant amount of the uncertainty associated with it. A presentation that contains no assumptions in the important-uncertain quadrant is highly suspect. A group making such a presentation invites the question Whom do you think you are fooling? Indeed, each of the groups is explicitly instructed in Phase II to make sure they have some significant assumptions in the important-uncertain quadrant. If they do not, they will be accused of dodging the issue or of not having given serious attention to finding significant snaildarters. "Any position worth promoting has significant uncertainties associated with it. If you don't find these uncertainties, you can bet your competition will." This is the motto! One dramatic way for the facilitators to make the point is to state, "If we were a competitor to your group, we would hope that you wouldn't think

Exhibit 5-6   Most Damaging Assumptions Form

Date: Group:

Project:

Record below the assumptions made by each opposite group that are most *damaging* or *threatening* to your group's concept of the optimal plan or those that *conflict* most with your assumptions. Use a different form for each opposite group.

Opposite Group:

Damaging Assumptions:

---

about the snaildarters." Not knowing your vulnerabilities and uncertainties is a very poor bargaining position in which to be. This is why the SAST process is anything but a luxury. It is an exercise in tough critical analysis. If a strategy can survive an intensive SAST analysis, it is in a much better position to survive in the world. (For comparison, see Starlride, Greve, and Hedberg, 1978.)

After each group has made its presentation, each group meets alone to identify the assumptions from the other presentations that are most damaging to their own. After lunch, each group reports these assumptions to the participants as a whole. A list of all damaging assumptions across all the groups is made. These constitute in effect the final set of critical issues that must be resolved. Exhibit 5-6 is a form that can be used for this purpose.

After the participants feel they have listed all the critical issues they can, the discussion is thrown open for an unconstrained debate. After the somewhat demanding structure of the last few days, this is often a welcome relief. Participants take to it quite easily. The facilitators play the role of "traffic cops" and encourage the participants to exchange ideas.

A number of distinct debate patterns are easily discerned:

1   Two or more groups may share essentially the same set of stakeholders and the same set of assumptions; however, they may give very different ratings to the assumptions. For instance, one group may rank

an assumption relatively unimportant and certain, while another may rank it as relatively important and uncertain. The stage is thus set for an interesting debate. Such differences in rankings help to illuminate deeper background beliefs. Instead of regarding such differences as harmful, SAST therefore regards them as essential because they help to illuminate additional factors that must be considered.

2 Two or more groups can have the same set of stakeholders but different assumptions regarding them.

3 Different groups can have different stakeholders and hence different assumptions altogether.

4 Different groups can have the same stakeholders and the same assumptions but have different strategies derived from them, or they can have different ideas as to what kind of data is needed to remove the uncertainty surrounding an assumption, that is, to move it up into the certain quadrant.

For whatever reason, the debate proceeds until the groups feel that they have gotten the critical issues out on the table and that they have a better idea as to why they are divided on them—not that they have necessarily resolved all their differences or persuaded one another as to the correctness of their position.

PHASE IV: INTEGRATION OF ASSUMPTIONS AND THE PLANNING OF FOLLOW-UP ACTIVITIES

SAST is founded on a particular set of social psychological conditions that vary over the process. The initial conditions are the relative absence of *interpersonal* conflict *within* any particular working group and the deliberate creation of purposeful *intellectual* conflict *between* groups. Both these conditions are necessary for the effective application of SAST. At the point of synthesis, however, a different set of social psychological conditions is necessitated if an integrated policy is to result. This set of conditions can be described by means of Figure 5-5, which is due to Kilmann and Thomas (1974).

Figure 5-5 shows five basic ways of responding to a conflict situation—avoiding, competing, accommodating, compromising, and collaborating. Consider two persons, A and B, in conflict over something. The point (0,0) represents the case where both parties decide to avoid the conflict altogether. Neither party decides that the matter is important enough to risk the inevitably unpleasant feelings that accompany an open

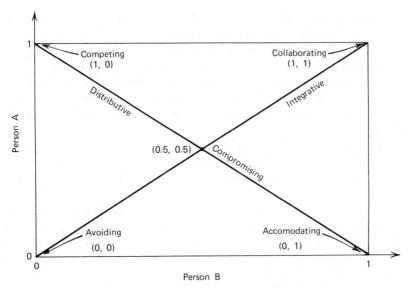

Figure 5-5   Ways of reacting to conflict.

contest of wills. Competition, on the other hand, is the case where one of the parties, for example, A, decides to get all he or she can at the expense of the other. Thus pure competition is represented by the point (1,0), signifying that A receives or strives to receive "1" or all of a perceived fixed pie of benefits. Accommodation, at the other extreme, signifies A giving in completely to B's wishes. Thus competition and accommodation are opposites. The state of accommodation for A is the state of competition for B and vice versa.

Compromise is the state where A and B both receive exactly half of what they would each receive in a state of pure or extreme competition. In fact, the point labeled compromise or (0.5, 0.5) is just one of an infinite number of points on a dimension that is called the distributive dimension. If A receives the amount X on the distributive dimension, then B receives $(1 - X)$ and vice versa. The distributive dimension regards the world as a "zero-sum" game or a "fixed pie." Whatever A receives (X), B receives a correspondingly different amount $(1 - X)$.

In contrast to the distributive dimension [in reality, there is an infinity of such dimensions described by the set of points $(X, n - X)$, where n is a variable "fixed-pie amount" such that $0 \le n \le 1$], the distributive dimension is described by the relationship (X,X). If the social psychology of the distributive dimension is that of "win-lose," so that whatever A wins (X), B loses $-X$, then the social psychology of the integrative dimension is that of "win-win." Whatever A wins (X), B also wins (X). The highest form of this behavior is the point labeled collaboration (1,1). Here the world is not conceived of as a fixed pie. Rather, the social psychological state of affairs is that of cooperation with one's fellow so that they may both "win," the so-called "win-win" point of view. The recognition is that the sum of the resources available is not necessarily fixed. This state is governed by the search for synergistic rather than conflictual solutions to problems.

It is important to stress that, depending on the situation, all these ways of handling conflict can either be appropriate or inappropriate. No single style is appropriate for all situations. However, individuals vary in their typical or characteristic ways of reacting to conflict situations. Indeed, Kilmann and Thomas (1974) have devised a short instrument that measures a person's characteristic style of handling conflict. Thus some individuals typically avoid conflict situations, while others adopt a competitive mode, no matter what the situation. That is, some individuals always compete whether competition is appropriate or not.

The SAST approach was designed for situations in which issues can not be avoided. It deliberately makes use of *controlled* conflict in that different groups are *purposefully* constructed to take competing views of issues. Indeed, in the early stages of the process the competition between groups is actually heightened by the various steps of the SAST process. As we have stressed repeatedly, the reason is that while conflict exists in all organizations and institutions, few know how to make *creative* use of their conflicts to produce new insights on problems.

The earlier stages of the SAST process presuppose the existence of creative conflict or competition; *the last stages presuppose collaboration.* The production of synergistic solutions to complex planning issues is as much a function of social psychology as it is of logic. Concepts do not synthesize themselves across groups; groups (i.e., people) synthesize concepts. The groups that are created in the very last steps of the SAST process reflect this.

In order to promote synthesis of ideas across the initial working groups, new groups are formed. The ideal arrangement is to select an individual from each of the initial working groups. In this way "synthetic" groups can be formed. Each synthetic group is now given the assignment to come up with the best plan that synthesizes or integrates the assumptions of the various groups. *Whereas before there was competition between groups based on widening the differences between them, now there is competition between the synthetic groups based on the integration of ideas.*

Integration or synthesis rarely occurs without encouragement. It must be explicitly sought after. Although there is no guarantee that SAST or any other process will produce synthesis, we have to do everything in our power to encourage it. Left to itself, it rarely materializes since the political and social climate of most institutions does not encourage it. In short, just as people must be encouraged and trained to learn how to disagree constructively, they require encouragement and training for synthesis, particularly in a culture that does not encourage systemic or holistic thinking.

As part of such training, the authors have found it worthwhile to give people very brief lectures on the model contained in Figure 5-5. At this point most people can profit from a discussion as to how the SAST process has been carefully designed to take advantage of Figure 5-5. The need for training for synthesis is especially emphasized. Furthermore, synthesis must be rewarded. Most organizations reward their members for thinking about the isolated parts and the surface concerns of issues. SAST rewards people for thinking about the whole of an organization and about the assumptions that lie beneath the surface of issues.

Finally, the day ends with the design of an action and/or follow-up plan to collect relevant information. The purpose of this information is to check on the critical or pivotal assumptions, that is, those assumptions that need continual monitoring so that the plan can be revised if the assumptions turn out to be misguided.

In Case Synthesis Is Not Possible: Assumptional Decision Theory

What should be done if a synthetic set of assumptions and a policy based on a common set of assumptions can not be achieved? Or, what if the groups as a whole feel that a compromise solution is not feasible or desirable? What does one do in this not untypical situation? We have found that it is useful to take the participants through a variant of the typical action-truth table that comes from statistical decision theory. Figure 5-6 illustrates the procedure. It is based on Savage's minimax regret or risk criterion.

Suppose that there are three policies such as the three identified in the drug company case described in Chapter 4. Furthermore, suppose it proves impossible to modify the assumptions in the three policies to make them acceptable to each of the other groups. Since some sort of action must eventually be agreed on at some point assumption examination terminates and action is taken. If we can not achieve compromise or synthesis between the policies, then one of them must be chosen to implement. The question is how that choice should be made.

Figure 5-6 reveals that the choice should be made by considering the effects of implementing any one policy with regard to each of the others.

Implementation/Action

	P_1	P_2	P_3	
P_1 Assumptions	correct	error RC = ? VC = ? R = ?	error RC = ? VC = ? R = ?	Lower price
P_2 Assumptions	error RC = ? VC = ? R = ?	correct	error RC = ? VC = ? R = ?	Raise price
P_3 Assumptions	error RC = ? VC = ? R = ?	error RC = ? VC = ? R = ?	correct	Middle price

Figure 5-6 Assumption decision table—comparison of the costs of implementing different policies. RC = the real cost of a policy assumption, VC = the visible cost of a policy assumption, R = the reversibility of a policy assumption.

Suppose, for example, that policy P_1 turns out to be "true" (i.e., a set of assumptions that were judged to be important but uncertain at the time of the choice of a policy ultimately turn out to be "correct" or certain in the sense of being verified by resultant market data, say within 3 to 6 months of putting the policy into action). Figure 5-6 asks what errors are made by implementing policies P_1, P_2, and P_3, in turn. If P_1 is true, and P_1 is implemented, then there is no error. If P_2 and P_3 are implemented, however, then there will be certain costs associated with these two cases. We have split these costs into two parts: a "real" cost (RC) and "visible" cost (VC). In addition, there is another factor to be considered: the "reversibility" (R) of an action or error. By "real" cost we mean a cost that is easily determined through normal market data.

In the case of the drug company example in Chapter 4, there were three policies facing the company: $P_1 =$ "lower the current price of one of its most important drugs," $P_2 =$ "raise the current price of the drug," and $P_3 =$ "steer a middle course between P_1 and P_2." By taking the representatives of all three policies through Figure 5-6, we were able to get common agreement between them as to the RC's, VC's, and R's associated with the off-diagonal cells. The RC for any P_i is the estimated real losses in profits that would occur if one adopted P_i and P_j were "true."

The VC's, on the other hand, are a bit more subtle and hence a bit trickier to determine. They are best explained as follows. Suppose that the policy P_2 is, in fact, the correct one. That is, suppose that because of competitive conditions, the quality of the product, advertising, and so on, one can actually raise the price of one's product—an action that many executives would be afraid to do. Because of this fear, suppose that it was decided to adopt policy P_1. There would then not only be an obvious real cost associated with this action (the obvious loss of profits), but we contend that there would be a less visible cost as well. If one lowers the price when one could have raised it, then it may be impossible for management to ever know this. By lowering the price, one has precluded the opportunity of finding out whether this action was possible. One precludes the availability of the data, so to speak. By the same token, the reversibility of this action may also be rather low. It may be very difficult to come in later and raise prices once one has lowered them. That is, the VC of P_1 is low or, conversely, the invisible cost of P_1 is high. Visibility thus refers to the ease and possibility of observing the cost of a policy if some other policy is in fact correct. By means of this reasoning process, it was decided (counter to initial intuition) that the "best" policy from the company's point of view was to recommend price increases!

If the process in Figure 5-6 is so valuable, why, one might ask, did we not proceed directly to it? The answer is that all of the data in the Assumption Decision Table derives from the previous steps. Each of the various cost estimates are made with respect to the assessment of the assumptions that have come before. The presumed "truth" of the policies is with respect to the key assumptions underlying each policy. The actions are with respect to what it takes to implement the assumptions, to act on their truth—indeed, to make them come true. The costs are determined relative to the assumptions by asking what is the cost of considering one assumption as true or false when another is true or false? To the authors' knowledge, this is very different application of conventional statistical decision theory.

There is also another reason for not proceeding directly to the risk table. Figure 5-6 not only embodies but also reinforces a win-lose competitive mentality between the various strategies. Although we do not want to preclude the possibility that one of the pure strategies is actually best, we wish to ensure that every serious consideration will be given to the search for a synthetic policy before opting for any pure policy. *Only after serious consideration has been given to synthesis do we wish to fall back on one of the pure strategies.* This derives from our basic belief that in complex social and managerial problems rarely will any one pure strategy pick up and integrate the multitude of considerations necessary for successful problem management.

Methods of Forming Working Groups

The procedures for forming working groups discussed under Phase I described the Nominal Group Technique for generating issues. There are several other options. In total, we have employed five different methods for forming working groups. These are:

1 Problem-solving style.
2 Basic philosophy.
3 MAPS.
4 Policy preference.
5 Issues.

The relative efficacy of these methods depends on the problem being considered and the people involved.

We usually face one of two general possibilities. Either *no* alternative policies have been identified, or several competing alternatives are available. If there are no previously identified policies, then each group must evolve its own policy. In this situation, we have found it best to form the groups by means of some projective technique such as the problem-solving style, basic philosophy, or MAPS methods. Each of the working groups is formed so that it has a different worldview or psychological approach. They are asked to specify the stakeholder assumptions that seem most reasonable to them and then to derive the most effective policy from those assumptions. Experience shows that the groups generally come up with significantly different policies and assumptions.

If one policy has been proposed and the purpose is to examine and test this policy, then any of the methods, except the policy preference method, can be used.

Whenever there are two or more policies that have been proposed for solving the problem, the designer is generally well-advised to form the groups around those policies. Extreme or ''pure'' forms of the policy alternatives are most effective for surfacing assumptions. Each group is given a policy and then asked to identify the assumptions under which their policy is optimal. The policy preference method works best for this purpose; however, any of the other four methods can be used as well. A brief description of each method follows.

Problem-Solving Style   The problem-solving style method proceeds from the assumption that different psychological types view a problem differently and therefore will surface different assumptions and assign different importances and certainties to them.

We have found that an effective approach is to form four groups according to the psychological types of Carl G. Jung (1971). Jung theorized that individuals take in data from the inner or outer world by one of two processes: sensation (S) or intuition (N). People who rely on sensation tend to focus on details, specifics, hard realistic facts, and the "here and now." Those who rely on intuition glean information from their imagination. They focus on the "whole," the entire gestalt, and what "might be."

Jung further theorized that there are two basic ways of evaluating the information recieved and using it to reach a decision: thinking (T) and feeling (F). People who rely on thinking tend to employ impersonal, formal, or theoretical modes of reasoning. Thinking types generalize. They look for the common dimension in things and express it in abstract and theoretical terms. They are logical and scientific. People who rely on feeling, on the other hand, use their own unique, personal value judgment to evaluate information. Feeling types particularize. They are sensitive to people and to individual differences. They tend to focus on judgments of good or bad, ethical and unethical, pleasing or unpleasing, and likable or unlikable.

These distinctions define four basic personality types: sensing-thinking (STs), sensing-feeling (SFs), intuition-feeling (NFs), and intuition-thinking (NTs). We have used these four types to form working groups. STs tend to be analytical and scientific in their approach and to attend to details. NTs tend to be conceptual and theoretical in their approach and to reason about ideas. NFs tend to be humanistic, conceptual, and general in their approach and to focus on social and cultural ideas. SFs tend to be humanistic but particularistic in their approach and to focus on the plight and concerns of individuals. Thus, each of these groups tends to generate different stakeholders and assumptions. A short form of the Myers-Briggs Indicator (1962) is adequate for separating the participants into effective working groups.

Basic Philosophy   In some organizations there are different philosophies and beliefs among the people about the nature of the business. For example, in one insurance company, we found that there were some people who believed that the purpose of insurance was to indemnify, that is, to repay the insured for losses or damages; however, another group believed that the purpose of insurance was to prevent a risk from occurring in the first place. These two sets of beliefs provided natural groupings for forming the working groups. Their basic philosophies led them to different stakeholders, assumptions, and policies.

MAPS   MAPS is the acronym for a group forming method developed by Kilmann (1977). It stands for Multivariate Analysis, Participation, and

Structure. The MAPS method asks people to respond on a scale of 1 to 7 (a) the degree of interest they have in participating in each of a series of identified organizational tasks and (b) the degree of interest they have in working with each of the other participants in the SAST session. Computerized cluster analysis techniques are then used to form groups of people who agree on their companions and on the tasks on which they would like to work. This method has been used successfully where a group of people from different parts of the organization have come together to plan the use of a new facility or service. Sessions conducted with high-level executives are usually not as conducive to the full use of the MAPS method.

Policy Preference The policy preference method is simple and straightforward. The drug company case and the U.S. Bureau of Census undercount case described in Chapter 4 are examples of this method in use. Two or more alternative policies that appear to be feasible and acceptable are identified. Working groups are formed on one of two bases. Either (1) participants are asked to rank order the policies in terms of their current preferences or (2) participants are asked to rank order the policies in terms of their willingness to make a case for it. The latter method is generally more effective, because the participants tend to "role play" the positions and not get trapped into defending personal preferences.

Issues The issues method was summarized in the discussion of Phase I. In the next section it is described in detail.

FORMING WORKING GROUPS ON THE BASIS OF ISSUES: THE FACET APPROACH

Purpose

The purpose of this process is to form n groups (usually about four) out of N individuals (usually about 20–30) in order to promote active dialogue among the groups on a complex problem such as a new strategy or plan. The groups are formed on the basis of two principles:

1   The members within each group should have as much agreement on the issues among themselves as possible.
2   The groups should be as different as possible from one another (i.e., maximal disagreement between groups).

Each group should contain approximately N/n members.

Exhibit 5-7   Issue Sheets—Instruction

On the Issue Sheets attached to this cover sheet, please summarize the issues that, in your opinion, need to be discussed or decided on with regard to the plan. An issue is any question, important point, matter, variable, factor, or event that may be disputed or needs to be resolved. The following questions may help you think about issues with respect to the plan:

1. If I were suddenly given total responsibility for implementing this plan, what questions, points or matters concerning this plan would be the most important to me *personally*?

2. If I were on the corporate staff and was reviewing this plan, what questions would I ask about it, especially if I wanted to be "tough-minded"?

3. If I worked for a competitor, what parts of this plan would I be most thankful for?

Generating Issues

Bring the group of N concerned individuals together. After a brief introduction, the group is asked to take 10 minutes of silence during which each individual is requested to make a list of central issues to be dealt with in the problem area. Instruction sheets such as that shown in Exhibit 5-7 may be used to facilitate the process.

At the end of the silent period, the group is polled in round-robin fashion and each individual is asked to contribute one issue in turn. Only clarifying questions are permitted during the round-robin polling. Individuals are encouraged, however, to add to their list during the polling.

Each issue is numbered and recorded on a board or flip chart where it is clearly visible to everyone present.

When an individual is polled and he or she has nothing to add to the list he or she simply says "pass." A "pass," however, does not prevent one from contributing an issue during a subsequent round.

The polling is completed when everyone has passed and there are no issues left to be recorded. Sometimes, however, it may be useful to cut off the polling at some predetermined number of issues (say 60). In any case, everyone should be given at least three opportunities to contribute issues, and no "burning" issues should be left off the list. Frequently, in order to get at some of the really deep issues in the situation, it is useful to ask everyone to try to get in touch with their emotions concerning the situation and to "dig deeper," "cast out more broadly," or "reach inside" to come up with additional issues.

Voting on Issues

When all the issues have been generated, numbered, and recorded on the board, the session is then opened up for discussion and clarification. Direct debate should be avoided, because that will take place later. Wherever possible, issues should be combined and restated.

At this point, each individual is asked to write down the numbers of the X issues he or she thinks are the most important or crucial. Five issues are usually the optimal number to list, because the number of choices is large enough to provide dispersion, yet small enough to force choice. A larger or smaller number of issues can be picked, depending on the circumstances.

Technically, the absolute minimum number of issues to be voted on X_{min} may be arrived at by using the formula

$$\log_2(N/4)^+ \leq X_{min} \leq \log_2(N/7)^+$$

where N = the total number of individuals
      4 = the smallest group size
      7 = the largest group size
      $N/x = n$, the number of groups
      $\log_2(n)$ = the number of binary distinctions necessary to assign individuals to n groups
      $+$ = rounded to next higher integer

Usually X_{min} should be increased by 2 or 3 in order to get dispersion and variety. Consequently, the actual will generally be larger than X_{min}.

When all of the votes are in, they are tallied. The top X issues are selected for further refinement.

At this point each of the remaining X issues should be restated, if necessary, as either/or choice issues. For example, an issue concerning the appropriate channel of distribution to use for a new product line might take the form How should we distribute our product, through direct sales or through wholesalers? An either/or statement contains two possible resolutions to the issue. Exhibit 5-8 illustrates the concept with five binary issues concerning the planning problem of a professional school.

Position on Issues

Each individual is now asked to state his or her current position on each issue (or the position he or she would like to take for purposes of dialogue)

Exhibit 5-8   Five Basic Professional School Issues

---

1. What should be the *scope* of the school's research and teaching concerns, *broad-gaged* or *focused*?

2. Should the school stress *theory* or *practice*?

3. Should the school strive to train as many qualified people as possible, or should it concentrate on a smaller number of highly selected, highly trained people: *(Quantity/Quality)*

4. Should the school emphasize its *stability* and *tradition*, or should it be flexible and adaptive to *change*?

5. Do students learn best through *self-directed experience* or through *systematic presentations* and exercises prepared by the faculty?

---

by indicating for each issue whether they prefer the first resolution or the second resolution. Preference for the first resolution is shown by recording a zero (0); preference for the second is shown by recording a one (1). Exhibit 5-9 illustrates the method using the professional school example.

PROCEDURE FOR FORMING GROUPS

Groups are formed using the following steps:

1. Each position sheet is assigned a binary code to reflect the individual's response on each of the X issues (i.e., 001100, 00110, 00000, 11111, etc.).

2. All the sheets are sorted by code and a count is made of the number of individuals who responded for each code.

3. An m by m matrix is formed where m is the number of different codes with one or more responses ($m \leq 2^x$). The matrix is used to make pairwise comparisons.

4. For each cell above the main diagonal, calculate and enter the following "dialectical factor" F_{ij}

$$F_{ij} = C_i \times C_j \times D_{ij}$$

where C_i, C_j = the counts for codes i, j, respectively

D_{ij} = the binary distance between the two codes (e.g.,

Exhibit 5-9   Issue Position Sheet—Professional School Illustration

Date:	Project:	Name:
Issue	0	1
1	Broad-Gaged X	Focused
2	Theory	Practice X
3	Quantity	Quality X
4	Stability X	Change
5	Self-Directed X	Systematic present
6		
7		
8		
9		
10		

Code: 01100

00000 and 11111 have a D_{ij} of 5; 01100 and 00110 have a D_{ij} of 2, 00000 and 00001 have a D_{ij} of 1)

5   Find the largest entry in the matrix, $\max_{ij}(D_{ij})$. This represents the greatest source of difference among the individuals. Assign all individuals with code i to Group 1. Assign all individuals with code j to Group 2.

6   Now find the next largest entry in the matrix.

    a. If both its i and j are different from the groups already assigned, then form two new groups using these two codes.

    b. If either its i or j is the same as a previously assigned group, form one new group using the new code.

7   Repeat Step 6 until the required number of groups is formed.

8   The remaining unassigned individuals are assigned to the established groups in order to:

a. Balance the size of all the groups, generally keeping them between 4 and 7.

b. Minimize the binary distance D_{ij} between an individual and the group to which he or she is assigned.

Exhibit 5-10 illustrates the process for the professional school case.

Creating the Dialogue

Each of the newly formed groups is given their primary formulation code, generally as a set of premises. The code indicates their initial resolution to the key issues. The group is asked to review their code, to discuss it, and to give themselves a name or label that captures their main theme. In the professional school case, for example, the groups gave themselves the names of existing schools that were following a strategy consistent with their code. Exhibits 5-11 and 5-12 illustrate some premise sets that emerged from the professional school case.

At this point the groups are given their SAST policy tasks. Examples of tasks are (1) to devise a new pricing policy for a new product line, (2) to uncover the underlying assumptions in a current plan or proposal, or (3) to develop a position paper on a particular problem area. Each group is instructed to take its code as "given" and to use the code as a set of premises for carrying out its task.

A SUMMARY OF SAST OUTPUTS

The outputs of the SAST process may be briefly summarized as:

1 The surfacing of a set of critical assumptions that underlie a policy or a plan.

2 Shared prioritization of critical assumptions, that is, consensus on the relative importance and certainty of a set of critical assumptions.

3 Identification of the pivotal assumptions, that is, those assumptions that are of high relative importance and high relative uncertainty; these assumptions identify the most dangerous risks associated with a policy.

4 The formation of an *information action* plan, that is, a clearly formulated plan for monitoring the status of the pivotal assumptions over time (e.g., the formation of a market research plan for collecting information to check on the status of the pivotal assumptions).

Exhibit 5-10 Matrix of Codes, Counts, Distances, and Dialectical Factors—Professional School Example*

Matrix:

Count C_1	Code	Code: Count C_j :	A 4	B 6	C 7	D 5	E 1	F 3	G 2
4	A	00011	X	5 / (120)	3 / 84	2 / 40	3 / 12	3 / 36	2 / 16
6	B	11100		X	2 / 84	3 / 90	2 / 12	2 / 36	3 / 36
7	C	10110			X	5 / (175)	2 / 14	2 / 42	3 / 42
5	D	01001				X	3 / 15	2 / 45	2 / 20
1	E	10101					X	2 / 6	5 / 10
3	F	11111						X	3 / 18
2	G	01010							X
= 28 Participants									

Group Formation

Initial Groups		Supplements	Total Count
Group C (175) = 10110 (7)			7
Group D (175) = 01001 (5)	+	01010 (2)	7
Group A (120) = 00011 (4)	+	11111 (3)	7
Group B (120) = 11100 (6)	+	10101 (1)	7
			28

*The circled entry in cell C,D is a dialectical factor of 175 calculated on the basis of a binary distance of 5 and counts of 7 and 5 ($5 \times 7 \times 5 = 175$). The other circled entry, in cell A,B is calculated similarly.

Exhibit 5-11   Code and Premises—Group A

---

1. Many different research and teaching foci directed by faculty interest. (0)
2. Emphasis on rigorous development of theory. (0)
3. Desired to serve community through rather large programs. (0)
4. Attempted to accommodate change by adding new educational programs. (1)
5. Assumed that students learned best through systematic presentation and planned exercises. (1)

What Guarantees the SAST Process?

A response to the question, What guarantees the output of the SAST Process? was presented in Chapter 2. This response was given in terms of what Churchman (1971) has labeled the "guarantor" concept. The guarantor is that component, albeit a very special one, of a system of inquiry that guarantees the workings of the entire system. Thus the guarantor validates the basic inputs to the system, the outputs, and the processes that transform the input to output. As Churchman shows, characteristically different systems of inquiry have very different kinds of guarantors.

The SAST process was carefully formulated for "messy" problems such as those described in Chapter 1. The guarantor for such problems is very different than that for well-structured problems. The guarantor for well-structured problems is that of logical consistency or agreement. This does not apply to ill-structured problems, which by definition emerge in a

Exhibit 5-12   Code and Premises—Group B

---

1. Focus research and teaching in one or two areas in which the school can excell. (1)
2. Emphasize the application and implementation of useful knowledge. (1)
3. Admit relatively few, highly qualified students. (1)
4. Build a tradition and more elements of permanence and stability in the systems. (0)
5. Stress self-directed, tailor-made experiential learning methods. (0)

---

context of conflict. In contrast, the guarantor of the SAST process is manifold. One part is the systematic or controlled conflict between differing viewpoints. Such conflict is necessary for exposing the real source of the difficulty, the underlying disagreement over assumptions. Another part of the guarantor is the ability to inspect and challenge assumptions. The third part is that of managerial judgment itself. The role of conflict is so basic to the process that it bears repeated emphasis. Unlike other planning processes, SAST works better, the more extreme the intellectual conflict between points of view. The reason is that the more extreme the underlying assumptions between positions become, the easier it is to surface and examine them.

Unlike other processes, which regard conflict as bad, signifying the breakdown of natural discourse, SAST regards such conflict as necessary to the emergence of a natural, synthetic policy. However, for this very reason, the participants often have to be encouraged to "role play." Frequently we have instructed them to carry their positions to a position more extreme than the one they believe in. Unless this is done, the positions become "so reasonable" that they are acceptable without adequate debate by all parties. In effect, suppressing the extreme differences inhibits the entire examination of real alternatives.

It should be noted that the SAST process is not intended to replace one of the most important functions of management, the exercise of creative managerial judgment. Rather, it is intended to check on and complement the exercise of such judgment. Ultimately there is no substitute for sound or creative judgment. The trick, however, is to know when judgment is indeed sound or creative. An even bigger trick has been to discover a methodology that is appropriate for aiding the exercise of judgment in the realm of messy problems.

_____ Part Three
Dialectical Debate

Chapter Six _____

Structured Dialectical Debate Concepts

_____

The concept of dialectic is central to all of the methods developed in this book. In previous chapters we have argued that a dialectic should be a fundamental part of any planning process designed to deal with ill-structured problems. A dialectic debate is an integral part of the SAST process. It is also a method that can be used directly when dealing with a policy, planning, or strategy problem. Chapters 6 to 8 expand the concept of dialectics developed thus far in the book.

In this chapter we begin by illustrating the application of dialectic thinking to a well-structured problem. The example shows that even in the seemingly most well-defined problem assumptions are critical. We have chosen a highly simplified inventory problem in order to illustrate this point. Later a more complex case is discussed.

ASSUMPTIONS IN A WELL-STRUCTURED PROBLEM

One of the important assumptions underlying an inventory stocking decision is the one that specifies the financial theory used to determine the value of the "holding cost" coefficient. At least two different theories can be employed.

Suppose, for example, we observe that a corporate treasurer maintains a quantity (q) of \$5773 in a 1 year revolving cash fund for the purpose of paying part-time workers in cash. We judge him to be a rational man.

Most of the chapter is reprinted by permission from Richard O. Mason, "A Dialectical Approach to Strategic Planning," *Management Science* **15,** No. 8 (April 1969), Copyright 1969 The Institute of Management Sciences.

Inquiring into the data on which he based his decision (i.e., his plan to carry $5773) the following is noted:

1   Each time funds are withdrawn from the bank to reimburse the fund, a lump sum charge (C_1) of $10.00 is levied.
2   The total cash demanded (B) over a 1 year period is $100,000.
3   Management's announced goal is to minimize costs.

The question we might pose is: Given this plan of q = $5773, the goal, and the data, for what view of the world is this an optimal policy?

In this case we can assume that the treasurer, being rational, drew on inventory theory and formulated the total cost equation

$$TC = \frac{B}{q}(C_1) + \frac{q}{2}(C_2)$$

where C_2 represents "holding costs." The well-known "optimal" solution to this formulation is

$$q = \frac{(2BC_1)^{\frac{1}{2}}}{C_2}$$

Since the cost of holding cash (C_2) was not explicit in the data bank, it can be inferred by solving

$$C_2 = \frac{2BC_1}{P_2} = \frac{(2) \times (100{,}000) \times (10)}{(5773)^2} = 0.06$$

Thus the treasurer imputes an approximate cost of 6 cents to each dollar he holds idle in cash inventory. For what view of the world is this the optimal policy?

Six cents would appear to be the appropriate rate if, in the treasurer's overall conception of his business, the relevant rate for financial evaluation is the external rate of return. There is a very credible and plausible theory of finance that essentially says that money is worth what it costs to borrow it. Given this assumption, the treasurer's plan to carry $5773 is optimal. But is this the correct assumption to make?

A contrary view of the world exists for which the treasurer's plan is definitely not optimal. For there is also another credible theory of finance in which the opportunity cost of assets is determined by the earning power of these assets when they are employed within the business itself. In this case, the relevant rate of return is the internal rate, which may be, for example, 25%. Conceiving the business from this point of view, the same goals and data can be interpreted to arrive at a new (or "counter") plan:

$$q = \left(\frac{(2) \times (100,000) \times (10)}{0.25} \right)^{\frac{1}{2}} = \$2830$$

These two different concepts of the business logically (and mathematically) imply strikingly different plans. Which should the treasurer adopt? Perhaps neither. The important point of this illustration is not to resolve this problem in financial theory. It is, rather, to demonstrate the intrinsic role that worldview assumptions play in deriving plans. Once management is made aware of these assumptions, they can reconsider and, perhaps, reformulate them. What we have seen demonstrated in this simple illustration, of course, is accentuated many fold in the complex, ill-structured problems of policy, planning, and strategy making. For in strategic planning the assumptions are of an even broader and often more implicit nature.

There are a variety of organizational designs that have been used to cope with the strategic planning problem. One is to establish a planning department to serve as the "alter ego" of management. We call this the "expert" approach. Another, frequently used in divisionalized organizations, is to have the policymakers and planners of an organizational unit submit plans for extensive cross-examination by top management. This is a "devil's advocate" approach. In the next two sections these "ideal types" are discussed in relation to two criteria for a good organizational design for planning:

1 It should expose the assumptions underlying a proposed plan so that management can reconsider them.
2 It should suggest new and more relevant assumptions on which the planning process can proceed.

The Expert Approach to Planning

Some managements, recognizing the gravity of the planning problem, have established planning departments or turned to consultants to secure expert advice on the plans they should follow. It is the task of the planner to make a study of the organization's environment (opportunities and threats), its resources (strengths and weaknesses), its personal values, and its ethical and social responsibility. The study concludes with a recommended plan that is usually presented to management in the form of a strategic briefing session.

However, the planner, like the policymaker, possesses a world view through which he interprets the organizational data to arrive at the recommended plan. These assumptions are "hidden" behind the arguments contained in the "staff paper," management report, or other planning documents and are infrequently communicated to management.

Often the expert planner is an economist. The economist (as is true of practitioners in any discipline), by virtue of his training and perspective, abstracts and considers only certain aspects of the total planning problem (e.g., "costs," "benefits," "efficiency").

"With deft analytical fingers, the economist abstracts from the untidy complexities of social life a neat world of commodities."

This was Kenneth Boulding's (1956) picturesque way of describing his chosen profession. Policymakers, however, cannot take such a limited view. They have the broader responsibility of determining the organization's plan from all points of view—social, political, psychological, and cultural.

Moreover, there is a tendency for some expert advisers to bury many of the assumptions of their plan within the jargon of their trade. Sophisticated techniques (such as mathematical programming) and complicated computer technologies tend to obscure the assumptions that underlie their use. Indeed, the aura of "mystic" that surrounds the technological solution can serve to give a plan more credibility than it deserves.

The point of this discussion is to show that the expert adviser also has a particular way of viewing the organization and that his method of communicating to management can serve to conceal the assumptions that underlie his recommended plan. Thus this approach to planning does not meet the requirement for exposing assumptions and bringing them to management's attention. It does not serve as a test to check the criticality of assumptions, nor does it serve to suggest to the policymaker a new managerial world view.

THE DEVIL'S ADVOCATE APPROACH

One technique that some organizations employ can be referred to as the devil's advocate approach. ITT employed the approach successfully under the leadership of Harold Geneen (Brown, 1966). In this procedure (which is normally used internally rather than with consultants), the planner appears before the organization's management and advocates a plan in a manner similar to that of the expert approach.

Management, however, assumes the role of an adverse and often carping critic. It attempts to determine all that is wrong with the plan and to expound the reasons that the plan should not be adopted.

Those who employ the devil's advocate approach assume that truly good plans will survive the most forceful opposition and that a sound judgment on a plan occurs when it is subjected to censure. These assumptions are partially valid, but there are several disadvantages inherent in the devil's advocate approach:

1 Although it exposes some underlying assumptions, it does so in the context of what is wrong with them rather than what they should be. It does not serve to develop a new managerial world view.

2 If the censure prevails and the plan is rejected, there is nothing to replace it.

3 There is a tendency for management's attitude to be destructive rather than constructive.

4 There is a possibility that the planner's psychological response to extended criticism results in his demoralization and, at best, in a tendency for him to develop "safe" plans rather than progressive ones.

The dialectical approach presented in the next section retains the advantages of the devil's advocate approach, but it also purports to eliminate these disadvantages.

A DIALECTICAL APPROACH TO POLICY, PLANNING, AND STRATEGY MAKING

A system may be said to be dialectical if it examines a situation completely and logically from two different points of view. The dialectical approach begins by identifying the prevailing or recommended plan and the data that were used to derive it. The question is posed: Under what view of the world is this the optimal plan to follow? This results in an attempt to specify a set of plausible and believable assumptions that underlie this plan, assumptions that serve to interpret the data so as to logically conclude that this plan is best for achieving the organization's goals.

In order to test the underlying assumptions, a search is initiated to find another plausible and believable alternative—the counterplan. It may well be one of the alternatives considered and rejected in the original planning process. This counterplan (as well as the plan) should have the attributes of being feasible, politically viable, and generally credible in the

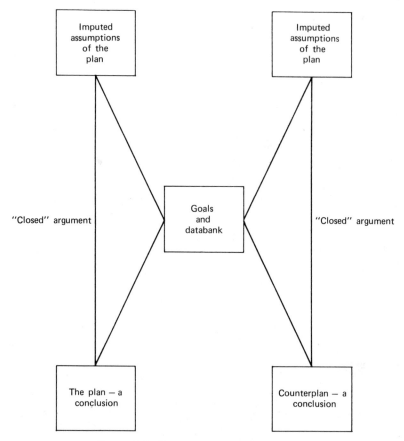

Figure 6-1 Inverse optimal logic.

organizational context. The view of the world for which the counterplan is "optimal" is then specified. Figure 6-1 summarizes the process.

The principal theme of dialectical advice is that policymakers, planners, and strategists learn about the plan's fundamental assumptions and come to understand them by observing the conflict that emerges between the plan and the counterplan and between their attendant world views. The vehicle for inducing this reflection is a structured debate.

Contrary to the "well-staffed paper" or the traditional management briefing, the structured debate consists of the most forceful presentation possible of the two opposing plans, given the constraint that each side must interpret, in its entirety, the same organizational data bank. Following a statement of the problem, the structured debate begins with the advocate of the plan stating his world view or model of the situation. The advocate of the counterplan does likewise. Then, as each item of data is introduced it is interpreted by each advocate to demonstrate that it can be interpreted as supporting evidence for his plan and negative evidence for his opponent's plan. The process continues until the data bank is exhausted.

In this dialectical design we are following a scheme suggested by Churchman's (1971) and Mason's (1968) interpretation of Hegel. The plan (thesis) is opposed by the counterplan (antithesis) both of which are constructed and argued for from the same data bank (the essence). Hegel's theory leads us to predict that the policymaker—observer of the conflict—will integrate and form a new and expanded world view (the synthesis). The synthesis includes exposing hidden assumptions and developing a new conceptualization of the planning problem the organization faces. The results obtained in applying the theory of dialectical advice to the strategic planning problem of a major U.S. corporation are summarized in the following section. Chapter 7 contains a copy of the dialectical report that resulted and two other dialectical reports.

RMK ABRASIVES: A FIELD STUDY/EXPERIMENT IN DIALECTICAL ADVICE

With the cooperation of the management of RMK Abrasives the dialectical technique was applied to their strategic planning problem. The firm had settled on two primary goals:

1 To increase after-tax corporate earnings by a minimum of 10% per annum (compounded) over the 10 year planning period.
2 To be earning a rate of return on assets (ROA) of at least 8% by the terminal (tenth) year of the plan.

Faced with the problem of devising a strategy to achieve these goals, the planning department collected considerable data—market trends in the abrasives industry, demand forecasts for the next 10 years, studies identifying their customers and factors influencing purchase, a determination of nonabrasive products that could be substitutes for their product, those technological and economic factors influencing customers, figures on the current and future use of abrasives in a variety of foreign countries, tables of manufacturing costs in various world-wide locations, transportation costs, and general sociopolitical data.

On the basis of a thorough analysis of this data, the planners concluded that the existing strategy would not result in the accomplishment of the corporation's goals. They recommended that a new strategy be adopted.

This new strategy essentially involved the firm's becoming an international, marketing-oriented organization. Within the framework of this strategy various particular countries and product-market relationships were explored. These recommendations and the supporting analysis were compiled in a strategic planning document and were also presented to management orally in a briefing session. It should be noted that this procedure is basically the expert advice approach to the planning problem—one point of view (the planning department's) analyzed the data, considered alternative strategies, and recommended a "best" course of action.

Several weeks following the presentation, the dialectical study began. Given the data, the goals, and the planning department's recommended plan, a set of assumptions was attributed to the planner to bring "closure" to the argument underlying the plan. Figure 6-1 shows the logical relationship between the goals data and plans and the assumptions imputed from them. The "inverse optimal" question was posed and a set of assumptions was derived. These assumptions had the property that, when used to interpret the data, they led to the recommended plan as a logical conclusion. For example, one apparent assumption underlying the recommended plan was that most of the inhabitants of foreign countries are basically motivated toward improving their own standard of living and that each country viewed the company's entry into its economy as satisfying this need. Another imputed assumption was that most abrasive user problems were similar and the strategic decision accordingly hinged on finding additional markets for existing products. With the aid of these assumptions and others, it was possible to interpret the data to conclude that the international, marketing-oriented plan was best for achieving the corporate long-range goals.

In general there were 10 basic assumptions underlying this international plan. They are listed below in postulate type form:

1-1   RMK Abrasives is a seller of abrasives products and services supplying the steel, metal working, and woodworking industries.

1-2   All abrasives problems are basically similar.

1-3   Management techniques are translocatable.

1-4   Host countries are xenophilic, riskless.

1-5   RMK's competitors are quantity, expansionist oriented. They will cut prices.

1-6   RMK's customers are conservative, slow to change.

1-7   R&D is a "necessary evil" required to keep up in the business.

1-8   Merger opportunities are available, receptive.

1-9 Other companies will not integrate into the abrasives business.

1-10 RMK's parent corporation will supply adequate financial, administrative, and managerial support for a program of expansion.

In order to establish the credibility of these assumptions, a study was made of the corporation's communication stream. By reviewing statements made in interviews, interoffice memos, corporate directives, magazine articles, and public announcements, considerable evidence was found to substantiate the fact that many members of the corporation did indeed believe (or at least espouse) the point of view set forth by the plan's imputed assumption set. Thus this was a set of plausible and credible assumptions for this organization. However, the study also revealed that there was not complete unanimity in these beliefs. This divergence of opinion served as a clue for developing a counterplan.

There were indications that some executives favored the firm's concentrating its efforts on the domestic market and emphasizing technological innovation. Thus a domestic technologically oriented counterplan was formed and a set of assumptions was sought that closed its argument. The counterplan's world view included several assumptions that were contrary to those of the plan. One counterplan assumption was, for example, that the inhabitants of most foreign countries are motivated primarily by strong nationalistic tendencies and that this would make doing business abroad risky. Another assumption was that each abrasive user has unique problems and, accordingly, that a successful company must broaden its product line to meet the varying needs of its customers. Again, it could be demonstrated that this new set of assumptions could be used to interpret the data and to conclude that the counterplan was best for achieving the corporate goals.

The 10 basic assumptions for this domestic counterplan were as follows:

D-1 RMK is in the business of applying special skills directed towards solving the problems of shaping, forming, and smoothing materials.

D-2 Every abrasives problem is unique.

D-3 Management techniques are specific to a particular environment.

D-4 Host countries are xenophobic, risk laden.

D-5 RMK's competitors are quality-product oriented. They will seek to produce a better product.

D-6 RMK's customers are dynamic, responsive to technological innovation.

D-7   R&D is the "heart and lifeblood" of the firm and is required to keep ahead of competition.

D-8   Merger opportunities are available, receptive.

D-9   Other companies will not integrate into the abrasives business.

D-10   RMK's parent corporation will supply adequate financial, administrative, and managerial support for a program of expansion.

Having established the plan, the counterplan, and their supporting world views, the next step was to prepare a structured debate. This structured debate was presented to RMK's management in both written document form and orally in a strategic planning briefing session. In order to eliminate variances in personality and persuasive ability, the role of both the advocate of the plan and the advocate of the counterplan were assumed by one person. An excerpt from the actual structured debate follows:

Data-Item

Ferrous Industry

The ferrous and iron and steel metal working industries account for a large percentage of the domestic abrasives business today. By 1980 it is anticipated that this percentage will decline. Some important factors are:

1 Continuous casting will replace soaking pits and will grow in importance. This process requires hot cutoff and hot grinding capabilities.
2 There is an increased demand for finer, microscopic tolerances, faster removal rates of excess stock, and reduced fixturing and set-up costs.
3 Steel companies are spending about $2.4 billion this year (greater than their cash flow) on revolutionizing the steel making process.

International Plan Advocate's Interpretation:

Our international manager sees the reduction in abrasives sales to the domestic iron and steel industry as a good reason for RMK's not depending as heavily in the future on this source of income as it has in the past. He also views technological changes, such as the switch to continuous casting, as imposing greater cost burdens on RMK's new product development without substantially increasing revenues. Many of these costs could be absorbed if the market were larger. For example, he sees a need for pilot plants to develop and test new products, but a firm must be large to afford a pilot plant. Expanding into the international market appears to be the best and fastest way of gaining the necessary size.

Once RMK increased its overall size of operations, then it would be in a better position to cope with the problems of technological change within the domestic ferrous industry. A source of increased revenues and a "listening post" for new ideas is the role of the foreign subsidiary in keeping the company competitive in the iron and steel market.

The manager fears that the domestic plan places far too much reliance on the somewhat unstable domestic ferrous metals market.

Domestic Counterplan Advocate's Interpretation:

Our domestic manager interprets the ''leveling off'' of sales to the ferrous industry and that industry's change in iron and steel making processes as a response on their part to increased competition from abroad (Japan, for example) and from domestic plastics, brick, and aluminum. They are now more cost-conscious and are willing to pay for products which have a higher ''worth'' in their operations. These users want higher tolerances, faster operations, and reduced abrasive costs. The abrasives supplier who can develop a ''package'' of products and services which solves these steel industry problems will capture a much greater market share.

The domestic manager believes that these changes in the domestic ferrous industry are occurring now and are going to take place rapidly. Hence, he asserts that RMK must concentrate on R&D and on devising new services for the iron and steel industry immediately. He believes that once one falls behind in the R&D race it is almost impossible to catch up. Instead of looking for foreign acquisitions, he would seek domestic acquisitions which would add new skills and help build RMK's technological base rather rapidly.

He fears that the international plan does not adequately provide for improving the company's position in light of current changes in iron and steel. The domestic market will not wait for foreign successes to provide the R&D funds that are needed now. Failure to become a leader in the domestic ferrous market today, in his opinion, means that this important market may be irretrievably lost to RMK tomorrow.

The central hypothesis of the study at RMK was that the manager-recipients of the debate form a new, more encompassing conceptualization of the problem—the synthesis. Evidence gained from questionnaires, interviews, and a recorded log of events supports this hypothesis. For example, the six top RMK executives all reported that the presentation had forced them to reconsider the assumptions of the corporate strategy and each of the executives mentioned at least one implicit assumption that had been exposed to him. Each, in some way, mentioned the assumption of timing in the execution of the final plan. A consensus began to grow among these executives that the plan and counterplan were not really mutually exclusive alternatives but rather should be considered as part of a more grand strategy that involved a well-timed execution of both domestic and international expansion. One executive, who articulated a rather detailed new strategy, said that he devised this new strategy in order to ''get the best from both sides of the dilemma'' presented by the structured debate. This timing concept was not made explicit in either the original plan or the counterplan; however, approximately 6 months after the structured debate presentation it had become an integral part of RMK's (still evolving) strategy. Several executives attribute that change to the counterplanning presentation.

In addition to exposing underlying assumptions, the structured debate also suggested new alternative courses of action (plans) to the recipients. One executive who proposed a rather complete new plan described the mental process that led to its development:

It (the dialectical presentation) structures creativity by stimulating thought. The two well developed points of view pull you both ways at the same time. You begin to ask yourself, "How can we get the best of both?" It becomes the vehicle for amalgamating the best plan you know how to develop.

All interviewees indicated that the presentation had caused them to reconsider the corporate goals (subsequently RMK modified its original goals) and that it had caused them to reevaluate the relevancy of the data bank. In particular, several studies were initiated in order to obtain information that was not available previously but that now seemed critical. All executives reported that they had developed a new and improved conceptualization of the problem, and each provided specific incidences to support his statement. Thus we can infer that a synthesis did occur. This synthesis had the effect of providing a new set of planning assumptions that ultimately led RMK abrasives to a new strategic plan.

CONDITIONS FOR THE EMPLOYMENT OF DIALECTICAL ADVICE

Every organizational design has advantages and disadvantages in its use. The dialectical approach to strategic planning is no exception. However, there are at least four circumstances that, if they are present in an organization, make the dialectical method very effective. These are:

1 Management is unaware of some important assumptions and is in doubt as to both the appropriate assumptions to adopt and the particular plan to choose. In this case there is no basic agreement on assumptions between the policymaker and the adviser (staff planner).
2 Management acknowledges the possible existence of multiple interpretations of the data, each of which indicates a different relevancy of the organization's data bank to the choice to be made. Consequently, the dialectic's alternative interpretation of the data is meaningful.

3 In cases of decision making under uncertainty, management looks to the advisor to point out the incidence of the uncertainty or the key assumptions on which it turns instead of resolving or "absorbing" the uncertainty inherent in the situation. Thus in the dialectic the advisor communicates different conclusions that are derived from different assumptions. Management then relies on its own judgment to formulate a synthesized set of assumptions on which the validity of his ultimate choice will depend.

4 Management believes that the expected cost associated with (a) developing both a plan and a counterplan and (b) involving itself in the development of a new set of assumptions (a synthesized world view) is less than the expected cost of an adviser's error in assumptions.

Expert advice, the devil's advocate approach, or some other organization design may be more effective than the dialectical approach if these conditions are not met.

SUMMARY

This chapter began by asserting that an organization's plan is based on the policymakers' assumptions about the world in which they operate. Specifically, these assumptions were said to include predictions, a value system or ends, and a choice from among available behavior patterns or means. This point was demonstrated by showing the role of assumptions in a simple inventory model.

We concluded that there is a need for a planning technique that serves to "test" the assumptions of a plan by exposing "hidden" assumptions and, ideally, by suggesting new and potentially more relevant assumptions on which the policymaker can base his future plan. It was argued that the traditional "expert approach" to planning fails to adequately test assumptions and that the devil's advocate approach, while in a sense testing assumptions, also tends to destroy the plan without replacing it with an improved plan. Hegel's triad—thesis, antithesis, and synthesis—was drawn on in order to design a dialectical approach to planning that averted the deficiencies of both the expert and devil's advocate approaches. It was proposed that the resulting counterplanning problem technique would stimulate a new and broadened concept of the planning problem—the synthesis. Evidence obtained in a field study/ experiment at RMK Abrasives supported this hypothesis. Since this evidence was obtained in the context of a real and ongoing organization, it is necessarily sociological in nature. Chapter 7 contains three cases in which the dialectical structured debate method was used.

Chapter Seven ────────────

Dialectical Debate Cases
────────────────────

This chapter contains three cases in which structured dialectical debate methods have been used to deal with complex problems of policy, planning, and strategy. The first case is a business planning case. It also illustrates one of the techniques for designing a structured debate. With this technique, facts or data items are presented and then interpreted by each point of view. The second case deals with a public policy problem. The technique used to design this debate is to present the plan with its supporting arguments, and then to present the counterplan with its supporting arguments. The third case is a dialogue in the form of two scenarios designed to penetrate the deeper metaphysical assumptions underlying a policy choice. This debate was prepared to show how data coming from the Earth Resources Technological Satellite might be interpreted from different points of view for making land use policy.

RMK ABRASIVES MANAGEMENT BRIEFING

THE PROBLEM

Situation

RMK is an established manufacturer of abrasive materials. New, aggressive management has actively pursued a program of increased growth in earnings and improved profitability in operations. A major step taken by management in initiating this program was to establish a department of corporate planning. Among the planning department's responsibilities was the setting, with management's assistance, of the corporation's financial goals and the development of a 10 year strategic plan for achieving these goals. This study is concerned with determining the general character of the 10 year strategic plan RMK *should* adopt.

Industry

Abrasives are materials of extreme hardness that are used to shape other materials by a grinding or abrading action. They generally assume one of three forms: (1) loose grain, (2) grinding wheels, or (3) coatings on cloth or paper. The primary function of an abrasive product is to remove waste or unwanted material in the shaping or forming of materials such as metals and woods, and in the precision grinding of these materials. Because of their superior hardness and ability to withstand high temperature, they have advantages in speed of operation, depth of cut, and smoothness of finish.

Abrasive products are used for cleaning and machining all types of metal; for grinding and polishing glass; for smoothing wooden surfaces, such as in the manufacture of furniture; for grinding logs to paper pulp; for cutting metals, glass, and cement; and for the manufacture of many miscellaneous products such as brake linings and nonslip floor tiles. They are, in general, industrial products that are employed in the manufacturing and processing of other products.

The raw materials used in the manufacture of abrasives are both natural and synthetic. Natural abrasive materials include diamonds, corundum (a form of Al_2O_3), emery (a ferrous-laden Al_2O_3), and silicon oxides (SiO_2) such as quartz. The synthetics include silicon carbide (SiC), which is made from 60% quartz sand and 40% carbon coke, abrasive aluminum oxide, which is made from calcined bauxite by fusion in an electric arc furnace, and synthetic diamonds.

There is a variety in abrasive products. RMK produces some 40,000 different types of coated abrasives such as sandpapers, each with a different grain, texture, or backing. Also, some 250,000 different shapes and compositions of grinding wheels are produced. Grinding wheels vary as to abrasive type, grain size, grade or hardness, bond type, and porosity. A wheel is a combination of abrasive, bonding agent, and air. Its hardness is a function of the type and amount of bond and the density of the wheel. In application, it is important to select the proper wheel for the grinding job to be performed. It must not be too soft or too hard. Thus the abrasives industry can be characterized as being very technical in nature.

The industry is oligopolistic in its market form, being dominated by Norton Corporation (approximately 25% of the total market), Carborundum Company (approximately 25% of the total market), and 3M Company, which accounts for over 30% of the coated abrasives market. The buyer's market also is characterized by a small number of firms. The steel and nonelectric machinery industries account for over 25% of the abrasives sales, while the balance of the sales is derived from a number of industries, including foundry, electrical, automotive, chemical, aerospace, furniture, and nonferrous metals.

Financial Summary

RMK Abrasives manages approximately $40 million in assets. The 1980 year-end balance sheet is summarized below:

Assets (in millions)		Liabilities	
Cash and securities	$ 6	Current	$ 5
Inventory	24	Debt	7
Net fixed assets	20	Common stock	
		and surplus	28
	$40		$40

Sales in 1980 were $40 million, and a profit after tax (PAT) of $2.5 million was earned on that volume. Depreciation allowances of $1.2 million were charged. Dividends of $0.9 million were declared and paid in keeping with a longstanding policy of paying out 36% of earnings as dividends.

Historically, RMK has carried a debt/equity ratio of 1:4; however, recent financial negotiations will permit RMK to borrow at a much heavier rate in the future. It is estimated that new borrowings may be floated at close to a 1:2.5 ratio.

As a consequence, RMK expects to generate funds for expansion approximating $2.44 million in 1981 and continuing at that order of magnitude or larger for the 10 year planning period. The $2.44 million figure was calculated as follows:

Funds from internal sources		
Profit after taxes (PAT) 1980	$2.5	
Depreciation	1.2	
Less dividends	−0.9	
Total		$1.80
Funds from debt sources		
Profit after taxes (PAT) 1980	2.5	
Less dividends	−0.9	
Retained earnings	1.6	
Debt equity at 1:2.5	×0.4	
Total		0.64
Total funds for expansion		$2.44 million

RMK's Strategic Planning Problem

The management of RMK Abrasives has adopted as its overall objective "to provide for a continual increase in the *value* of the corporate stock for its shareholders." This has been translated into the financial goal: "To increase *after* tax corporate earnings (PAT) by a minimum of 10% per annum (compounded)." The goal is spelled out in terms of actual dollar amounts as follows:

PAT 1980	$2.5 million
10% Compounded growth	
Rate $(1.10)^{10}$	$\times 2.594$
Target PAT 1990	$6.5 million (approximately)

A second corporate objective is to secure this earnings growth with a minimum of investment in assets. This objective has been operationalized as the financial goal: "To be earning at least 8.0% on assets (ROA) by 1990." (This is calculated as PAT divided by total assets.) Current ROA is ($2.5/$40) or 6.25%.

Finally, a third objective is to insure that the programs and projects undertaken do not involve too great a risk of the corporation's resources. This goal is realized by careful evaluation of expansion and investment proposals.

Studies of the domestic abrasives industry, which RMK currently serves, indicate that the total dollar volume of demand for the industry's products will essentially remain constant during the 10 year planning period. Forecasts for domestic abrasives sales in 1981 are for $350 million and in 1990 are for $380 million, a mere increase of $30 million during that period.

RMK's strategic planning problem can be more clearly pinpointed by comparing its expected earnings from domestic abrasives sales in 1990 with its targeted earnings for 1990 (figures in millions):

Domestic abrasives market forecast 1990	$380.00
RMK's market share (1980 = 11.5%)	12%
Expected RMK revenue 1990	$ 45.60
RMK expected PAT as a percent of sales (1980 = 6.25%)	7%
1990 expected PAT from domestic abrasive sales	3.2
RMK's target PAT 1990	6.5
Difference to be made up from new sources	$3.3

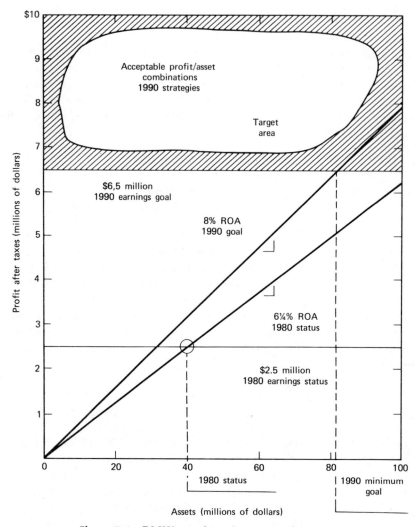

Figure 7-1   RMK's profit and asset requirements.

Thus RMK's strategic planning problem is to plan for new sources of income that will provide for an additional $3.3 million PAT by 1990 from markets other than RMK's traditional domestic abrasives market. Total 1990 PAT should be $6.5 million, and an ROA of 8% should be realized. (See Figure 7-1). It is important to notice that assets will probably more than double during the 10 year period, from $40 million in 1980 to approximately $81 million in 1990. Figure 7-2 displays RMK's planning problem using "gap" analysis.

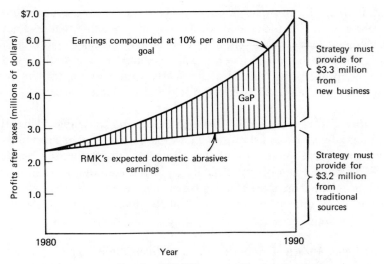

Figure 7-2 Graph of RMK's strategic planning issue.

Alternative Strategies

It is clear that in order to meet its goals, RMK Abrasives will have to undergo some rather substantial changes during the next 10 years. The corporate planning staff has identified five alternative strategies or courses of action that RMK can follow. Although these alternatives are not mutually exclusive in the long run, the planning staff feels that due to funds limitations and the heavy initial fixed investments required to embark on each of these plans, they are to a large extent mutually exclusive in the short run, especially during the first 4 to 5 years of the 10 year period. It is believed that each of these strategies, if it is to be successful, will require the better part of the $12 to $15 million in expansion funds, which can be generated over the first 5 years of the planning period. (Expected funds for 1981 are $2.44 million, as shown previously.)

Complete Domestic Abrasives Supplier This strategy would entail an increased development of the present product line and expansion into new abrasive products in an effort to increase the domestic market share. It would require more research (both basic and applied), increased technological orientation, and investment in new manufacturing facilities. An important part of this strategy would be the development of allied products and services, such as machining systems that employ abrasives.

Limited Domestic Abrasives Supplier   This strategy would be patterned after 3M's success in the coated abrasives field. It would involve selecting either coated abrasives or grinding wheels and focusing marketing and R&D efforts in that area. Unprofitable products, plants, and personnel would be pruned. By this strategy RMK would attempt to increase profitability and market share in the selected products markets.

International Abrasives Supplier through Export and Licensing   This strategy essentially involves establishing new markets for existing products by finding the right combination of foreign agents, export houses, brokers, and RMK-owned-and-operated facilities in foreign countries. Emphasis would be placed on marketing, advertising, sales training, packaging, transportation, and insurance skills and facilities for serving the world abrasives market.

International Abrasives Supplier through Investment   This strategy essentially entails taking existing managerial and technical know-how into new market areas and establishing or acquiring new foreign operations. A world-wide, multinational organizational form would be adopted to direct the personnel and capital resources located abroad.

Diversification into Related (but Nonabrasives) Fields   Under this plan, RMK would concentrate its efforts on diversifying into related nonabrasives fields. This program of concentric diversification might include acquisitions and investments in ceramics, marketing to heavy industries that RMK now supplies, mining, and/or materials handling and processing.

MANAGEMENT BRIEFING

A Structured Debate between the International Plan and the Domestic Counterplan

The planning department has identified two fundamentally different plans by which RMK might expand in order to meet its goals:

1   To become an international abrasives supplier through acquisition and original investment (described in the previous section, hereafter called the *International Plan*).
2   To become a complete domestic abrasives supplier through acquisition, R&D, and technological expansion (described in the previous section, hereafter called the *Domestic Counterplan*).

These two basic strategies or plans are stated more precisely in the statements of strategy.

STATEMENTS OF STRATEGY

International Expansion Plan

RMK Abrasives will seek to become *the* international supplier of abrasives. Its management will adopt a multinational orientation with interests in the major abrasives markets throughout the world. RMK will engage in an active program of acquisition, licensing, or original investment in order to establish raw material sources, processing plants, and marketing organizations in foreign countries throughout the world. Diversification opportunities will be considered wherever and whenever they are compatible with international operations.

Domestic Integration Counterplan

RMK Abrasives will seek to improve its position in the domestic market by becoming a well-integrated, quality supplier of products and services designed to solve problems related to the shaping, forming, and smoothing of materials. This will be accomplished by (1) backward integration into new sources of raw materials, especially synthetic abrasive materials, (2) forward integration into warehousing, distribution, and customer services, and (3) horizontal integration into related product areas based on RMK's acknowledged skills and suitability for existing users. RMK will strive for technological superiority through a customer needs, problem-solving, marketing-oriented, and R&D program. Diversification will be considered where it is compatible with domestic skills and organization and as it is necessary to meet profit goals.

As can be seen, the international plan and the domestic counterplan represent two quite separate and distinct strategies for accomplishing RMK's goals. One plan would change the overall character of the company during the next 10 years into a multinational organization that supplies the abrasives user wherever he is located. The other proposes a much more technically oriented company that is bent on improving the scientific nature of its management, products, and operations and on using its skills and knowledge of domestic requirements to establish leadership and ensure profitability. The talent required, the acquisitions made, and the programs initiated would all be substantially different depending on which plan was adopted. This is especially true during the early phases of the 10 year period.

Both plans have in common that the domestic abrasives business will serve as a foundation, supplying the profits and know-how on which expansion programs can be based. However, whereas the domestic plan intensifies activities within the domestic market, the international plan seeks to extend the market itself. In addition to internally generated funds, both plans further assume the availability of administrative support and managerial backing from the corporation necessary to embark on a program of expansion, acquisition, and diversification.

The question before us then becomes, *Which plan should RMK adopt?*

The answer to this question depends very much on how *you,* the people who are responsible for carrying out and living with the final decision, view your organization, its people, its environment, and, in particular, the future prospects for the world in which RMK will operate during the next decade. In order to address this question, let us begin by painting two pictures of the "world of RMK abrasives"; two "stories" that convey the outlook and perceptions of two imaginary managers who have decided on each of these plans.

Each manager's story will be broken into a sequence of episodes. Each episode describes his view of one of the basic factors that underlie the decision. These basic factors are:

1   View of RMK's business and growth possibilities.
2   View of abrasive problems in general.
3   View of generality of management techniques.
4   View of a foreign country's acceptance of RMK.
5   View of competition.
6   View of the domestic customer.
7   View of R&D.
8   View of merger and acquisition possibilities.
9   View of outside influences.

We begin with the world view of the international plan manager.

INTERNATIONAL PLAN

The rationale of an executive who adopts the international plan may be something like this. First, he sees RMK as a seller of *abrasives* products and services, one that supplies the steelworking, metalworking, and woodworking industries. The basis of RMK's business is raw materials such as bauxite, diamonds, and silica sands, and the knowledge of how to process them into products such as grains, grinding wheels, and coated papers. The growth that divisional goals call for should come from the application of this traditional know-how to an expanded market area. Since there is little opportunity for this expansion to take place in the domestic market, he is led to consider international expansion. The industries to which RMK sells are established in all the more economically developed countries, and they seem to be on the "up-swing" in some of the other less-developed countries. The profitable company of the future, in his mind, will be the one that has the flexibility and opportunities that broad geographical scope provides.

The similarities among abrasives problems predominate, in his opinion, and a good management should be able to adapt or modify its operations to satisfy a particular customer's, *or* a particular country's, needs.

Although he is cognizant of the fact that each user has a different production process, basically "smoothing is smoothing" and "grinding is grinding" to him, and he thinks that a common solution to a large number of industries' abrasive problems, regardless of their geographical locations, should exist.

He sees the industry as moving into an era where increasing use of mass production techniques can be economically employed in abrasive processing. Raw materials are still the key inputs. He believes that an abrasives firm should continue to seek out and secure new sources of these vital raw materials that are of economical scale in size.

Here in the United States, during the postwar period, he has seen the development of a considerable number of new managerial techniques, new methods of marketing and distribution, better and tighter methods of control, new systems of incentives, and new concepts of general organization, many of which RMK has been able to employ effectively. In his opinion, there is a good opportunity for RMK to introduce and apply these more efficient techniques abroad.

As far as he is concerned, a kind of "enlightenment" has occurred among the free-world countries in recent years, and they are far more receptive to American-based companies entering into their market areas. To be sure, there will be some cultural and ethnic animosities. These animosities will always exist, but this simply means that a company must plan for periods of mutual adjustment and "getting to know each other." However, in the long run, he believes that people in other countries are seeking to improve their standards of living and ways of life. Despite all the United States' shortcomings, other countries tend to see the economic prowess available to them through a company such as RMK as a means for securing a better life for their own people (e.g., Norton's Lillesand, Norway, plant). He believes that the risks of doing business in a foreign country have been overstated. He points to the fact that abrasives are vital inputs to a country's basic industries. This accords the American-based abrasives manufacturer a kind of leverage in a foreign community, by virtue of his control of the influx of the managerial, distributive, technical, and financial expertise that are unavailable locally. Geographical dispersion and large size would allow RMK to "self-insure" itself against an occasional disturbing influence in any one of the countries in which it was located. In general, there are a variety of techniques for protecting the company against the hazards of multinational operations, and the "international plan" manager would assume that RMK can develop the managerial talent necessary to employ them effectively.

Our "international plan" manager is concerned about what he perceives to be increased competitive activity abroad. Norton and Carborundum have both been especially active in foreign markets, and the recent mergers will enhance their abilities for foreign expansion. RMK's opportunities in foreign countries are diminishing rapidly. Norton is active in 77 different countries; both Norton and Carborundum are now selling over one third of their gross overseas. Thus it appears to him that if RMK does not establish itself in the foreign market almost immediately, it will have forsaken its opportunities there for some time to come. Meanwhile, the competitors, spurred on and financially supported by foreign successes, will be in a position to threaten the profitability of RMK's domestic operations. They will be able to engage in price cutting and in offering additional services in an effort to expand their own share of the domestic market.

In his opinion, the company will be able to satisfy the domestic customer's needs while it embarks on an international expansion plan. He sees the typical abrasives customer as a large industrial firm with a long tradition and investment in its own internal production processes, a firm that is historically committed to the market share system in purchasing from suppliers. A good marketing program and a reasonable rate of technological innovation are all that is required to maintain the domestic business while the company concentrates a good portion of its resources on developing its international operations.

From his point of view, research and development is merely one aspect of the overall activity of the company. It is important that it be maintained at a level adequate to insure that RMK keeps abreast of new developments as they occur and that the company does not fall behind in new product development. However, the "international plan" manager is also aware that it is possible to spend money for R&D without gaining much in the way of new and profitable products. Some important aspects of the abrasives business are still in the "black art" stage and *cannot* be subjected to completely technological solutions, in his opinion. He would rather invest more heavily in foreign countries now and let the revenues gleaned and the know-how acquired from these foreign operations support future R&D expansions. In general, he sees the increased size gained from world-wide operations as the key to achieving economies of scale in R&D, as well as in production and in distribution.

Acquisition and merger opportunities are available, in his opinion, on both the domestic and international scene, and these companies are generally receptive to proposal offers as long as the mutual benefits of combination can be spelled out to them.

As he looks at other possibilities, he is convinced that other companies, such as the big chemical firms, will *not* decide to integrate into the abrasives business.

On the basis of these considerations, he has concluded that RMK should adopt the international expansion plan as its strategy for the next 10 years.

Our second imaginary manager, the one who would adopt the domestic counterplan, holds a much different view of the "World of RMK abrasives." The contrasts between his view and that of the international plan manager become more clear as his "story" unfolds.

DOMESTIC INTEGRATION COUNTERPLAN

The rationale of an executive who adopts the domestic counterplan may be something like this. To begin with, he visualizes RMK as a collection of special skills directed towards solving the problems of shaping, forming, and smoothing of materials. The growth that corporate goals call for should come, then, from RMK's ability to improve its capacity to solve these types of customer problems. In order to do this, the company must expand and build on its existing "core of skills" so that it can provide better and more useful services to its customers and offer a wider selection of quality products. The profitable company of the future will be the one that is a leader in "imagination"—the one resource that, once established, cannot be readily duplicated by competition.

The safest assumption to make, in his opinion, is that abrasive problems are unique. Every steel firm, every furniture manufacturer, in fact, every abrasives user has its own peculiar operating characteristics. The problems of a foreign-based industry are even more diverse because of the differences inherent in their different cultures and business traditions. The well-managed company, to his way of thinking, differentiates its product line and provides related services so that it might offer the best "package" for each individual abrasives situation.

He recognizes America's industrial might and the very efficient methods and procedures that have made our country's economic growth possible. But he believes that this is due, to a large extent, to a national philosophy that does not necessarily prevail in other countries. American management techniques are *not* transferable, tit for tat, to a foreign operation. An attempt to transfer those techniques would be both naive and costly, in his opinion. Instead, if a company wants to operate in a foreign country, it must make a fairly heavy investment in developing new processes and techniques that are attuned to the local conditions.

The "domestic counterplan" manager is concerned about a return to a stronger nationalism now that many countries have improved their production and trade capabilities. He fears that these countries would much prefer to develop their own indigenous capacities, and not be dependent on another country for help, especially a "Yankee Imperialist." The foreign customer will switch his allegiance to a local supplier as soon as it is economically feasible for him to do so. He is *not* the kind of customer on which a sound long-range program can be based. The world political situation, over which RMK can exert very little control, bothers our domestic manager. So do the possibilities of devaluation, or even revolution, that one must take into account when doing business abroad.

Despite all the risks involved in doing business in a foreign country, he thinks that the international market does present many profitable opportunities. But there is one thing he is convinced of: the best insurance policy against risks of international business is to be technologically superior, to continue to lead in the development of skills and know-how that cannot be duplicated elsewhere. In his opinion, RMK abrasives has not reached this position of leadership yet, and hence it should not venture abroad until it has secured its technological position here at home.

Our "domestic counterplan" manager is much more alarmed at the fact that Norton recently purchased the National Research Corporation as an R&D diversification and that Norton, Carborundum, and 3M all devote considerable resources to R&D than he is at any international activity on their part. As a consequence, RMK can expect to compete against better, more durable, higher-quality products, special services, and, perhaps, "packaged abrasive programs" in the future. The company must be able to meet this competition.

The "domestic counterplan" manager views the domestic abrasives customer as "ready" for these new innovations. In his opinion, the abrasives customer has become a much more intelligent purchaser who is "sharpening his pencil." The customer is much more fickle than he used to be, and much quicker to recognize and accept the technological and economic superiority of a product—witness the impact of continuous casting in the steel industry and of Carborundum's ability to provide the requisite hot cutoff and hot grinding capacity. RMK Abrasives must recognize and respond to the changes that are occurring within the abrasives business. "The day of the supersalesman is over—*now* is the day of super abrasive systems." In light of the dramatic changes that are taking place here in the domestic market, the company simply cannot afford to divert its efforts by going abroad.

"From whence you start is research" is the belief of our "domestic counterplan" manager. He believes that the stream of products and services emanating from R&D is the "lifeblood" of the firm, that investments in research are prerequisites to new markets and new sources of demand. It is becoming more important in the abrasives business for a supplier to "qualify" in the eyes of the customer by virtue of its innovations and its leadership in research. However, it takes time, management's dedication and support, and an investment in facilities and personnel to put together the right combination of talent and skills to be successful in R&D. He feels that the company must continue to improve its R&D program, including a closer liaison with the user and more research into his needs, before it tackles problems in foreign lands.

In his opinion, acquisition and merger opportunities are available both on the domestic and the international scene, and these companies are generally receptive to proposal offers as long as the mutual benefits of combination can be spelled out to them.

As he looks at other possibilities, he, too, is convinced that other companies will *not* decide to integrate into the abrasives business.

On the basis of these considerations he has concluded that RMK should adopt the domestic integration counterplan as its strategy for the next 10 years.

Thus there is a rather substantial difference between these two opposing views of the "world of RMK abrasives." The success of the strategic plan for the next 10 years depends, in great measure, on which of these views turns out to correspond most nearly to that of the "real" world.

It is helpful in approaching this problem to consider some of the key facts we have available concerning the abrasives business and how each of our two managers might interpret them.

FACT

Little growth in domestic total *dollar volume* of sales of abrasives is expected during the next 10 years. The predicted volume of sales for 1981 is $350 million; for 1990, it is $380 million.

Industry studies classify domestic grain, grinding wheel, and coated abrasives markets as "topped out" for the 10 year period. This fact summarizes domestic market forecasts.

International Plan Interpretation

Our international plan manager would say that this forecasted leveling off of total abrasives demand is an indication of limited growth opportunities in the domestic market. To achieve earnings growth goals, RMK should seek new sources of demand for our products and current technology. He believes that competition and the institutionalized market share system will prohibit any significant increase in domestic sales volume. Thus international markets are needed to meet our goals.

He would point out that the domestic plan does not adequately take this into account. If RMK were to remain in the domestic market alone, he foresees considerable price cutting, free services, and other oligopoly-type responses that would impair the company's profit picture. The competitors could support this activity because of RMK's failure to challenge them in the international market.

Contrary to the domestic manager, he would point to the possibility that RMK's increased activity in R&D might "trigger" an intense R&D "race" within the industry, which would be costly for all concerned. Furthermore, it is very likely that these new developments are not required (or even desired) to satisfy the customer's needs. Some abrasives consumers, for example, have expressed doubt that new bonding agents and new coating techniques (e.g., resin, electrostatic coating) will be justified on a cost-performance basis in their applications.

Domestic Counterplan Interpretation

Our domestic counterplan manager would disagree with that view. He would say that the relevant consideration was not "leveled-off" total volume but the *reason* for this occurrence—technological change. Customers requiring more durable abrasives and changing to processes with a lower abrasives consumption are major reasons for this stabilization of demand. RMK must respond rapidly to this change by continuing to develop better products and more customer-oriented services such as installation, application, and maintenance programs. This is where the real future revenues lie.

He is afraid that the international plan takes the total market's level volume at "face value" and does not see the turbulence taking place *within* the industry. In his opinion, these gross volume considerations lead the international plan manager too quickly into higher risk situations in foreign countries. Moreover, the international plan, in diverting its efforts abroad, does not provide the level of protection needed to secure the domestic market.

FACT

The abrasives industry is reasonably well-defined in that its producers and customers are easily identified. Demand for its products is derived from the demand for the abrasives user's products (steel, metals, automobiles, furniture, etc.). Abrasives serve as input factors in their production processes. In the past, abrasives products have not been vulnerable to substitution from sources outside the industry (aluminum and wood, for example, can be substituted for steel), although improved products produced within the industry can be and are substituted for less effective ones. Moreover, abrasives products have not been competitive in other markets. An important exception to this is that recent developments have permitted the substitution of abrasives for cutting and milling tools in some processes and vice versa. This data item refers to the economic nature of the abrasives industry itself.

International Plan Interpretation

The international plan manager sees international expansion as a means of enlarging the market definition in geographical terms. He notes that abrasives are a necessary (currently nonsubstitutable) input into the user's production process. RMK's experience and know-how must then be broadly applicable to abrasives problems in other countries as well. In addition, foreign operations serve as good training grounds for executive talent and also provide for a "cross-fertilization" of ideas among the countries of the world.

He believes that the domestic plan constrains the market area too severely, and he foresees a period of "dog-eat-dog" competition in the U.S. market as a profit squeeze "shake-out" of marginal firms occurs. Without foreign operations to serve as a "buffer," he doesn't believe RMK could continue to generate the funds necessary for growth from the domestic market alone.

Domestic Counterplan Interpretation

On the other hand, the domestic manager sees R&D and well-planned operations as the only way to survive in the important U.S. market. Since abrasives products and services are necessary inputs in the user's production process (ones for which there are very few known substitutes from outside the abrasives industry), he believes that the customer will turn to the technological leader for his abrasive supplies. Hence R&D investments are rewarding. In this competitive industry, technological development is the most effective way of differentiating your product.

He notes that when the metals manufacturing process is viewed as a system, there are several "critical" points where improvements in the cutting, milling, or grinding operations would improve the overall performance of the process. An abrasives-machinery combination securing these improvements would be extremely valuable to the users. It can be sold at its "worth" to him (the user) rather than its cost of production; hence there are profits to be made here if the right products are made available. As long as RMK can develop products and other services that "make money" for the customer in his plant, it can thwart any competitive threats arising in the domestic market. By acquisitions and mergers, which enhance existing domestic skills and bring in new skills to correct weaknesses, RMK can hope to grow even more rapidly.

He would be concerned that the international plan is concentrating on new markets, not new skills, and hence may fail to provide the necessary R&D and management know-how to maintain the domestic market, on which all expansion must be based. The well-defined nature of the business allows competitors to focus their research on the key problems of abrasives users and thereby increase their market share unless RMK matches or exceeds them. The international plan does not weigh this factor heavily enough, in his opinion.

FACT

The ferrous and iron and steel metalworking industries account for a large percentage of the domestic abrasives business today. By 1990, it is anticipated that this percentage will decline. Some important factors are:

1   Continuous casting will replace soaking pits and grow in importance. This process requires hot cutoff and hot grinding capabiliities.

2   There is an increased demand for finer, microscopic tolerances, faster removal rates of excess stock, and reduced fixture and setup costs.

3   Steel companies are spending about $2.4 billion this year (greater than their cash flow) on revolutionizing the steelmaking process.

International Plan Interpretation

Our international manager sees the reduction in abrasives sales to the domestic iron and steel industry as a good reason for RMK's not depending on this source of income as heavily in the future as it has in the past. He also views technological changes, such as the switch to continuous casting, as imposing greater cost burdens on RMK's new product development without substantially increasing revenues. Many of these costs could be absorbed if the market were larger. For example, he sees a need for pilot plants to develop and test new products, but a firm must be large to afford a pilot plant. Expanding into the international market appears to be the best and fastest way of gaining the necessary size.

Once RMK increased its overall size of operations, it would be in a better position to cope with the problems of technological change within the domestic ferrous industry. A source of increased revenues and a "listening post" for new ideas is the role of the foreign subsidiary in keeping the company competitive in the iron and steel market.

He fears that the domestic plan places far too much reliance on the somewhat unstable domestic ferrous metals market.

Domestic Counterplan

Our domestic manager interprets the "leveling off" of sales to the ferrous industry and industry's change in iron- and steelmaking processes as a response on its part to increased competition from abroad (Japan, for example) and from domestic plastics, brick, and aluminum. The industry is now more cost-conscious and is willing to pay for products that have a higher *"worth"* in its operations. The users want higher tolerances, faster operations, and reduced abrasive costs. The abrasives supplier who can develop a "package" of products and services that solves these steel industry problems will capture a much greater market share.

The domestic manager believes that these changes in the domestic ferrous industry are occurring *now* and are going to take place rapidly. Hence he asserts that RMK must concentrate on R&D and on devising new services for the iron and steel industry immediately. He believes that once one falls behind in the R&D race, it is almost impossible to catch up. Instead of looking for foreign acquisitions, he would seek domestic acquisitions that would add new skills and rapidly build RMK's technological base.

He fears that the international plan does not adequately provide for improving the company's position in light of *current* changes in iron and steel. The domestic market will not wait for foreign successes to provide the R&D funds that are needed now. Failure to become a leader in the domestic ferrous market today, in his opinion, means that this important market may be irretrievably lost to RMK tomorrow.

FACT

Market research shows evidence of a customer trend in preference for:

1 Guaranteed abrasive replacement cost.
2 Guaranteed removal rate of waste metal, wood, or other material.

This data item reveals that the customer is considering requesting more guarantees from his abrasives supplier.

International Plan Interpretation

The international plan manager believes that the company can reduce the risk inherent in offering guarantees by growing, having more installations, and being exposed to more problems and solutions. Since a malfunction or mishap can occur at any time, the customer's manufacturing process is basically unpredictable. A larger number of installations would increase the actuarial soundness of the guarantee program.

Domestic Counterplan Interpretation

On the other hand, the domestic manager points to a need for closer relationships with customers and for acquiring a more intimate knowledge of their processes and their operating practices. This means more technical support—located in the field (at the customer's site if necessary), which works directly with the customer to solve his problems and make his guarantee good.

Moreover, the guarantee should be based on a sound knowledge of the properties of RMK's products and of how they will stand up under different types of applications and utilization. The R&D emphasis of the domestic plan provides for the technological knowledge on which these guarantees can be based.

FACT

A proprietary product lasts until competitors can match it. In the abrasives industry, patent protection is becoming less effective (e.g., synthetic diamonds). Competitor reaction times are shrinking.

A conventional abrasive will usually last until the customer industry changes its practice. The estimate is that 50% of today's product line will be extant in 1990. The product life of a commercial item seems to be diminishing, as shown in this data item.

International Plan Interpretation

Changing technology has made the abrasives industry volatile. The international manager believes that the best way to absorb the shocks of these quick changes is to become bigger, that is, to become a multinational supplier. He is afraid that the domestic plan places all of RMK's "eggs" in the R&D "basket." A competitive "breakthrough," or a big price cut in a conventional product, could severely cripple you if you remain domestic and count almost exclusively on R&D to keep you in business. Furthermore, difficulties in obtaining patent protection allow the competitors to catch up with you when *you* get the "breakthrough." The intent is to have markets at various degrees of development so that when a product becomes obsolete domestically, there is still a market for it in another country. Generally speaking, foreign countries lag 5 to 10 years behind the United States in their use of abrasives, so there is an opportunity to sell at a level adequate to keep you abreast with new developments as they occur. This can be accomplished *without* committing substantial amounts of new funds to an R&D program, if careful attention is paid to management of the activity.

Domestic Counterplan Interpretation

The domestic manager views this fact very differently. When product lives are short, you must turn to R&D as the source of a stream of new products. This customer will not have a long tradition of having purchased newly developed products from any supplier. The company that is the leader can obtain more than its market share. This is one of the objectives of the R&D and domestic acquisition programs in the domestic counterplan.

Suppliers who do not gear themselves to the fast-changing technology may soon be out of business, because they will no longer be able to solve the consumer's problems. In a field where patents are of limited effectiveness for protecting your market position, skills and know-how become the soundest source of growth.

FACT

Small companies play a larger role in continental markets. A trend to consolidation is apparent.

Strong ties, caused in part by cultural preferences, exist between customers and suppliers. Relatively less importance has been attached to new product developments.

Different product mixes are found in Europe, reflecting the different raw materials resources and the different manufacturing practices employed there.

General conditions of overcapacity, obsolete equipment, and labor intensive manufacturing practices prevail. Until 1980, somewhat excessive amounts of labor were employed, but conditions are improving due to actions taken by abrasives producers and buyers. This data item summarizes the European abrasives market picture.

International Plan Interpretation

The international plan manager reads the European situation as an indication of a growing awareness of the need for abrasives suppliers to become larger and to become abrasives specialists. He thinks that RMK must avail itself of acquisition and new entry opportunities *now*, while they are available and before a reconsolidation of abrasives suppliers takes place in Europe. He sees some of these changes as reflecting Europe's recognition of the need for new and improved abrasives for their expanding industries.

He believes that excessive labor, obsolete equipment, and a tendency toward overcapacity are all indications of the need for the better management that RMK Abrasives can provide. The presence of these inefficiencies probably affords RMK an improved bargaining position when the terms of acquisition are negotiated.

Domestic Counterplan Interpretation

The domestic manager sees conditions of overcapacity and obsolescence as indicating the kinds of difficulties RMK would encounter in trying to employ American processes abroad. Certainly, acquisition would be RMK's only reasonable entrée into a market that is experiencing overcapacity. But it has many drawbacks. Many of the companies are small (difficult to expand in a saturated market), and they traditionally have many special "arrangements" and contracts with customers, workers, and local communities that RMK must honor.

Acquiring local management can alleviate some of these problems, but these are the same managers who are responsible for the inefficiencies prevailing in Europe today.

In short, the domestic manager believes that acquiring a European subsidiary or establishing a new operation in Europe at this time would be a substantial drain on RMK's resources. He believes that RMK's resources would be better spent in acquiring a domestic abrasives company or a related or compatible (with respect to skills or know-how) domestic firm that would serve to reinforce RMK's domestic position.

A STRUCTURED DEBATE ON AIRPORT CONGESTION REGULATORY POLICY*

This case shows two different points of view on the public policy problem of congestion in airports. The method employed here is a structured debate in which each world view is presented in terms of its view of the problems and its plan for solving it. The two prospectuses were presented to a group of people playing the role of commissioner in a planning session that contained the following schedule of events.

Schedule of Events

2:30 P.M.	Commissioners submit position papers.
2:35 P.M.	Planner presents the plan.
2:50 P.M.	Counterplanner presents the counterplan.
3:05 P.M.	Planner presents his rationale.
3:25 P.M.	Counterplanner presents his counterarguments.

*This case is abstracted from an unpublished dissertation "The Nature and Extent of Long-Range Planning in the Transportation Regulatory Agencies" by Burton Ross Pierce (Stanford University, 1971). Reprinted by permission.

3:45 P.M.	Moderator distributes copies of plan and counterplan papers to "Commissioners."
3:50 P.M.	Planner and counterplanner entertain questions.
4:10 P.M.	Planner summarizes.
4:15 P.M.	Counterplanner summarizes.
4:20 P.M.	Planner and counterplanner leave. "Commissioners" redraft position papers, making any changes they desire to make as a consequence of the debate.
4:50 P.M.	Break for 10 minutes.
5:00 P.M.	Distribute questionnaire to "Commissioners."
5:30 P.M.	Collect completed questionnaires.

AIRPORT CONGESTION: PLAN

The Problem

The growing congestion of major U.S. airports has shown up in recent years as a worsening of daily delays and extended holding-pattern traffic. To anyone who has waited 30 minutes or longer for his airplane to take off or land, the congestion is real. For business travelers it is a critical problem. The very heavy traffic at O'Hare International Airport and Washington National Airport, as well as at the three international airports in the greater New York City area, has been well publicized, and most people would agree that something needs to be done to relieve the peak congestion here and at several other major airway nodes. In the case of New York City, capacity is truly strained, and authorities are searching for a site for a fourth and even a fifth jetport. Even if a site were chosen immediately, however, it would take years to get an airport designed, financed, constructed, and operational. At points other than New York City, total airport capacity is probably not nearly fully utilized. Washington, D.C. has two major airports in the region besides National, both superior in facilities to Washington National, and both carrying significantly lower levels of traffic. Chicago has Midway Airport, which is more convenient to the city, but which is having only a moderate degree of acceptance as a revived airport. The immediate intuitive response to airport congestion is the building of more airports. However, are there other alternatives that must be considered, both in the short and long run? Although more airports are eventually needed, and planning efforts toward them must proceed, both an immediate plan of action and a long-range policy toward airport use and construction are needed. Otherwise, regulation will not reinforce public policy arrived at by an economic and efficient solution to the problem of airport congestion.

The Public Policy Issue

What are the major alternatives available to relieve airport congestion? Probably the most important alternative addresses the issue of free public access to airport facilities. Traditionally, an airport has been viewed as a public facility available to aircraft on a first-come, first-served basis. Any aircraft could use any airport at any time. Some critics maintain that the United States must abandon this policy in favor of segregated use of airport facilities. Proposals have been advanced for banning certain types of traffic at some airports, having airports serving exclusively general commercial or military aviation, and even for segregating short, domestic, long-haul domestic, and foreign flights. Some have advocated separate airports for supersonic or "jumbo" jets. Allocation of facilities by use has been instituted quite recently at the most congested major airports. Should such segregation become a matter of long-term public policy? Or should we regulate so as to perpetuate unrestricted use of the nation's airports? This section presents the argument that we should, in the long run, pursue the latter alternative. It then proposes a complementary interim solution to the problem of airport congestion.

Interdependence of Various Classes of Aircraft

By the nature of the services they offer, different classes of aircraft and air travel complement and depend on each other. Regional air carriers feed the national carriers, which feed international carriers, and vice versa. Airtaxi and corporate aircraft gain a large part of their usefulness from their ability to interchange passengers with commercial aircraft. Private for-hire carriers and supplemental carriers likewise depend on connections with scheduled air carriers, as do cargo carriers. In fact, some of the scheduled carriers run cargo operations on the same aircraft that, at other times of the day, are used for passenger operations. Segregating such operations would only add to the expense and time required to make the conversion from passenger to cargo and back. An aircraft might be required to deadhead from one airport to another when changing over, adding to the operations at each airport.

Ecological Considerations

In the foreseeable future, airports will continue to be major sources of air and noise pollution in a region. Twice as many airport neighbors subjected to half as many flights (each) per day is not desirable. All airports within the region served contribute to the air pollution of that region. Therefore, it is not desirable to build another airport until the existing capacity within a region is *fully* utilized. Even then, segregated airports, which would enable concentration of specific types of air traffic at specific airports and would enable more passengers than ever to crowd into some airports, would only take the congestion from the air and put it on the ground. Excess airport construction can be compared to the great quantities of freeway construction that were believed to be the answer to automobile congestion in the 1960s. By segregating different types of traffic (through and local, fast and slow) and providing enough capacity to handle the peak volume of traffic, planners believed that traffic congestion would not occur at any time of the day. Congestion at peak travel times continued to occur, as people swarmed to take advantage of the new facilities, and rational alternatives such as mass transit were abandoned. Despite their capacity to handle former peak loads without congestion, the new freeways invited even higher peak loads, greater congestion, and as a result, much worse pollution. A plan for leveling peaks and spreading traffic across existing airports would enable the country to avoid a similar trap in air travel.

Military Users

Establishment of military facilities at civilian airports means that during peacetime the large facilities are maintained and paid for by large volumes of commercial and general aviation, but that in a national emergency extensive, well-maintained facilities that have been in continuous heavy daily operation can be placed at the disposal of the military. Since such sharing is frequently done, the military aircraft have their own parking, servicing, and boarding areas, separate from civilian areas. Runways, tower, ground transportation, and some taxiways are shared. Military flights, in general, have the ability to operate at off-peak hours, since training flights, and so on, can often be made at any hour of the day. As a result, the sharing of civilian facilities with military users presents some special benefits for both. Segregation would remove the possibility of these benefits.

Airport Density

The most convincing reason for continuance of the open-use principle is the airport density concept. In order to develop this concept, a number of preliminary observations may be made. First, because of the air and noise pollution problems connected with the operation of any airport, even one with light traffic, it is desirable to utilize fully existing airports where possible and to build new airports only when the total air traffic of the region in question is too great for the airports of that region to handle (or, better, when the traffic will become too great to handle in the near future). Second, ground traffic consumes a substantial part of American air travelers' time not only because of congestion near the airports, but also because of ground traffic congestion all through our population centers and the surrounding areas. Therefore, it is desirable that each of us have all types of air traffic available at the airport nearest us. A policy of segregated traffic at various airports guarantees that any person will *not* have all air services available at the nearest airport and that driving to the second, third, or even fourth nearest airport will be necessary for some types of air transportation.

Since the number of airports within a given area will be the minimum required to handle the traffic of that region and that number will be the same whether the traffic is segregated or open-use, the airport density is determined by the amount of air traffic within a region. Diverting the user of air transportation to airports farther from his home or place of business will lengthen his trip time, and detract from that unique advantage of air travel—speed. More ground travel will add to the air pollution and ground congestion of a region, and such a policy surely is not in the best interests of the public. Traffic segregation represents an avoidance of public responsibility and as such should not be an acceptable policy.

The Public Policy Posture

This plan proposes that a long-range policy of open airports be continued and promoted. In those areas in which another all-purpose airport is required, a short-term answer is needed that will still be within the spirit of such a policy and that will enable the safe and efficient handling of traffic to be accomplished on a fair basis. The following plan will be workable for current and future instances of congestion.

The Immediate Plan

The peak traffic at this country's major airports occurs during the late afternoon and early morning hours. The middle of the day and the evening hours have considerably less traffic, even at the busiest airports. In addition, as mentioned previously, there are other available facilities in many metropolitan areas that are presently underutilized. In other words, today's capacity is adequate to handle today's traffic and expected traffic in the near (and finite) future. The problem, then, is one of allocation of landing and takeoff times. The allocation could be made by application-and-award procedure, but such a procedure would be time-consuming, complex, distasteful to operators who are already complaining of over-regulation, and burdensome to the regulators. With the present plan of unregulated scheduling of time and number of flights, the airlines find that enough travelers wish to fly at peak hours to compensate for the extra expense of congestion delays. There is a need for change, and, fortunately, a system is available to us that represents the American way of free market transactions and that will at once level traffic and bring an increased value to the traveler.

Let us begin with the premise that a flight from LaGuardia Airport to O'Hare at 8:00 A.M. is a product different from either a flight from LaGuardia to O'Hare at 9:00 P.M. or a flight from Newark to Midway at 8:00 A.M. We can see that offering all three flights at the same price, with supply adjusting to try to meet any demand, is bound to lead to clustering at preferred flight times and airports, even if the preference is relatively slight. Since the maximum number of flight operations per hour at each airport is fixed, ticket prices should be allowed to reflect relative desirabilities of various combinations. The traveler to whom price is relatively important will accept less desirable departure times and/or airports to achieve the lower fare, while the traveler to whom time and airport location are more important will pay a premium in exchange for a higher probability of on-schedule flights than he currently has at those times. Such freedom of choice, with the consumer paying a price based on the desirability of the product (flight), could be administered as follows. A maximum safe number of flights per hour would be set for each airport and reduced by a percentage to allow for slightly increased loads following temporary suspensions or obstructions of traffic. If the maximum number of operations were determined to be 70 per hour for a particular airport, then 60 or 65 per hour would be scheduled. Quarterly auctions of the 65 time slots would be held, with the award of each going to the highest bidder. A successful bid would entitle the bidder to that time for each of the 91 days of the following quarter, with the right to sell or transfer any or all of the time slots to another airline for each or any of the days on notification of the airport traffic control. The bidding would be open to all, with corporations, air-taxi services, and so on, eligible to bid. If there were no bids for a time slot, bids would be accepted for that slot on individual days, or the times could be sold at a predetermined low rate on a first-come basis.

Conclusion

The best interests of the American public and the users of air transportation will be served by a long-range policy of open use of our nation's airports. At airports with heavy traffic loads, an open market system of user fees can be employed to adjust the price to reflect demand and thus to allocate fairly the commodity that an airport offers—runway minutes.

AIRPORT CONGESTION: COUNTERPLAN

The Problem

The plan is at best a whitewash of a very complex problem. Unfortunately, its authors neither understand the problem nor clearly identify it. They offer solutions that will only further institutionalize a second-rate airport system. Before we proceed, it is essential to comprehend the meaning of the problem, airport congestion.

The plans for today's airport facilities were designed 10 to 15 years ago. During the planning period, growth in "air" travel was moderate. Thus the capacity of today's facilities was largely based on forecasts that understated the actual volume. Between 1957–1962, U.S. domestic and international passengers grew at an average rate of 2.9 million per year, and in the 1962–1969 period the rate was 15 million per year. The former period was the planning era. The latter was the utilization era. As a result of insufficient capacity, and despite expedient "catch up" programs, today's air passenger is being exposed to varying degrees of a great variety of inconveniences and delays.

These inconveniences include: delays on access highways, delays and congestion in approaches to the terminal, distant and/or unavailable parking, lack of adequate information and communication channels in the terminal, delays in check-in lines, congested boarding gate areas, delays in aircraft departures, stacking delays while aircraft await clearance to land, delays while aircraft await parking positions, lines while waiting for customs or other clearances, and finally, congestion delays while awaiting baggage returns.

The Segregated Airport

Considering the nature of the problem and the aviation industry, the most practical and effective solution is the "segregated airport concept." In brief, the concept is that airports should be "segregated" by some criteria, for example, aircraft speed, airport facilities, or airport-aircraft safety interface. This concept will now be supported by analyzing it with respect to the issues raised in the plan.

The Need for Segregated Airports

According to the plan, the problem is the allocation of landing and takeoff times. This same "problem" is also given as the solution. The author is treating the symptoms of congestion and not the disease. Even his intuition about the necessity of building more airports is not supported by a reasonable diagnosis of the disease. Nevertheless, let us examine the feasibility and merit and meaning of the short-run solution of allocated landing times.

First, under the 1938 air legislation such interference with regulatory authorities is explicitly illegal. Thus present feasibility is doubtful. Route structures are awarded by government authorities with the stipulation that the route be serviced. Service means one or more flights. Supply and demand of the passenger traffic essentially sets the number of flights from one point to another. Local airport authorities establish, according to safety, speed, and facilities criteria, the number of movements per hour that their airports can handle. In most cases, arbitrarily selected percentages of these movements per hour are given to commercial, general, air taxi, international, and cargo aviation.

Thus in addition to supply and demand requirements, there are localized criteria whose purpose is the proper allocation of a scarce resource and effective management of the facility. Though federal authorities cannot limit the number of flights, the local authorities do limit flights via localized criteria. No type of aviation has 100% freedom in selecting times and numbers of flights.

The solution proposed by the planner has been in effect for many years. His "American way of free market transaction" is a hoax. Allocation of takeoff times is and has been a matter of public safety—not something to be thrown into an auction among large commercial airlines. But let us assume flight times were bargained for among airlines and the cost passed on to the consumer. Over 80% of the flights made by domestic passengers are for business reasons. Thus this group would be assessed the most for a price increase. Given that 37% of the businessmen who fly domestically make over 24 trips per year, the additional cost would be enormous. In effect, the passenger would be paying more with no guarantee of reduced congestion, as historically demonstrated. Furthermore, the businessman might easily shift his mode of transportation, given a changed cost/benefit ratio. The commercial airlines would certainly not want this to happen. This auction market system lacks merit. Also, though it is suggested that the bidding be open to all, it is doubtful that the private owner is going to win against American Airlines. Yet this is precisely the individual whom the system is supposed to protect. Airlines and passengers alike lose as a result of airport congestion. There are no benefits from a congested airport; that is why movement restrictions have existed for several years.

So far only short-range plans have been discussed. The planner also makes several sweeping and false generalizations about long-range planning. Rather than defending the "an airport is an airport" concept, he attacks the segregated-airport concept.

First, he is concerned about limiting or impairing flight connections. Take, for example, New York City, which in 1967 had 44% of all international air passengers and 55% of the international air cargo originate or terminate at its three area airports. Many domestic connecting flights service the international airlines. The result in New York is chaos. Yet there is no reason for 100% of these connecting flights to go through New York. The Boston and Philadelphia airports are just as useful for much of this international business, and they would assist in reducing New York area congestion.

He also mentions pollution as being a problem, which it is. Currently, air transport manufacturers are struggling with this problem. There is little that an airport authority can do to expedite what is already happening. Somehow the author confuses the building of more airports with pollution. The first demand of the segregated-airport concept is to use to their fullest *all* present facilities.

Maintaining the high level of facilities utilization is important. It is a two-way street, but the author is going only one way. Traffic levels and mixture are good for facilities support. Yet, over 95% of general aviation does not need the multimillion facilities of a Logan, a Dulles, a Kennedy, or an O'Hare airport. General aviation accounts for over 50% of the movement in the country. The cost of specialized private airfields is a private, not a taxpayers', cost. Furthermore, the neighborhood or company airfield does not need the facilities of an urban airport.

The military use of civilian airports is insignificant. The only military planes at Logan airport are eight Air National Guard planes. The remaining planes are maintained at specialized military airfields in the state. All taxpayers pay for these every year.

The planner's final confusing argument concerns the density concept as the most convincing reason for continuance of the open-use principle.

What is the density concept? This argument is full of inconsistencies and contradictions. The author wants to fully utilize existing airports but with no segregation of aviation. How can a 747 land at Worcester airport? Why should a Cessna 500 land at Logan airport? He concludes that the density concept is also a convincing argument for specialized airports. Finally, the traveler who flies in his private plane, uses the company jet, and is a member of the Air National Guard is almost unique.

The authors of the plan plead their case in terms of the inconvenience of a hypothetical individual being unable to carry on all his flying activities at the nearest airport. Probably the nearest airport is an open field for single engine prop planes. It is doubtful that the National Guard or the hypothetical individual's company would keep their jets there for his convenience. Furthermore, distance from his home to several airports is insignificant and this same hypothetical individual would be unable today to fly a private plane from certain airports such as Logan. In short, the entire example is a poor one.

The Segregated Airport Summary

Segregated airports exist today. Washington's National and New York's LaGuardia, for example, are used for local flights within a 500-mile radius. Dulles and Kennedy handle long-haul and international aviation. Logan does not allow private prop planes, while Midway Field in Chicago is essentially for general aviation.

Why are airports segregated because of traffic congestion? A Cessna 500 lands at 80 mph and a 747 lands at 240 mph. Thus the former uses up three times as much air time as the latter. That is, three 747's could land in the time it takes one Cessna 500 to do the same. Quantitative analysis of the difference in cost, passenger movement, and facility use is beyond the scope of this paper, but a common sense estimate of the difference is substantial. The same Cessna 500 does not have the equipment for instrument landing, which is required for safety and ease of management at most large airports.

Airport segregation by type of plane, speed, and function is a realistic solution that addresses itself to the entire scope of the problem of airport congestion. In a city like Washington, D.C., most air cargo is shipped via truck outside the city, yet most arrives at National Airport in downtown Washington. This traffic could be segregated to Dulles, situated on a highway similar to Route 128 in the Boston area. Segregated facilities deriving funds from their users is much closer to the American way of doing things than the present policy of "'open use,'' which is in reality a poorly organized de facto segregation.

The Proposed Segregated Airport

Airports in the United States could be segregated according to the following criteria: approach speed, airport/safety interface, destination, and cargo. This is currently being done on the local level, but a federal policy is needed for this nationally oriented business.

Aircraft with approach speeds of less than 175 mph should be banned from major metropolitan airports such as Logan, O'Hare, and National. This policy should be further carried out for intermediate, moderate, and small size airports. There is an optimum match between aircraft and airport vis-à-vis speed requirements. While a slow plane could not land at an airport above its speed category, a fast plane could land at an airport below its speed category if other constraints such as runway length were met.

The airport/aircraft safety interface is another criteria aimed at matching the aircraft with the proper airport on a graduated basis. Less sophisticated and slower aircraft are not legally required to have extensive operating and navigational instruments. However, larger airports are required to use very sophisticated equipment. The result is that smaller aircraft are not always in full communication with the airport authorities. Holding and landing management for highly sophisticated aircraft differs considerably for less capable aircraft. This additional variable to airport congestion is an unnecessary risk. Therefore, aircraft such as the Cessna 500 should fly from airfields geared to handle this class of aircraft.

International flights offer a subfunction by which airport use can be segregated. There are several ways in which this can be accomplished. The purpose would be to relieve the New York area. International departures that originate at Kennedy would be eliminated. These movements would be portioned out to Logan, Philadelphia, Friendship, or Dulles. Thus only arrivals and through flights to other U.S. cities would be allowed. Or, all through flights to other U.S. cities would go through the group previously mentioned and not Kennedy. These movements account for about 25% of the total. If such a federal policy were instituted, it is most likely that supporting flights to and from the group mentioned would be established. Kennedy is already the predominant international airport in the New York area. This newer segregation would further utilize the international capacity of other airports. Remember, international flights do not have the same rush hour characteristics as domestic flights.

Most cargo flies on commercial passenger planes at "off-hour" times. However, companies like Butler, Flying Tiger, Air America, and Airborne own aircraft and operate from presently congested airports such as

Logan. This group should not be allowed this privilege; it should be segregated to less congested airports. The National-Dulles problem previously discussed is an example. Removing this type of aircraft would also free up large amounts of real estate for passenger movement use. Truck facilities and small warehouses would still exist, but the cargo using these facilities helps keep the price of a passenger ticket down. Air cargo company hangars, maintenance facilities, runways, and parking areas can be used more effectively with a congestion reduction program.

AN EARTH RESOURCE DEBATE

PROLOGUE

What is the true value of the Earth Resources Technological Satellite (ERTS)? There is no ultimate answer to this question but it is important to consider how one might go about answering it. Some would say that the answer is essentially simple but computationally insuperable. That is, in principle all one needs to do is to calculate the benefits or savings accruing from snowpack estimation, more efficient water management, blight detection, forest fire detection, new mineral discovery, improved cartography and land-use mapping, and so on for each application. Then, merely sum up benefits from all applications and, by subtracting the actual opportunity costs, obtain a figure representing ERTS' value.

However, others, on reflection, find that the answer is more elusive and complex than that. Such a simple method raises some doubts. When one takes a broad view of resource and environmental problems (the problems that in the long run ERTS is to help us solve), one sees that these problems are interwoven closely with our governmental, industrial, and cultural institutions. The very way that we think, live, and view the world is an integral part of the resource problem. If we can only find the right perspectives and institutions for nourishing the earth and ensuring its survival, then, in a most essential way, the resource problem will have been solved. A "solution" of this type is not measurable in benefit-cost terms, since benefit-cost analysis must assume a certain institutional framework to make its procedures work. However, there is immense value to be gained if we can find the right perspectives and institutions to aid man in solving the earth resource management problem.

There are three fundamental components to the earth management problem. First, there is the physical nature of the earth itself. Second, there are the institutions, that is, the laws, customs, practices, and organizations that man has devised for dealing with the earth. Finally, there is the psychological outlook or perspective of the earth that each person, especially those in decision-making capacities, possesses. These components work together to determine the final dispensation and utilization of earth's resources. Dysfunctional uses, such as pollution, result from breakdowns or misunderstandings in any of the three dimensions.

If the ERTS program is to achieve its ultimate goal of solving mankind's food, water, and mineral resource problems, it must deal with all three components of the earth resource management problem. This debate takes this perspective.

Perhaps what is most intriguing about the ERTS program is that it shows great potential for producing value in the sense of developing new perspectives about the earth. To be sure, there will be cost-effective "applications," but these will flow naturally from the creation of a more lasting impact—a sobering realization of man's place in this "fathomless universe" (Whitman, "O Captain! My Captain!"). The astronauts' descriptions and the awe-inspiring space photographs perhaps only herald a new world view to come. At least, there is some evidence of this. Take, for example, John Caffrey's letter to the editor in *Science* (March 20, 1970) in which he related the profound effect that the space photographs had on him. He then went on to say:

Looking at the blackness beyond the sharp blue-green curve, trying to see even the place where the thin envelope of atmosphere and the solid Earth meet, the curious word "fragile" comes to mind. To be on Earth and think of it as fragile is ridiculous. But to see it from out there and to compare it with the deadness of the Moon! I suspect that the greatest lasting benefit of the Apollo missions may be, if my hunch is correct, this sudden rush to inspiration to try to save this fragile environment—the *whole* one—if we still can.

Such are the potential benefits of ERTS, but, more importantly, this fresh perspective sheds new light on our opening question. The "true value" of ERTS is not now of primary concern; rather, the question becomes How can ERTS best be used to secure the value inherent in a more appropriate perspective toward the earth? What follows is an initial response to this question.

A METHOD

ERTS imagery is only data—a set of basic observations of the world. Information is the "meaning" one derives from data. In order to produce information, data must be interpreted from some perspective or point of view. Data are inert, but information becomes the basis for action. It is information that determines what decisions will be made and what actions will be taken. Any notion of value must be based on total short- and long-range effects of these actions. Consequently, it is vital that we always consider the point of view that was used to interpret the data, as well as the adequacy and completeness of the data-bank itself. This is the only way to evaluate the ERTS program in any ultimate sense. This kind of evaluation will require an approach that is different from the one employed to review data-capturing and processing systems, because perspective is psychologically based.

Our research has led to the development of a new approach for exposing and examining points of view, or *Weltanschauungen* (world views). It is patterned after the dialectic. Using this approach the data are systematically and logically interpreted from two opposing points of view, which are, in turn, debated for the policymaker. The policymaker, then, must reflect on both the data and the point of view. The assumption is that, on witnessing the thesis-antithesis debate, the policymaker forms a new, broader, more encompassing perspective from which to view the data and the situation—the synthesis. In the context of the ERTS program the synthesis may result in a "better" way of viewing earth, one that pressing environmental, resource and population problems seem so desperately to call for.

The dialectical method involves determining opposing positions, writing empathic scenarios for each, and placing these positions into conflict over the data and issues via debate. The next section represents the beginnings of such an Earth Resource Debate.

Background for the Debate

Our studies have shown that one of the early and perhaps most productive uses of the Earth Resources Technological Satellite will be to prepare comprehensive and comparable land-use data. These data will then be interpreted by policymakers to evaluate past usage and to make decisions about future usage. Their evaluations and decisions will depend principally on the perspective they take in interpreting the land-use data.

In order to expose these perspectives for conscious consideration, a debate has been prepared between policymakers possessing two different points of view. The sample data for this debate show land-use trends in Los Angeles County from 1940 to the present and as projected through 1990.* In the future one might assume that the data would be produced

*The authors are indebted to Herbert Libow who helped collect this land-use data. Our study revealed a definite lack of consistent, coherent, and comparable land-use data for L.A. County over the last 30 years.

from an analysis of ERTS imagery. Overlaying the photographic image would be a land-use map prepared by computer analysis of digitized data obtained from various sensors and augmented by inputs from trained human observers. However, for the present we will use the available data as the basis for the debate. The data are displayed in Exhibit 7-1.

Exhibit 7-1   Land-Use Trends in Los Angeles County, 1940–1970

Land Use[a,e,f]		1940	1970	1985–1990
Urban used[d,p]	southern county	25.1%	73.6%	82.0%
Urban vacant[c]	southern county	10.1	5.3	
Nonurban used[d]	southern county	45.3	7.3	
Nonurban vacant[c]	southern county	19.5	13.8%	
		100.0%	100.0%	
Urban	southern county	35.2	78.9%	
Nonurban	southern county	64.8	21.1	
		100.0%	100.0%	
Used[d]	southern county	70.4	80.9	
Vacant[c]	southern county	29.6	19.1	
		100.0%	100.0%	

Land Use[b]	1940	1960	1970	1985–1990
Recreation and parks[c,g,h]		0.83%[q]	1.6%	2.3%
Agriculture[c,i]		9.2%	3.6%	
Crop acreage[c,j,k]	12.7%	5.8%	3.1%	2.3%
Range and[e,l]		7.9%	8.0%	
Freeway mileage[m]		6	405	1045
Sand and gravel production[n,o] (in millions of tons)		7.0[r]	23.2	
Gold production[n,o] (in dollars)	258,000	7200[q]	3200[q]	

[a]The figures represent the percentage of southern Los Angeles County acreage devoted to the particular land use.
[b]The figures represent the percentage of Los Angeles County acreage devoted to the particular land use unless otherwise indicated.
[c]"Vacant land" has possibilities for future development.
[d]"Used land" has minimal possibilities for future land development and may or may not have a current land use. Most land in this category is in use. Vacant land and used land are mutually exclusive categories.
[e]Revised Land Use Acreages by Statistical Area, Los Angeles County Regional Planning Commission, April, 1971.

THE DEBATE

Two policymakers—Adam and Bud—debate the "correctness" of the land-use policy reflected in the foregoing exhibit by interpreting the data from their respective points of view. Adam begins the debate.

Adam Well, our land-use policy as reflected by these land-use data looks pretty good to me. From the standpoint of regional and national goals it demonstrates much of the great accomplishment of humanity. We have identified great new resources and have been able to employ them for the betterment of our ever-growing population. Just look at the extent to which we have been able to expand our cities as reflected in the increased urban use. This means that more people may have their own private homes and their own place to work. There is smog, crime, and some congestion, to be sure, but we are making progress and our agricultural land is still adequate to satisfy food needs for some time to come.

Contained here in this single table is a message of great inspiration. We have discovered our earth, subdued it, and put it to work for us. Truly earth is now resting comfortably under the dominion of man.

---

*f*Land Use Survey, Los Angeles County Regional Planning Commission, July 1940.

*g*Building for Tomorrow: The Community Improvement Program for Los Angeles County, Los Angeles County Department of Parks and Recreation, 1957.

*h*Los Angeles County Regional Recreation Areas Plan, County of Los Angeles, 1965.

*i*Land Uses, Los Angeles County Regional Planning Commission, 1960 (based on Los Angeles Regional Transportation Study and U.S. Bureau of Census).

*j*Southern California Agriculture: 1969 in Review, Los Angeles Regional Chamber of Commerce.

*k*Southern California Agriculture: A Look Ahead to 1970 and 1980, Los Angeles Chamber of Commerce, 1961.

*l*1970 Crop and Livestock Report, Los Angeles County Agricultural Commissioner and County Veterinarian.

*m*Verbal information obtained from Los Angeles Regional Planning Commission, Mr. Ron Mayhew, September 1971.

*n*Mineral Information Service* **21** (1968) and **6** (1953).

*o*California Journal of Mines,* **50**, Nos. 3 and 4 (1954).

*p*1990 Land Use, Los Angeles County Regional Planning Commission, Sept. 1971.

*q*Estimated from available data.

*r*Earliest available information indicates that production was 11.1 in 1947; however, a trend line projection indicates that 1940 production was about 7 million tons.

Bud   Oh, the treachery of it all, Adam. The data show that our policy has obviously been to consume and destroy our land and its resources through too much urbanization. Man can never really be superior to his environment, he's a *part* of it. What the data show is that we are in the process of breaking the basic harmony man must have with his world. Man is such a recent arrival here on earth—a few thousand years is nothing considering the billions of years that the earth has been around. Don't our predecessors, successors, and partners have rights? Flora, fauna, and minerals have a rightful place in a harmonious world, too. We are offending these rights and may *not live* to regret it.

Sure, we derive a lot of pleasure and comfort today from our expansive sprawling urban areas, the products of our mines, our transportation system and so forth; but, the cost of depleting our environment is very high. We must learn to "give and take" with nature, take a little "bitter with the sweet," if man and this earth are both to survive.

Maybe now is the time for man to start looking inward a little more to find himself and his place in the universe. Earth is not an object to be conquered, but a *partner* with which to live. If man could only understand this he would learn to understand himself. After all, that's the real purpose in life.

I believe that 73.6% of our land in urban use is far too much. The projections are for it to get worse. Let's cut it down to 20% and let's cut down on the transportation usage as well. Return the rest to wilderness where it belongs.

Adam   Come on now, Bud. We have to *use* our environment to our own advantage. Nature changes the environment every day of our lives, right? Why shouldn't we change it? Make it work for us? Besides, I'll never understand your concept of returning land to wilderness. Do you mean that you want us to take large sections of land and just set them aside, never to be touched evermore?

Bud   Certainly.

Adam   How ludicrous. I agree with you that we must plan the ways in which we use our land very carefully. We have made mistakes in the past and chopped up wilderness areas much too quickly and too rambunctiously. Certainly we aren't making the most efficient use of what we have. Some realignment and forethought are most assuredly needed. But to return to primitive times? Ridiculous!

In my view, the best land-use principle is quite simple. Take a region of land. Survey it well and make a comprehensive plan for its use. Then make part of it accessible for human use and part of it inaccessible. Don't touch the restricted portion until it's absolutely necessary. The 1990 projections seem consistent with this kind of planned land-use policy.

Bud   Would you preserve those restricted portions forever?

Adam   No, not forever. You can't take a large area of this country and keep it the way it was a thousand years ago. Nor can man afford to retreat from the most productive lands. We cannot continue to deny man's urgent needs by trying to create useless wilderness.

Bud   Wilderness is not *useless*. A wilderness area is worth saving or creating in its own right. Man has no business disturbing what lives there naturally. The pollution problem has shown that it doesn't take much to destroy ecological balance. In other areas our land-use policy literally is driving some species into premature extinction. That's just not morally right. These species are partners in the universe. They have their rights, too. Only the forces of nature can sentence a species to extinction. It is not within man's moral purview to do so.

But, there is another reason for maintaining wilderness areas that perhaps you'll understand more readily. Wilderness represents a bank for the genetic variability of the earth. It's our "gene pool," as it were. We are depleting this reserve at a very alarming rate. Now is the time to stop. What is wild, leave wild. Then let's take the land we've unwisely developed in the past and start a genetic investment program by rebuilding our wilderness "capital." Wilderness is a place where natural forces keep working essentially uninterrupted by humankind. Humanity should not interfere constantly in the process of natural selection and adaptation, because the long-range survival of earth depends on it. Earth always seeks an ecological balance. Everything is connected with everything else. Once man materially disturbs the balance the whole thing can go out of control. Puff! No more earth. Let's protect man from his ignorance now, if it's not already too late. As Pogo says, "We have met the enemy and he is us!" The wilderness reserve is our best policy for protection against ourselves and our ignorance.

Man has taken enough for himself already. He needs to start paying back his debt. We should pretend that these wilderness areas don't exist. Don't ever disturb them. They are there for a different purpose—one that will ensure the ecological variety that will ultimately save humanity. But that's not the only point. The important point is that we must learn to be humble with our land and its creatures and show respect for them. That's the proper thing to do; it's part of our obligation to maintain a harmonious universe.

Adam   While you're maintaining harmony, what are we going to do about the people? Population pressures seem to be irresistible. This population growth simply will not permit the kind of policy you're proposing. During the next 20 years we can expect the earth's population to increase from 3.5 billion people to at least 5.5 billion people, perhaps to 7.5 billion people. The Southern California region alone (60 counties) is expected to increase from a present 10 million people to nearly 16 million in 1990 and 22 million in the year 2020. That's a lot of people to feed, clothe, house. They all need an acceptable standard of living. Where's it going to come from? Not from wilderness, that's for sure. It will have to come from the continued exploration and development of the land and eventually of the sea. We will have to discover and develop new resources continually in order to satisfy the demands of this ever-increasing population.

Bud   Just a minute, now. Those population figures are projections, not fact; I don't buy them. Indeed, the Washington Center for Metropolitan Studies suggests that there is a distinct possibility of achieving zero population growth within this century. We still have a *choice* in this matter. Population growth is not inevitable; in reality it's only an artifact of the extrapolations you make. But, if your crowd keeps talking that way, you'll come to believe it and then you'll go ahead and make it happen. Then we'll really be in trouble. The worst thing about all these population forecasts is that they tend to become self-fulfilling prophecies.

We have the knowledge and wherewithal today to control population growth and to level it off. It's naive merely to predict the population in the year 2020 and then plan how we are going to respond to it. The intelligent thing to do is to intervene now. We will have to intervene to reestablish the balance we have destroyed by excessive population growth. Within the limits of those already born, we can have any population we want in 2020. When we come to improve our understanding of the basic equilibrium of the universe, we will realize that this continued reproduction of man destroys the balance. Human population growth makes just too many of one resource-grubbing species.

Adam   Well I'm not as optimistic as you. History tells us that we just cannot put our "head in the sand" on this population growth issue. Any way you look at it the species is going to reproduce. Furthermore, we know that human wants are insatiable. Elementary economics tells us that we are going to require more resources to satisfy the wants of this ever-increasing population.

This means we need to plan for earth-resource and land use development. Resources exist where you find them and their quantities are finite.

178 Dialectical Debate Cases

Perhaps the most criminal thing in the world is to waste resources or to let them stand idle when people need them. Our standard of living depends on them. The trouble with your wilderness policy is that it doesn't take into account some basic facts about resources. Their original source is fixed by nature. So man must go to them, seek them out and develop them, no matter where they are.

Bud Do you include the beaches, the Santa Monica Mountains, and Lake Arrowhead? The sequoias, the saguaros? Grand Canyon, Yellowstone, the Tetons, Yosemite? King's Canyon? Lassen? Shasta? Lake Tahoe?

Adam Yes, if necessary. If that's where the vital resources are. You have to go to the resources. They don't come to you. But they are the ultimate basis of our standard of living. That's where we get our foodstuffs, houses, furniture, televisions, telephones, electric lights, autos, and airplanes. Everything.

If we need lumber we should cut down those trees that provide the greatest yield for the cost of procuring them, but never more than we need. If that's the sequoias, O.K. If Mt. Shasta has an economical deposit of an ore that is needed, mine it. That ore may improve the standard of living for 100 years to come.

Bud Adam, you're all costs and no aesthetics. In the long run you'll have to pay for this excessively economic view of things. You know, there isn't much natural world left now. What there is, is *all* men will ever have, and all their children will ever have, too. Somewhere, sometime, we must learn to revere our sanctuaries of beauty. The most impressive thing about ERTS space photographs is that the natural magnificence of earth comes radiating through what is at best a cumbersome technology. But even now we can see the flaws, man's defiling of the splendor that once was the earth.

No Adam, your concept of value has you trapped. What's the worth of Yosemite? Fifty billion dollars? No! There's no price on it. The price of beauty has never been evaluated. Look at El Capitan! What would it cost to replace it? If we destroy it, what is the "cost" to those who will never thrill to it, who will never know its beauty?

Adam Bud, modern society has developed a very good method of arriving at such prices. It's called the market system. In it everything has a price—each commodity and each service—and is available for free exchange. Everyone receives money for what he sells and uses this money to buy what he wants. If you're short of a good the price goes up; if you're long, it goes down. This way an equilibrium between supply and demand is maintained.

Now producers, such as mining companies, continue to compare the prevailing price of their inputs, such as ore, with the cost of its extraction and the market price of its final product by means of a profitability calculus. As long as the enterprise is profitable they are interested.

So, the time may come when Yosemite becomes profitable for ore mining. El Capitan will go into ore production if the mining companies outbid the other competitors for its use.

Bud   There's a limit to the utility of the market system when it comes to natural resources, a flaw which goes much deeper than just market imperfections or information lags. As you've defined it, only the producers bid, and only the *living ones* at that. We need to be sure that the aesthetic value, recreation value, peace-of-mind value are cranked into these market decisions. In large measure, these prices are beyond estimation.

But, it's not just the beauty, Adam, it's sustenance as well. The universe is infinite. We know nothing of its beginning or its end. There will (we hope) be many, many generations after ours. Where will *they* turn for the resources *they* need, when we have depleted them? There are the other creatures who inhabit and will inherit the earth. How does your market system take these other kinds of bids into account?

Adam   I am not going to penalize people today for the sake of future generations. But, my friend, "a bird in the hand, is worth two in the bush." Let me prove it to you. Suppose I offer you a choice between a dollar for certain today or a dollar a year, or say, 100 years from now. Which would you take? The dollar today, wouldn't you? Why? Because the future is uncertain. Other things being equal, the longer we wait, the greater the possibility that conditions will change and the dollar will be worthless, or may never be paid back.

There is a second important reason why this is the right thing to do. The dollar received today can be invested to grow to more than a dollar a year from now, compounding year after year. The man who gets a dollar now and invests it wisely will have more money a year from now than the man who waits a year or more for his dollar.

Now, it's very much the same with resources. Their future value is less than their present value. An oil field, for example, is not worth very much a hundred years from now when we desperately need petroleum for energy today. For each year we fail to discover and develop new resources the world is losing some of this oil's value.

Bud You're always thinking about just yourself, Adam, the all-powerful individual, the conquering hero. Never do you consider all of the others. You always place immediate needs ahead of those of the future generations and the other creatures. Remember that Noah took all species, not just man, on the Ark. He saw the need to preserve an ecological balance.

Consider, also, the needs of future generations. What's our obligation to them? Shouldn't the generations of the year 3000 "participate" in our resource decisions? The year 4000?

We should follow the advice of Theodore Roosevelt: "The nation behaves well if it treats the natural resources as assets which it must turn over to the next generation increased and not impaired in value." If we take him seriously then your idea of value is topsy-turvey. Resources are worth *more* in the future. We should at least be compounding forward rather than discounting backward. The future value of a resource is always higher than its present value. And the "true value" of resources is very, very high. When we pump oil, mine ore, or in any way spoil the beauty of nature, we change something *forever*. The recipient should at least pay a price equal to the cost of replacing the resource, of restoring nature to its original state, or he should pay the cost of depriving future generations of the resource.

Adam Bud, those costs are unreasonable. They are astronomical.

Bud Well, that's the true value. If you *really* need these resources, you'll be willing to borrow the money and amortize the debt over a few thousand years.

Adam, your version of the market system had made the cost of resources appear too cheap in the past. Consequently, we've become a society that is addicted to resource consumption. We had better "kick the habit" before it's too late.

Adam Bud, you don't know what you are saying. If we place large amounts of land into wilderness and charge the fantastic prices you suggest, we'll be headed for an economic tailspin. Stagnation. Depression. Disaster.

The great accomplishment of the last 200 years has been our incredible ability to increase per capita real income despite an ever-increasing population. This is, undoubtedly, humanity's most singular achievement.

Bud And, alas, it may be his very last!

Adam But economic development wasn't accomplished with the kind of mystical, religious, and fuzzy kind of thinking I've heard from you so far. No, it only was achieved through a rational, goods-centered concept of personal and social welfare. It was accomplished because we were dedicated to procedures for accumulating "factual data" and for measuring progress (such as the GNP). But what a blessing the resulting economic growth has been for us. It has enabled the members of our society to look forward to an ever-rising standard of living. Economic growth, moreover, is a great social solvent. When everyone can look forward to raising levels of well-being, the pressure of redistributing the existing pie is reduced. Bud, not to be in favor of economic growth is as heinous a crime in our society as hostility to dogs and little children.

Bud   I note that you don't include the buffalo or the bald eagle. Was what we did to them in the name of economic growth a crime?

Adam   That's not the point, Bud. Economic growth is the way we satisfy people's wants and needs. Demand for goods and services is the basic force that keeps the system running. People want better meals, new clothes, more comfortable living, automobiles, TV's, washers, dryers, stoves. This consumption is made possible by the productive output of capital stock and the labor force and through technical progress. As long as we increase capital and the labor force at a propitious and proportionate rate and as long as we continue technical progress, we'll achieve full employment. Thus we will enjoy steady per capita income growth.

Bud   The theory of economic growth is doomed. We live on a finite planet with an infinite time horizon. Earth resource management must now take this into account. The rate at which our natural resources are being ravaged in our present frantic attempt to keep growing is frightening. As Thoreau said, "What is the good of a house if you don't have a tolerable planet to put it on?"
The trouble with technical progress is that it leads us down Richard's "road to oblivion." It increasingly forces us to use our more marginal resources. Take the case of copper, for instance. Early in this century if an ore wouldn't yield 2 to 3% copper it was bypassed. Today 0.7% ore is mined as a matter of course. Soon it will be 0.35%. Then what? Will we dig huge open pit mines anywhere an infinitesimal trace of copper is to be found?
This specter is only too clear today in the strip-mined hills of Kentucky. In the quest for coal to support our nation's growing need for energy we have literally denuded a good part of 11 counties of the state. Sure, strip mining is less costly than deep mining and safer, in part because it employs fewer miners. But it has destroyed the terrain and led to erosion,

landslides, pollution, and, alas, now that the coal is nearly gone, economic depression.

And there seems to be no stopping. The U.S. Geological Survey says that 3000 square miles in 26 states already have been "stripped" and that 71,000 more could profitably be gouged out in the future. But, it's not just the surface area that needs to be considered, it's the insides as well. Stripping has gone as deep as 700 feet in Germany. In the United States it could eventually go as deep as 2000 feet.

An alarming aspect of the L.A. County land-use data is that we are rapidly depleting our precious metal resources, as shown by the decrease in tonnage. Meanwhile, our sand and gravel consumption goes up to construct our sprawling cities and expand our freeways. How much longer can we keep this up, Adam? When our mining resources and vacant land are gone, what then?

Adam Of course, we must practice conservation to ensure the maximum use of resources for the benefit of all people. But stop exploration and development as you suggest? That's unthinkable.

There are some practical ways in which private enterprise can discharge its responsibility for conservation. Coal sells at about $7 to $10 a ton. Why not spend 5 to 15 cents a ton for general conservation and restoration? These funds could be used for developing and financing new mining techniques in which topsoil would be stripped off and saved, the minerals would be extracted, "clean" atomic explosives would be used to level the land, the surplus earth would be distributed and compressed, and the topsoil would be redistributed on the surface and treated with fertilizer. This program would be backed up by additional conservation policy to ensure that the land was reclaimable, that the vegetation would grow, that proper drainage patterns were maintained, and that the atomic blasting was not hazardous to the residents of the area. In the future we will have to follow these conservation policies more strictly.

Bud Conservation is humanity caring for the future, Adam, not technology and cost effectiveness. This must become the age of man's service to man. Personal service can continue to grow with a static population and without destroying nature. We don't have to continue to think in terms of increasing production and consumption, supply and demand. We must come to realize *scarcity* is the nature of the world, now and forevermore. All resources are limited; nothing is superabundant. Man must cherish and live with his environment the way it is and *not* consume it excessively.

We must begin to take the "right view" of our world. All things are interconnected with everything else. Everything we do affects other things; everything goes somewhere. Pollution. DDT. They all go some place; they all affect something. In nature there are no "bottomless ponds." What is irrevocably destroyed or disturbed when we implement our plan, Adam? Aren't there many unintended consequences from leveling the land, destroying habitats and valleys?

No, we must cease this craving for consumption. We must begin to live in a way that is least harmful to other living things, their habitat, their means of survival. In this way we will come to understand ourselves a little better, too, dispel some of our more evil thoughts, arouse and maintain some good ones. The alert mind of the future must pay close attention to every state of the body, feeling, and mind and attempt to place them in eternal harmony with the environment. This will require reflection and concentration. But the rewards are worth it. In this way we will find the infinity and pleasure we seek. Not an infinity of material resources, which doesn't exist, but an infinity of freedom from excessive passion and desire.

Adam Bud, it sounds like you are placing restrictions on man that even nature does not place on any carnivorous species. Man has a right to live, to eat, to seek shelter, to protect himself, and to grow.

Bud Yes, but for the sake of harmony he should take only his share. These land-use data indicate that he has gone too far. With the intelligence man has gained as a species there comes a moral obligation. He must strive to live in harmony with his environment. This means that our land-use policies must be changed.

Adam Your plea is eloquent, Bud, but on the basis of the data and this debate I can only conclude that our past land-use policy has not been that bad. With intelligent planning for the future, and with the ERTS data, man will be able to make better use of earth resources and to continue his dominion over nature. The future of man is assured if he follows this approach.

Bud No, Adam, from the debate one must conclude that our land-use policy has been disastrous. Man must stop thinking in terms of his dominion over the earth and begin to consider his moral obligation to all of creation. He must strive for harmony and ecological balance among all species and things. The hope of ERTS is that its imagery may provide some insights as to how to accomplish this. Humanity's survival hangs in the balance. The future of human kind is *not* assured. It is in great jeopardy. We must adopt a new approach.

Chapter Eight

Dialectical Debate Procedures

We have developed several different designs or sets of procedures for carrying out the dialectical process on problems of policy, planning, and strategy. Each of the designs incorporates the following steps:

1 Issue and problem identification and statement.
2 Identifying three roles:

   a. Thesis role, T.
   b. Antithesis role, A.
   c. Synthesis role, S.

   The designs assign people to play out these roles in different ways.
3 Argument and world view generation.
4 Presentation and debate.
5 Synthesis and conclusion.

Four basic designs that incorporate these steps have proven to be useful.

1 Dialectical advice—staff presentation.
2 Formal policy debate—one-shot decision.
3 Formal policy debate—routine decision.
4 Real time planning session with facilitator.

Each of these four designs are described in this chapter.

DIALECTICAL ADVICE—STAFF PRESENTATION

The dialectical advice design was employed at RMK Abrasives. There the planners had already devised a plan—the international marketing-oriented plan—and they had written a report recommending that the plan be adopted. At this point the chief executive officer wanted a review and test of the proposed plan. This is a typical situation in which dialectical advice can be used by staff and/or consultants working together. The procedure is generally as follows.

Defining the Thesis and the Common Databank   The proposed plan becomes the thesis T. The plan is reviewed carefully, and the factual data on which it is based is identified. Often this will require some additional research and interviewing. This data becomes the common databank.

Inferring World Views from the Thesis   Once the T position has been identified, the question is posed: Under what views of the world is this the best policy to follow? Or, How would one view the business's, problems, technology, geography, competition, customers, research and development, and other dimensions of activity so that he would interpret the data and the goals as supporting this particular plan? Viewing this proposed plan as a conclusion drawn from data interpreted by warrants, the quest is for a set of warrants that tend to "close" the argument logically. These warrants are statements of values and beliefs that serve in the interpretation of the data. When articulated, they approximate the world view that underlies this plan.

In the warrant-seeking process one may find many warrants, all of which lead to the same conclusion. Here the rule is to choose the one that is most plausible in the context. For example, consider the belief that a foreign country's inhabitants are friendly toward an American firm. This may lead to the conclusion that the firm adopt an internationally oriented plan. However, this assumption may appear to be too strong and dogmatic to have been held by a reasonable man in the context of this organization. Another, perhaps more credible, warrant would be that the inhabitants are motivated to improve their standard of living and that they view the potential activities of this company in their nation as a means to that end. This would also lead to the same internationally oriented plan. Generally speaking, one can easily find extreme, dogmatic warrants that support the recommended plan but are too extreme to be convincing. The principal task is to find less extreme warrants in support of the same plan that are maximally credible to the organization as a whole.

More reasonable statements can often be heuristically obtained from the extreme ones by introducing terms of qualification, contingency, probability, and modality: "Unless x . . .," "Under condition y . . .," "In all likelihood . . .," "Will tend to do . . .," and so on, are all qualifying clauses and phrases that render a statement less extreme. Our interpretation is that they decrease the degrees of intensity in the original statement. The following simplified example and diagram illustrate this process:

Let

X = the extreme form of a statement, such as "foreign countries are friendly"

$\bar{X}$ = the polar opposite of X, such as "foreign countries are hostile"

Further assume that the statement X in this situation concludes the thesis T. A line drawn from X to $\bar{X}$ can be considered to represent decreasing degrees of intensity X brought about by the addition of more qualifications.

X			$\bar{X}$
Plan T region			Plan A region

As we move from X and $\bar{X}$ the balance shifts at some point in favor of Plan A, the antithesis. Conceptually this is analogous to finding probability regions in the theory of games for which each act maximizes expected return and finding the points at which the change occurs. The thesis role player's task is to find the point in the region that concludes Plan T and is most *credible* in the organizational context. This generally requires moving away from the extreme statement by the addition of qualification and interpretation. What evolves is another story about how one views the item of interest rather than a set of postulates (which, of course, are also a story). However, the story should retain the property of logical interpretation of the data to conclude with the adoption of the same plan.

In the region that does not conclude Plan T, there may be a variety of A's or antitheses. In order to obtain dramatic opposition, the A role should select the plan that is most opposed to Plan T.

Of course, not all situations will be as "well behaved." Consider the beliefs X = "this task is exceedingly difficult" and $\bar{X}$ = "this task is exceedingly easy." Kurt Lewin originally suggested and Atkinson subsequently determined empirically that Plan T = "do not attempt the task" will be concluded in ego involvement situations at *both* extremes. As shown following, in decreasing degrees of intensity in statement X, the counterplan A = "attempt the task" would be supposed in the mid-ranges.

X		$\bar{X}$
Plan T region	Plan A region	Plan T region

One can envision more complex situations. In any event, however, the procedure is the same. Given Plan T, the thesis role seeks to find that point in the region concluding Plan T that has the highest degree of organizational credibility. As will be discussed later, one way to secure this credibility is to ascertain what has actually been said about the item by an individual or a group within the organization. Speeches, memos, reports, interviews, and the like, are good sources for these more believable, storylike, statements.

Establishing the Antithesis Because debate, dialogue, and discussion often improve the soundness of the judgmental process, it is useful to develop an opposing point of view that will *test* the judgment on which the original plan was founded. The procedure here is to construct an antithesis, sometimes called a counterplan, with a supporting argument and view of the world in which the counterplan is the best policy.

The RMK example helps to illustrate this point. Recall that the following apparently credible belief or warrant was articulated: "Most of the inhabitants of foreign countries primarily desire to improve their standard of living, and the company's entrance into their economy could help satisfy this desire." This belief influenced the recommendation of a strategic plan for the company to become an international marketing oriented firm. However, another quite credible alternative plan for the firm was that it should concentrate its efforts domestically and emphasize technological innovation. This counterplan was partially based on another believable proposition: "Inhabitants of most foreign countries are motivated primarily by strong nationalistic tendencies that would make doing business there risky."

Having settled on an antithesis, A, the antithesis roleplayer seeks set of credible warrants that tend to close the argument with the conclusion that the counterplan is optimal, given the *same* data and goals. The procedure is the same as that used to find warrants supporting the thesis.

Developing an antithesis requires the operationalization of the concept of opposition. Dialectical drama is derived from the joint influences of opposition and credibility, that is, when two *Weltanschauungen* confront each other. In order to illustrate when a relationship of opposition may be considered to exist between two *Weltanschauungen*, we will focus our attention on an individual warrant (w_1), which is an element of the *Weltauschauung* W_1 and its counterpart in W_2, (w_2).

First it should be mentioned that many of these warrants are the same ($w_1 = w_2$) in any decision situation. These are the common underlying assumptions of both the plan and the counterplan. In addition, many of these are implicit (or unconsciously held). The equivalence of two warrants depends on the classification system employed by the person making the judgment; likewise the notion of opposition depends on the concepts employed.

Let us consider three relations of opposition that may exist between two warrants, w_1 and w_2.

w_1 is a *contradiction* of w_2

A relation of contradiction obtains when w_1 and w_2 are mutually exclusive and collectively exhaustive possibilities within the concept employed (i.e., they form a partition on the domain of the concept). In a truth value sense, if w_1 is true, then w_2 is false; if w_1 is false, then w_2 is true; w_1 must be either true or false. Within the concept of color, "*x* is not red" is the contradiction of "*x* is red." "Foreign countries are friendly" and "Foreign countries are not friendly" are contradictory statements that emerged at RMK.

w_1 is *contrary to* w_2

A relation of contrariety between w_1 and w_2 can obtain when they are at the polar extremes of a conceptual framework. The warrant w_1 is contrary to w_2 provided that: If w_1 is true, then w_2 is false; and if w_2 is true, w_1 is false, while it is possible for both w_1 and w_2 to be false. The excluded possibility is the conjoint truth of w_1 and w_2: "*x* is red" is contrary to "*x* is blue" within the concept of color. Of course, *x* may be neither (it may be white), but if it is one of the above it cannot be the other.

w_1 is *conceptually opposed* to w_2

In either of the two preceding cases, w_1 is not logically independent of w_2. There are, however, pairs of warrants that, while they are strictly speaking logically independent, are closely related within the larger frame of reference of a problem. They are *conceptually opposed* to one another. Since they are predicated from different systems, discussion of their joint truth or falsity is inappropriate.

If a firm is concerned about the tactics its competitor uses in the market place, then the statement, "Competitors will respond by cutting prices," is conceptually opposed to the statement, "Competitors will respond by producing a quality product." Although logically independent concepts (price-cutting versus product quality), given the purposes of the firm, they may lead to different market conditions and thus opposing strategies are suggested. In this sense they are in opposition. In the case of a conceptually opposed pair of warrants, one may be as credible as the other.

In order to make this more precise, we shall define w_1 to be conceptually opposed to w_2 if:

1 The subject of w_1 is the same as that of w_2.
2 w_1 and w_2 are logically independent and their predicates employ different concepts.
3 In considering these two warrants for a teleological entity, w_1 implies states of the world different from those implied by w_2 and the entity has a preference ordering on these states.

A *Weltanschauung* was defined to be the conjunction of a set of warrants. For the purposes of dialectical debate, two *Weltanschauungen*, W_1 and W_2, will be said to be in opposition to each other if:

1 The set of subjects in W_1 is equivalent to those in W_2.
2 At least one w_i in W_1 is contradictory, contrary, or conceptually opposed to a w_j in W_2 that attaches a different predicate to the same subject.

Contradictions are the strongest form of opposition in a purely logical sense but it is rare that a person or a group attributes high credibility to both X and its logical contradictory, not X. However, they may well ascribe high credibility to a positive statement Y that is contrary or conceptually opposed to X. Just as the counterplan is a positive counterproposal to the plan, its supporting *Weltanschauung* W_2 will be in a contrary or conceptually opposed relationship with the *Weltanschauung* supporting the plan W_1.

We have seen that an antithesis and its supporting *Weltanschauung* can be generated through a search for opposites and use of the logic of negation. Admission of these notions of opposition into the realm of possibility, however, means that several or many opposing views may be found. In addition, there is the question of the intensity of the statements. Theory indicates that we should select the most plausible and credible point in this multidimensional space of opposition. How does one go about finding this "most credible" antithesis and its supporting set of warrants?

The very term "credibility" connotes that the antithesis is the outcome of a subjective process. The process is, as with so many other intellectual endeavors, as much an art as a science. We can, however, suggest some guidelines for selection. These criteria appear reasonable for determination of the credibility of an antithesis or its warrants. Not all of these criteria will apply in any particular situation, nor will their relative importance necessarily be the same from situation to situation.

However, before developing these criteria, one important point should be borne in mind:

Any criterion that is used to evaluate the credibility of a plan and its *Weltanschauung* itself becomes *a common underlying* assumption of both the plan and the counterplan. As such, it too is ultimately questionable.

With this proviso, then, the proposed criteria for credibility follow.

The warrants must be capable of being explicitly stated in specific or concrete terms. This requirement may be more constraining than it appears to be on the surface. There are many vague notions of values and beliefs that underlie plans of action, but virtually defy articulation. Since the counterplanner's task is to inform and to communicate with management, the warrants and the plan must be verbalized. Moreover, it is important that the verbalized story form of the warrants carry with it some of the connotations of feeling that are difficult to express. This requirement for articulation forces us to bring in the organization's (or the culture's) language, itself already heavily laden with values and beliefs, as a common underlying assumption.

The warrants should *not* be analytically or tautologically true. It is not generally fruitful to refer to one's credence in a self-evident truth. The whole aim of our efforts here is to identify those subjective, synthetic statements on which a choice can be based.

The plan and its warrants must be feasible. At least they must appear to be possible and to be within the scope of our existing scientific and technological knowledge. Science and technology become common underlying assumptions.

They should be *legal* and *proper* within the culture to which they are addressed. This requirement, of course, already evokes a value premise for law abidance (natural law, as well as statutory law) and for observance of the proprieties of the culture. Here we are suggesting that a viable alternative, which adheres to the generally accepted canons of behavior for the society in which the organization is located, will be more credible than one that breaks with these standards. If one were a planner for a group of criminals, he would of course be forced to consider the ethos of that group in determining proprieties.

This point was brought out rather clearly at RMK. There were several economically attractive alternatives that would have involved acquiring control of firms in the same line of business (e.g., major competitors or customers). This would have invited antitrust or other Justice Department intervention. As one of the planners put it, "Our management simply wouldn't listen to any plan that might involve antitrust litigation." Thus antitrust legislation became a criterion for credibility in their view.

The sets of warrants and the counterplan must be politically *relevant* and significant in the context of the organization. This is determined by the interests and ideals of an actual person or persons within the organization's sphere of influence, including the industry and its customers. Viewing the firm as a coalition in the manner of Cyert and March, the counterplanner should look for those stakeholders who have beliefs differing from those ascribed to the plan and attempt to find out what sort of plan the stakeholders would have proposed had they not coalesced, and what sorts of beliefs they would have used to substantiate it. In this way we seek to find views backed up by commitment and conviction.

In order to secure this type of relevance, an effort should be made to become immersed in the firm's communication stream. This involves reviewing company documents: memoranda, articles, and speeches by company and industry personnel, trade journals, and the like. The focus of this research is to determine a cohesive line of thought in support of a plan other than the one chosen. We assumed that, by virtue of their having been expounded by members of the firm or the industry, beliefs and views discovered by this process would also be credible to the firm's decisionmakers.

An important aspect of assessing the relevance and significance of a counterplan and its supporting *Weltanschauung* is to determine the relative political power of the group supporting the opposing point of view. We should assume that the larger the group, the higher its position in the organizational hierarchy, and that the more dedicated its members are to their beliefs, the more credible a plan revolving around their world view will be for the decisionmaker. There is a "conviction" in the plan on the part of some coalition members. The counterplan then should not be merely contradictory to the plan, but rather its "deadliest enemy" (Churchman, 1971). It is an anticonviction at least as forceful as the conviction. In attempting to assess what sort of political support the counterplan would accrue and from whom in the organization this support would come, the counterplanner can begin to estimate the credibility of the counterplan.

Finally, an attempt should be made to make the *Weltanschauung complete*. We believe that the more complete the view of the world, the more credible it will appear to be. Any glaring gaps or oversights in the set of warrants will detract from the credibility of the plan or the counterplan.

The Structured Debate   Logic has been used to develop arguments and to produce opposition, and criteria have been offered to secure credibility. This effort was directed toward production of the drama necessary to awaken the synthesis roleplayers, policymakers, planners, and strategists to assumptions and to encourage them to challenge these assumptions. Drama, however, requires more than just logic—it also requires a literature, a rhetoric.

Balwin (1928) said that "the true aim of rhetoric—the energizing of knowledge—is necessarily correlated with inquiry and with policy." Inquiry to develop a policy or a plan is the purpose of the counterplanning design. The original plan is based on one view of the world, W_1. The role of the dramatic aspect of the debate is to awaken policymakers and to apprise them of the true conditional nature of the plan. That is, given a set of goals and data, the decision problem now takes the hypothetical form: *If* W_1 is your view of the world, *then* the plan is optimal; *if* W_2 is your view of the world, *then* the counterplan is optimal.

The policymaker's task has been elevated from a choice among alternative plans to a decision on a world view. The essence of the decision problem is judgment on the policymaker's *Weltanschauung* that warrants the conclusion of the plan. If the debate is dramatic and the policymaker's knowledge is "energized," then we propose that the stage is set for the "qualitative change" of Hegel that produces a synthesis or a new world view, W_3. This is why the theory of the dialectic is so fundamental to our theory of planning.

The proposed program for debate is styled after that used by Kant (1965) for "The Antinomies of Pure Reason." Kant's intent was to be skeptical and to reveal the "transcendental illusion" that besets unconstrained reason. He encouraged the reader to attain this "synthesis" by placing the thesis, "The world has a beginning in time," into juxtapositioned conflict with its contradictory antithesis, "The world has no beginning in time." He then proceeded to produce the most cogent argument possible for each side. The scheme adopted here is to use the notion of two opposing *Weltanschauungen* in Kant's framework as the layout or "structure" for the debate.

This debate takes on one characteristic, however, that most ad hoc debates and many formal debates do not have. Namely, both sides—the plan and the counterplan, both thesis and antithesis—are conjoined to refer to the *same* databank and the *same* problem. Each must interpret the entire databank according to the view taken regarding the problem. The purposes are to highlight and to emphasize the incidence of the opposing points of view by revealing for each item where they disagree and where they agree and on which aspects of the data their agreement or disagreement rests. This is done to simulate an important aspect of the Hegelian philosophy that is followed here. In Hegelian theory, the antithesis (counterplan) arises from the essence of the thesis (plan). We interpret this essence, in the light of a decision problem, to be the data or facts from observation, the stated goals to be obtained, and the dimensions of the problem to be considered. The plan and counterplan become "deadly enemies" by virtue of the fact that they take such contrary views of the data and the problem at hand.

A second aspect of the debate, one found more frequently in unstructured debate, is the role of the devil's advocate. The devil's advocate, which was described briefly in Chapter 6, draws attention to everything that is wrong, bad, or incorrect about the other side. In particular advocates of each position seek to argue and to demonstrate that every item of data not only supports their plan, but also does not support the opposing plan. They may even attempt to show that the data invalidate the opponent's plan.

The design for a debate to be presented to the synthesis roleplayer or policymaker is straightforward. The overall sequence is as follows:

1   The problem is stated.
2   The advocate for the plan announces his *Weltanschauung* by describing the warrants or the assumptions that, when conjoined with the data, conclude the plan. He does this in a "storytelling" fashion.
3   The advocate for the counterplan does likewise.
4   An item of data is introduced.
5   The advocate for the plan argues that this item of data can be interpreted as a piece of information in favor of the plan and against the counterplan. He produces a line of reasoning to demonstrate this.
6   The advocate for the counterplan now engages in Step 5 using the same item of data.
7   Steps 4 to 6 are repeated for every item in the data bank.

After hearing and reflecting on the debate, the decisionmaker must now make a judgment on the view of the world that will be adopted for this particular problem.

One might now ask, Since the executive merely develops a new world view, why haven't the advisors prepared as many world views as there are identifiable alternatives? The response is that once the executive reflects on the question of what view of the world he wishes to hold, he is *free* to formulate a new *Weltanschauung*. However, the key point is more fundamental and goes to the very heart of the philosophical concepts that underlie our work: The policymaker must not only observe the different world views, but he must also *observe* and *feel* the *opposition* if he is to achieve the higher perspective on the problem accorded the synthesis or new world view. He must involve himself in the dramatic.

The New Weltanschauung or Synthesis   The new *Weltanschauung* or synthesis is a new set of values, beliefs, or concepts—warrants supporting a plan as their conclusion—that the decisionmaker now elects to employ as the basis for his decision. Both the plan and the counterplan have organizational support or conviction; both are to some extent credible. The executive should attempt to discover the source of the disagreement and how the opposition arose and to resolve the observed conflict. He attempts to arrive at a *synthesis*. How and why he does this requires a psychological theory of decisionmaker behavior.

Such a theory of decisionmaker behavior begins with the assumption that the decisionmaker is strongly motivated to arrive at a conclusion or a plan of action, and thus he is in opposition to the very nature of the conflict between the plan and counterplan, just as a Hegelian observer of the conflict would be. Following the theory of conflict developed by March and Simon (1958), the decisionmaker perceives both the plan and the counterplan as "good" alternatives and credible views of the world. They meet or exceed the level defined as acceptable by the individual (i.e., they will accomplish his goals) and they are viable in the context. The decisionmaker regards the subjective probability of achieving a positive state of affairs as "high" for both cases. This dilemma results in a state of "incomparability" between alternatives, in which the decisionmaker cannot identify the most preferred alternative. This perceived conflict serves "as a generator of search behavior" because "the commonest reaction of an organism to a conflict situation is to look for a way out of the dilemma." The search is directed toward "clarification" of the issues and "new alternatives."

It is assumed in our theory that the decisionmaker's search consists of the formulation of a new *Weltanschauung*, in which the original conflict becomes understandable and explainable. With this new and higher-level view of the world, the plan/counterplan conflict is no longer the most relevant aspect of the decision problem. Both the plan and counterplan have, at the outset, some claim to plausibility and credibility, but both are defective as well. The search for the new *Weltanschauung*—their *synthesis*—is an attempt to reconcile and to harmonize the tensions created by opposition. The synthesis is the result of a mediation process that seeks to eliminate the defective aspects of both the thesis and antithesis by establishing a new intellectual model of the world. In this new view, the original plan and the counterplan become irrelevant.

This completes the procedures to be used for staff work development of dialectical advice. We have also found that for many policy, planning, and strategy issues the actual advocates of a point of view are effective in participating in the structured debate. One model for involving them follows.

FORMAL POLICY DEBATE—ONE SHOT DECISION

The Jet Propulsion Laboratory was asked by the U.S. Department of Energy to consider the question of R&D funding for roadway powered vehicle systems (RPVS). A formal, structured dialectical policy debate was designed to secure information on the problem. The JPL design featured extensive use of the policy argumentation concepts to be described in Part 4; however, it also illustrates the procedures for conducting a policy debate that involves real advocates for each side. The steps are as follows.

Problem Defining   First the problem to be studied was clearly stated. In this case the problem was: Is the RPVS system a promising technology for meeting the transportation and energy conservation needs of the United States? Which, accordingly, should receive increased R&D funding?

Role Assignment   Three roles were defined, and individuals were assigned to them. Four experts currently engaged in RPVS research were asked to assume the thesis role taking the positive or "pro" position. This team was called the T team. Four individuals who were experts in competitive technologies assumed the antithesis role. They are referred to as the A team. Four individuals who had generalized background in the broad issues involved formed a "third party." They were responsible for developing the synthesis and are referred to as the S team.

The teams were given several weeks to prepare their position statements. In addition a moderator was appointed.

Preparation for Debate   The afternoon before the structured debate was held, all parties met. Ground rules were discussed. The members of the T and A teams were told to rank all of the relevant issues surrounding the problem in order of importance and to select the six most important issues to be debated the following day. The results were as follows:

First Listing of Issues—for Each Team

T Team:
1. Technical
2. Social and institutional
3. Implementation
4. Preservation of mobility
5. Safety
6. Transportation
7. Energy
8. Resource requirements
9. Environment

A Team
1. Petroleum displacement
2. System energy efficiency
3. Transportation availability
4. Costs of petroleum conservation
5. Utility capacity addition
6. Electric, Hybrid Vehicle (EHV) mobility cost comparison

Second Listing—for Both Teams, Not Prioritized

Petroleum displacement—with utility implications
System-energy efficiency (later combined with A)
Economics
Transportation (availability, safety, intermodal, automation)
Implementation (social, institutional, infrastructure)
Comparison with alternatives (electric battery-operated vehicle, hybrid vehicle, synfuels)

Third Listing—Prioritized Listing of Issues/Agenda for the Debate

1   Petroleum displacement

    a. System energy efficiency
    b. Source fuel
    c. Peak demand

2 Economics

  a. Cost elements
  b. Cost allocation
  c. Comparison

3 Transportation

  a. Automation
  b. Modes
  c. Availability
  d. Safety
  e. Capacity

4 Implementation process

  a. Institutional
  b. Infrastructure
  c. Social and environmental
  d. Scenarios and time frame

5 Comparison with alternatives

  a. Electric, hybrid, and ICE vehicles
  b. Synfuels

Debate of Issues The specific time allocation for each of the following elements of the debate is shown in Figure 8-1. The debate takes a full day and is conducted as follows:

1 **Opening of the Debate** The *moderator* opens the debate by presenting:

  a. The basic question addressed. In this case, it is whether or not there should be further R&D funding of the roadway powered vehicle system (RPVS) within the DOE EHV program.
  b. The data base, that which is taken as a given or as the common assumption of all parties. For this debate, it would minimally include the conceptual design of the RPVS.

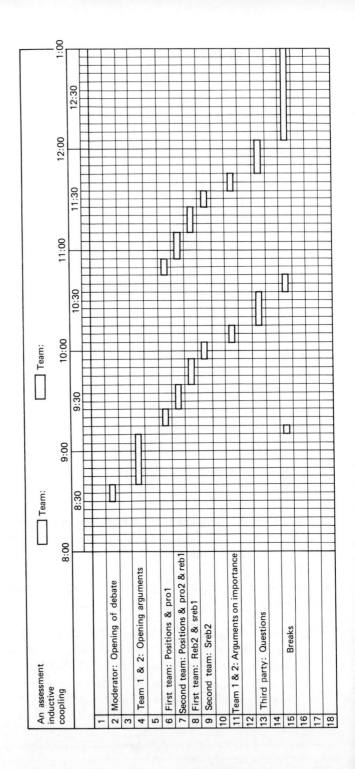

An assessment inductive coopling

Team: ☐   Team: ☐   Team: ☐

1	
2	Moderator: Opening of debate
3	
4	Team 1 & 2: Opening arguments
5	
6	First team: Positions & pro1
7	Second team: Positions & pro2 & reb1
8	First team: Reb2 & sreb1
9	Second team: Sreb2
10	
11	Team 1 & 2: Arguments on importance
12	
13	Third party: Questions
14	
15	Breaks
16	
17	
18	

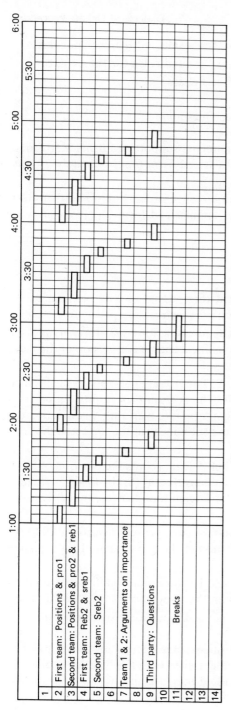

Figure 8-1 Structured debate schedule.

    c. The issue areas and the six issues selected the previous day.

    d. The format and any necessary ground rules for the debate.

    e. The principal rationale for the debate.

2 Opening Arguments on the Basic Question:

    a. The *T team* presents the arguments supporting further R&D funding of the RPVS, in a summarized form (approximately 20 minutes).

    b. The *A team* presents the arguments supporting no further R&D funding of the RPVS, in a summarized form (approximately 20 minutes).

3 Debate on the First Issue:

    a. Issue 1. The most important (first) issue and its boundaries are presented and defined by the *moderator.*

    b. Position T and Pro T. The T team presents its position on the issue in question and argues it as an inescapable conclusion of the data, logic, premises, and warrants.

    c. Position A, Pro A, and Reb T. The A team presents its position on the same issue and argues it. The A team then rebuts the position of the T team by presenting alternative warrants, invalidating the premises, and/or attacking the soundness of the logic and the relevancy of the data.

    d. Reb A and Sreb T (Pro T). The T team rebuts the position of the A team and may then present a surrebuttal (Sreb) to the A team's rebuttal of the position of the T team (and hence expand their pro T argument).

    e. Sreb A (Pro A). The A team may then present a surrebuttal to the T team's rebuttal of the position of the T team (and hence expand their pro A arguments).

    f. Arguments on the importance. The *moderator* called for summary arguments from both sides on the importance of the positions.

    g. The *third party* or S team may ask questions for clarification.

4 Remaining Issues in Order of Importance Steps 3a to 3g are then repeated for each of the remaining issues with the lead for each issue alternating between the T team and the A team.

Reflections on Debate   On the next morning all parties meet and engage in the following two processes:

1 **Third Party Questioning**   The third party, S team, asks questions for clarification of the debate issues, their importance, consistency, and underlying assumptions. This session should allow for a more open discussion than the previous day's session.
2 **Closing Arguments**   After reflecting on the debate that has taken place, and the third party questioning, both the T and A teams then present their closing arguments supporting the two sides of the basic question: Should there be further R&D funding . . . ?

Third Party Reporting   The third party prepares a list of the apparent warrants of each side and those premises that are not truly warrants but that could be validated or refuted through analysis. These are summarized in a report using argumentation analysis (see Chapters 9 to 11). The purpose of the report is to encourage a synthesis.

FORMAL POLICY DEBATE—ROUTINE DECISIONS

Many organizations have permanent committees or peer review processes that deal with repetitive policy decisions. Often the decisions can have a substantial effect on the performance of the organization. Personal budgeting and capital investment decisions are illustrations. In every case it is important that the committee obtain a comprehensive understanding of the assumptions underlying each decision in order to understand the precedents that the decision may set and the congruence of world views among decisions. Dialectical structural debated methods have also proven useful in these settings.

We are aware of at least two departments in leading universities that have employed these methods for purposes of faculty review. (One is at UCLA; the other at the University of Wisconsin, Milwaukee. See Nystrom, 1977.) The application of dialectical structured debate to collegial decisionmaking on personnel issues will be used to illustrate the procedures.

At the beginning of the year the committee meets and reviews its agenda. For example, there may be a series of promotion cases or a group of investment proposals to consider. A docket is established. The committee discusses its overall mission and the criteria it will use in evaluation cases. A committee chairman is selected to preside over all meetings.

A data collection procedure is established. The information that must be included in the vita and dossier is identified, and all interested parties are notified. In the case of capital investment decisions, the appropriate project information, cost data, and other analyses are specified. This information should be available to all committee members prior to consideration of the case. In order to prevent the use of surprise tactics or the introduction of unverified data or irrelevant data, a ground rule is established that permits only the use of this prespecified data. The data so identified becomes the common framework for the structured debate. All committee members are required to read the entire case file before the meeting during which it is considered.

An advocate is appointed to play the thesis role, T. The T role takes the positive or pro position for the case, for example, that Assistant Professor Smith be promoted to full Professor. A second person is appointed to play the antithesis role, A, and takes the negative or con position. All committee members including T and A are required to take the synthesis role, S.

Some useful guidelines for assigning roles are the following:

1 The overall work load of T and A roles should be evenly distributed over the academic year. Ideally, each member will play at least one T and one A role during that period.

2 Avoid assigning a T or A role to someone with a vested interest in the outcome. Such an individual will have an opportunity to present his views during the discussion period. The main purposes of this guideline are to avoid bias and vitriolics, to provide independent points of view, and to encourage deeper immersion in the case by less interested parties.

3 Attempt to match the T and A parties in terms of their abilities for argumentative analysis and oral presentation and their relative status in the organization.

At the meeting in which the case comes up on the agenda, the T role presents the pro side of the case first. Time limits are set depending on the complexity of the case, but, generally, 15 to 20 minutes is adequate. The presentation is made without interruption unless, at the discretion of the chairman, a question of clarification is entertained.

Following the T presentation, the A role presents the con case. Again a time limit is set, and only questions of clarification are permitted.

Both the T and A roles are told to make the most forceful case they can and to show how the common data is interpreted to support their cases.

Throughout their presentations, they are to present the assumptions under which their candidate is the very best choice.

After the presentations each of the T and A roles are given an opportunity for a rebuttal to statements made by the opposing party. This should not take more than about 5 minutes.

The meeting is now opened up for direct inquiries and statements by any of the committee members. Both A and T are permitted to drop their roles and express their own points of view. Open discussion and deliberation takes place. The amount of time devoted to this phase depends on the importance of the case. We have participated in sessions running anywhere from 10 minutes to several hours.

At an appropriate time the chairman requests that the members review the presentations and discussions thus far and formulate their own interpretations and conclusions. It is frequently useful to share these in a round-robin process. Then recommendations are called for. Sometimes these recommendations will include courses of action not previously considered, and they will need to be discussed briefly. Finally, a consensus emerges, a vote is taken, or some other method is employed to come to closure.

Our experience with this approach reveals several advantages. The meetings are generally more efficient. Better use of time is made since sensitive issues are typically uncovered early in the meeting rather than after prolonged discussion. Usually a more thorough and balanced review of the case is made. The relationship between this case and other cases decided by the committee is made more clear because assumptions are presented and can be compared. Finally a very significant advantage arises when the committee is required to write a report and is held accountable for its conclusions. The structured dialectical debate ensures that the facts, assumptions, and reasons, pro and con, for a decision have been stated and discussed. Consequently, the notes of the meeting become the basic material for making the report and for the documentation supporting the final conclusion.

There are several possible difficulties of which users of this design should be aware. Some members have difficulty playing a role or interpreting the real position of others who are playing a role. A frequent question is, Yes, but, how do you *really* feel about this case? This is a fair question after the presentations are made but should be avoided while the T and A roles are in effect. A second difficulty is that occasionally the advocates are mismatched and an unbalanced presentation ensues. We are aware of one case where a clever advocate in the A role presented a very devastating negative case against a rather weak T presentation for

the case. Prior to the presentation, all the members of the committee felt
that the case was very strong. In the open discussion period this much
stronger positive case emerged, and the promotion was awarded. However, this points out a danger that should be avoided.

A version of this procedure with three or more roles has proven to be
useful for educational purposes. We have used it as a method of analyzing
cases in executive training sessions and in regular classrooms. For example, the *Harvard Business Review* article "Decision at Zenith Life" (Collier, 1962) has been assigned, and individuals or groups were appointed to
make the strongest case for each of four candidates for the presidency of
the Zenith Life Insurance Company. Using other business and public
policy cases, individuals or groups have been appointed to present one of
the identified courses of action in the case. The class sessions are conducted following the procedures outlined previously. The sessions are
always lively and are favored by the students. Important educational
points are brought out dramatically.

REAL TIME PLANNING SESSION WITH FACILITATOR

The three designs discussed previously are useful for large, complex
problems and generally take a fair amount of commitment and time.
Sometimes, however, smaller problems arise that a group would like to
study quickly prior to making a decision. The real time planning session
with a facilitator has proven to be useful in these situations. It incorporates many of the concepts of dialectical debate discussed in this and
previous chapters. Given a general problem area, a meeting is called of all
relevant parties, and a facilitator takes them through the following procedures.

Some time is devoted to a discussion of the problem area and the events
leading up to its occurrence. All present are encouraged to share their
perspective on it. Usually not more than 30 minutes is devoted to this
sharing process.

The facilitator now moves to obtain a clear definition of the problem in
concrete terms. A preliminary definition is called for and is written legibly
so that all present can see. Flip charts with easels and newsprint are
effective media for this purpose. The preliminary definition is discussed,
debated, and modified until there is agreement on a definition. The problem must be stated in sufficiently concrete terms to allow it to be considered as a *real* problem, not a pseudo problem. The final statement of
the definition is written on the newsprint and placed in a prominent place
on the front wall.

Exhibit 8-1   Alternatives Form

Alternatives	
T	A

At this point the facilitator takes a new sheet of newsprint, writes the word "Alternatives" at the top, draws a horizontal line underneath it, draws a vertical line down starting from the underline to divide the sheet into two equal parts, and places a T (for thesis) on the left side and an A (for antithesis) on the right side. The result is a form like that shown in Exhibit 8-1.

The facilitator now asks the group to offer a candidate solution to the problem. This is the thesis. The proposed solution is written down on the T side of the form. Explaining briefly the notions of opposition and credibility described earlier in this chapter (under Dialectical Advice—Staff Presentation), the facilitator calls for an opposing alternative solution. This is the antithesis and is recorded on the right-hand side of the form under the A. At this point the facilitator reminds the group that these are merely suggested alternatives, not *the* solution to the problem.

The "Alternatives" sheet is placed to the right of the "Problem" sheet on the front wall.

The facilitator writes the phrase "T Assumptions" at the top of a fresh piece of newsprint. A version of the nominal group technique is now used in order to elicit the T assumptions. The group is asked to reflect silently for 5 minutes on the inverse optimal question What must I assume to be true for T to be the optimal solution to the problem? Then they are asked to write their answers down on a sheet of paper. Picking someone at random, the facilitator asks the individual to state a T assumption. The assumption is summarized in a concise, terse phrase and written on the newsprint, preceded by a short line. Using a round-robin procedure, the facilitator continues to ask for assumptions. During the first round everyone is required to state an assumption; however, redundant assumptions are to be avoided. Only questions of clarification are permitted. The assumptions are *not* to be evaluated. This comes later. During subsequent rounds a participant may say "pass" if he or she has no new assumption to offer.

The facilitator continues rounds until there are no new assumptions offered. Then the facilitator announces to the group: "Stop. Be silent. Close your eyes. Take three deep breaths. Now, think *deeply* about another assumption." The silence is maintained for about a minute. Then the facilitator says "O.K. Let's have one more round of T assumptions" and proceeds with the round robin. Frequently, new and creative assumptions will emerge from this last round. The group takes a break at this point.

When the group reconvenes, the facilitator writes A assumptions on the top of a fresh sheet of newsprint. The round-robin process is repeated.

At the end of this step the front wall contains: (1) a statement of the problem and two alternatives T and A for solving the problem, (2) a list of assumptions under which T is the optimal solution, and (3) a list of assumptions under which A is the optimal solution.

At this point the facilitator labels a fresh sheet of newsprint "S Assumptions" (for synthesis). He or she then leads the group in an evaluation, discussion, and debate on the assumptions.

1 Assumptions that are the same or similar between the T and A sets are identified. The question is posed "Is this a sound assumption for any effective solution? If there is agreement, the assumption is recorded on the S assumptions list. If not, it is debated until an acceptable statement of the assumption can be made.

2 Assumptions that are different are identified and debated. An attempt is made to arrive at a single assumption that captures the best of both the T and A assumptions.

3 Assumptions that are unique to either the T or A list are identified. They are discussed in terms of their distinctiveness. The facilitator asks, What is the companion assumption for this one in the other list? Is this really a unique assumption? The best statement of the assumption is now placed on the S list.

Processes 1 to 3 are continued until all assumptions have been debated and the result placed on the S list.

The S list is now reviewed, item by item. The question is asked Is this the most plausible assumption that can be made? If the answer is "no," the assumption is debated until a plausible assumption is stated. Sometimes it is necessary to mark an assumption as an "issue" and to go on with the review, returning to the issues at the end.

As the last step the facilitator turns the group's attention to creating a solution, one that logically follows from the S assumptions. Everyone is implored to create a solution consistent with the S assumptions. As solutions emerge, the facilitator writes them down and discusses them, pointing out their relationship to the S assumptions. Finally, the facilitator strives for some form of consensus on a solution.

If time is available this solution can be tested by making it the T alternative and assumptions, posing a "deadliest enemy" A alternative, generating its assumptions, and carrying out the rest of the process described previously.

Part Four

Policy Argumentation

Chapter Nine

Policy Argumentation Concepts

FAILURE AND SUCCESS

Top management for a large U.S. corporation was considering the release of a new product. During the product planning committee meeting, the Vice President of Marketing stated that he had just reviewed the latest market research data. It indicated that the market for the proposed product was not large enough to make it profitable to sell. His claim went unchallenged and his recommendation carried the day. The new product project was scuttled.

Meanwhile, the management of the firm's major competitor, using substantially the same market research information, was excited about their version of the new product. They released it, captured a substantial market share, and earned a large return on their investment in the area. For them it turned out to be a very profitable decision.

How can two companies with the same basic information arrive at such different conclusions? Because the market research data was subject to different interpretations. The key question in the market research questionnaire was Would you use the proposed product for function X? Most respondents said "No." Yet, under the comments section of the questionnaire, many of these same respondents said that they would, however, use the product for function Y.

The top management of the corporation that lost out made two grievous errors. First, they had an unexamined preconception that the product was intended for function X rather than function Y, and, second, they never challenged the claims being made by the Vice President of Marketing. Although this was one of the most important decisions the company was to make in a decade, the Vice President was never required to provide the facts and assumptions on which his conclusions were based. Nor, was he ever asked under what conditions his conclusions might *not* be valid.

211

In contrast, the top management at the competitive firm debated the subject at length. They kept inquiring as to the reasons for each conclusion presented. When the statements appeared to be weak or implausible they pushed deeper. In the process they discovered a potential strong support for the products in the market for function Y. Intuitively their management knew to challenge the important claims that were made and to demand a fuller statement of the underlying reasons for them. They only lacked a systematic method for doing this. Policy argumentation is such a method. It focuses on the concept of a claim.

ON CLAIMS

The complex and uncertain world of policy making is an unintelligible morass until someone makes a claim. "The market will grow at 7% per annum." "Physicians will subscribe to our drug at a higher price." "The installation of an electrified roadway system will substantially reduce petroleum consumption in the United States." Each one of these claims is an assertion made in order to infuse certainty into an otherwise cloudy policy decision situation. Claims are the supporting foundation of a policy, a plan, or a strategy. Every assumption that underlies a policy is a claim.

Once a policy claim is articulated it is proper, indeed sometimes mandatory, to call it into question. Why should a claim be believed? This basic question, so vital in policy making, requires a particular kind of response called an argument. When one calls for an argument, one demands a well-stated set of the reasons that support the claim. Each of these reasons itself is also a claim from some prior argument, and so the demand for supporting arguments may be continued to various levels of depth. Chains of policy arguments are thereby created. These argument chains can be quite intricate, reflecting the complexity of the world they seek to describe. But they are anchored at the bottom by two things—facts and judgments. Policy argumentation is a conceptual framework for dealing with the claims, facts, and judgments that arise in a dynamic, ever-changing policy-making environment. It serves as a tool for bringing order out of the chaos.

This chapter introduces a framework that is especially suited to handling the structure and the dynamics of complex policy arguments. The framework consists of two parts: a qualitative part and a quantitative one. The qualitative part has been designed to capture the structure of the reasoning processes, which proceeds from the grounds of an argument to the resultant claims or policies. The quantitative aspect has been designed to help evaluate the plausibility of the component parts of an argument and the plausibility of an argument as a whole.

This chapter also extends the SAST and dialectical debate processes. In effect, argumentation analysis is a supporting method that can be used to take these processes one step deeper. Policy argumentation is a structured way of exploring the complex linkages among various policy assumptions. Assumptions, it will be recalled, pertain to the properties of stakeholders and as such are the underlying bases on which policies, plans, or strategies are built. In short, assumptions may be conceived as the premises from which policy arguments and conclusions are derived. In this chapter we will learn how the structure of such arguments may be systematically examined and evaluated.

A word of clarification is in order before proceeding further. By the use of the term "argument," we do not necessarily mean a hostile, adversarial proceeding characterized by unbridled quarreling. Rather, by "argument" we mean a *process of reasoning,* a process that proceeds from the underlying basis of an argument to its conclusions. One way to think of an argument is to think of it as a "brief" for a policy position similar to the brief a lawyer builds for a legal case. Briefs are arguments for preferred outcomes. The purpose of the argument is to convince or persuade the audience that something is true. Thus in this chapter we are concerned with examining the "logical structure" of policy arguments and the "logical links" between stakeholder assumptions and policy outcomes.

THE QUALITATIVE ASPECT: A FRAMEWORK FOR ARGUMENTATION ANALYSIS

A framework for the structure of arguments is shown in Figure 9-1. It is based on the work of Stephen Toulmin (1958). Toulmin devised the framework to account for the complexities, subtleties, and dynamics of arguments that are not adequately handled by the classic structure of the simple syllogism. We have drawn on his concepts to create a theory of policy argumentation.

Toulmin describes argument basically as the *movement* from accepted *data* through a *warrant* to a *claim.* His model for the structure of an argument consists of five parts, as shown in Figure 9-1. The claim (C) stands for the *outcome* or *conclusion* of an argument, the merits of which one wants to establish. Claims are not true with absolute certainty. As Brockriedge and Ehninger (1960) put it, the claim "is the explicit appeal produced by the argument, and is always of a potentially controversial nature." In other words, any claim other than a tautology is never completely certain or necessarily true. In the market planning illustration in

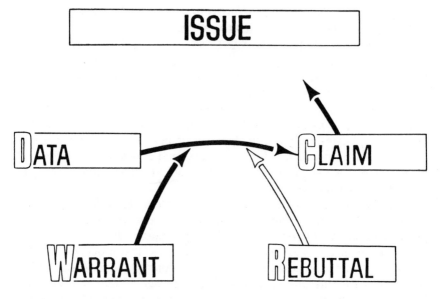

Figure 9-1 The structure of arguments.

the previous section the claim is that "the market will grow at 7% per annum." That statement like all policy statements is debatable. The doubtful policymaker may demand reasons for it and in so doing may inquire about the grounds on which it was made.

Data (D) consists of the facts presented by an advocate as grounds for the claim identified. It represents the evidential support for the claim. Data may be factual statements or claims from other arguments. Accounting records, survey results, scientific findings, testimony, analytical reports, or citations from authorities are illustrative sources of data. Data answers the question: "What do you have to go on?" Thus data are the "givens" in an argument. Data can be prefaced by the phrase "Given that. . . ." A statement like "the market has grown by at least 7% a year for each of the last 10 years" is a data item.

Warrants (W) are rules, principles, premises, or inference licenses that act as a bridge *between the data and the claim*. That is, a warrant is a *justification* for interpreting the data as support for the claim. In Toulmin's framework a warrant "authorizes the mental 'leap' involved in advancing from data to claim." Data answers the question: What do you have to go on? A warrant answers the question: How do you get there? A warrant generally takes the form of a universal hypothetical statement. Symbolically, a warrant may be represented as D → C (read "D implies C"; or, "If the data D is true, then the claim C is true."). Consequently, warrants form the underlying basis for an argument.

A warrant is the *because* part of an argument; it says C follows from D *because* of an "accepted" principle. For example, "the market will grow at 7% per annum" follows from "the market has grown by at least 7% a year for each of the last 10 years" *because* of the principle "past market growth is a good indicator of future market growth." It is important to note that the "because" part of an argument is often not made explicit. Consequently, warrants must often be inferred by the person doing the argumentation analysis.

Another illustration may help to cement the relationship between issues, claims, data, and warrants. Consider a policymaker who is concerned with the issue "What is the potential size of our market next year?" The claim may be: "60,000 units." The data: "From a population of 200,000 potential customers, a random sample of 500 were surveyed by telephone, and 150 (30%) said they would purchase our product next year (30% of 200,000 is 60,000)." The warrants for this argument are somewhat complex. They include (1) "The sample of 500 was of adequate size," (2) "The sample was representative," and (3) "What people say they will do during a telephone survey, they actually intend to do."

The W, D, and C of an argument are similar in structure to the traditional syllogism, with one important exception. The standards for judging their soundness, validity, or cogency vary from profession to profession. Different disciplines and functional fields use different warrants, data, and claims. The argument that the market will grow at 7% per annum is ultimately based on the judgment of an experienced marketer. The argument that the market size will be 60,000, on the other hand, is based on statistical theory and practice.

The claim C does not necessarily follow logically. For this reason, backings and rebuttals are added to the framework. The backing (B) is the underlying support for the warrant and is always "waiting," ready to come to its defense. Every warrant, no matter how strong it may appear on the surface, always rests on certain taken-for-granted, "self-evident," background truths or assumptions. A backing normally appeals to some established or generally accepted categorical statement of fact that supports the warrant. Backing systems include statistical principles, laws, categories in a taxonomical system, definitions in a language, or accepted methods of calculation. They also include the credentials of the person making the claim. The function of the backing is to certify or to legitimize the assumptions inherent in the warrant. It is called into play when the assumptions expressed in the warrant are questionable, when the audience is not willing to accept the warrant at its face value, or whenever a deeper rationale for accepting the claim is required. Backing answers the question What is the support for the warrant? It identifies the experience base, the theory base, social values, prior policy choices, or other beliefs that underlie the warrant. A marketer's experience and accepted statistical theory are examples of backings. Backings are often prefaced by "Since . . . ."

The rebuttal (R) serves two functions. First, it is a safety valve, an "out," so to speak. In this case, the rebuttal lists the conditions under which the warrant and/or the claim may not hold. For instance, the R may say "W holds *unless* . . . ." The statement following the "unless" is the R. In this case, the rebuttal serves as a contingency or face-saving device. The second function of the rebuttal is to indicate those outstanding challenges and objections to the argument that come from other sources such as from opponents of the argument, advocate of other policies, or other stakeholders.

Thus rebuttals are the contingencies or conditions under which the claim is not true. They may deny the data, warrants, backings, or they may present counterclaims. For example, the claim of a 7% market growth may be rebutted by the statement "Unless the market has reached the saturation point and no growth is left," or "Unless an entirely new segment enters the market expanding the growth rate to 15%." The data may be rebutted by stating, "Past market growth is based on sales data that include price increases and other factors that are no longer relevant to this market." The warrant may be rebutted by stating that "social change and structural change taking place in the market mean that the past is no longer a reliable indicator of the future."

One of the main functions of the rebuttal is to help qualify the argument and to assess its plausibility. If strong rebuttals can be adduced, the argument may be assessed to be relatively weak; if only weak rebuttals can be adduced, the argument may be considered to be relatively strong. As we will see subsequently in this chapter, rebuttals play a key role in assessing the plausibility of an argument.

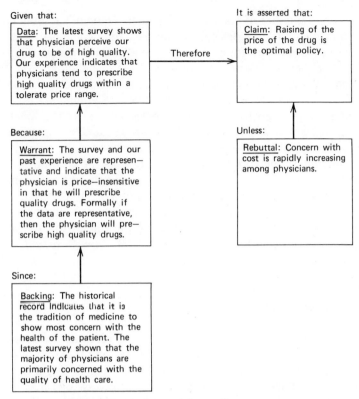

Given that:

Data: The latest survey shows that physician perceive our drug to be of high quality. Our experience indicates that physicians tend to prescribe high quality drugs within a tolerate price range.

Therefore

It is asserted that:

Claim: Raising of the price of the drug is the optimal policy.

Because:

Warrant: The survey and our past experience are represen—tative and indicate that the physician is price—insensitive in that he will prescribe quality drugs. Formally if the data are representative, then the physician will pre—scribe high quality drugs.

Unless:

Rebuttal: Concern with cost is rapidly increasing among physicians.

Since:

Backing: The historical record indicates that it is the tradition of medicine to show most concern with the health of the patient. The latest survey shown that the majority of physicians are primarily concerned with the quality of health care.

Figure 9-2   A drug pricing policy argument.

Figure 9-2 illustrates a full-blown policy argument. It is based on material drawn from the drug company case reported in Chapter 4. The issue, it will be recalled, concerned a major problem faced by one of the largest drug manufacturers in the United States, that is, What price should the firm charge for its drug line? An analysis less formal than that shown in Figure 9-2 of the structure of the argument of the high-price group was conducted. It showed that the status of the backing, warrant, and data was adequate to derive the claim. Unfortunately, neither the backing, the warrant, nor the data were judged certain enough to justify very much confidence in the resultant claim. On further inquiry it turned out that there was as much support for the rebuttal, as derived from the other policies, as there was for the warrant and backing.

Note that in the drug pricing policy argument the important assumption of the price insensitivity of the physician enters into the structure of the argument at a number of places, not just one. Toulmin's argument structure helps reveal the complex role of this assumption and clarify it. It also raises an important question. At what level are the assumptions being made? At the level of factual properties of the stakeholders, that is, the data; the level of resultant policy, that is, Is one justified in enacting a certain action?; the level of the warrant of the argument, that is, the movement of passage from the data to the claim; or the level of the argument's deep basis, its backing? Answers to these questions give the policymaker a deeper insight into the reasons for the policy.

The Toulmin framework is also a powerful tool for locating and exposing the weaknesses in policy arguments. It shows the extreme complexity of policy statements. Most arguments are not as simple as that just outlined but rather have a complex structure consisting of multiple chains of argumentation. Thus one finds in applying the framework that *the outcome or claim of one argument is often the data input, warrant, or backing of another.*

CHAINS OF ARGUMENT

Any time a claim, data, warrant, backing, or rebuttal is offered by an advocate, someone else may say "I doubt it!" and thereby demand the reasons behind the assertion. In response to this doubt, a supporting argument is produced at a lower level. Alternatively, one may move up the chain by asking of any claim What am I to make of this? What does it mean? How does it fit in the broader scheme of things? Hence the claim may become data, warrant, backing, or rebuttal in a higher level argument.

The Toulmin framework and the concept of chains of argument demonstrate in a novel manner the ways in which the structure of an organization affects policy, planning, and strategy making. As originally proposed by Toulmin, the framework contains the subtle, implicit assumption that the structure of an argument is contained entirely within a single person. In organizations, however, this is not generally true. In most organizations, claims, data, warrant, rebuttals, and backings are distributed to a variety of people and departments. In a large, complex organization, one dominant individual or group may literally own or control some of the backings and warrants (e.g., a belief in certain underlying business principles or expertise in statistical or cost accounting principles); another group may control the data (e.g., accounting or the market research data), while still another may control the claims (e.g., preferred policy outcomes) that derive from neither the data nor the warrants of the other groups (e.g., the board of directors). The framework is thus capable of serving as a paradigm for studying such topics as organizational communication, information flow, influence, power, and source credibility.

POLICY ARGUMENTATION AND SAST

Having presented both the SAST methodology and the Toulmin argumentation scheme, we may summarize their relationship to one another. Any policy statement, such as "Raise the price of the drug" is based on a series of assumptions made about stakeholders. These assumptions are data in an argument that concludes with the policy statement as a claim. One implicit warrant in any major policy argument is that all the stakeholders have been properly identified and their assumptions properly specified. The backing for this warrant is the theory of teleological systems and, of course, the assumption that the SAST method itself has been properly conducted. The rebuttal, then, is the case for one or more alternative policies. As such, the rebuttal constitutes the basis for a dialectic. Furthermore, a claim and its supporting argument taken together with all possible rebuttals constitute a specification of the whole system. Hence our application of the Toulmin argumentation scheme is holistic in nature.

An assumption uncovered by the SAST method is of the general form "Stakeholder S_i is assumed to have characteristics a_j." This assertion may be considered to be a claim in an argument. As such, it may be doubted. Then a policymaker may request the underlying reasons for it by applying the concepts developed in this chapter.

Our experience indicates that when arguments are requested for important assumptions, these assumptions are often found to be weak and implausible. Whenever this is the case one should engage in more research and inquiry in order to bolster the plausibility of the argument. For example, in one organization we worked on a strategy involving the release of a new medical product. A crucial assumption was made that the stakeholder "physician" was willing to pay a higher price than that charged for competitive equipment in order to get the increased speed of processing offered by the new product. In a planning session, one top executive openly doubted this claim. He asked the planner for the argument supporting his position. The planner responded "My brother-in-law is a physician, and he said that he was willing to pay more." Unimpressed by the quality of the data in this argument and the highly implausible warrant it requires to interpret the data as support, the executive was ready to throw out the entire recommendation. Remembering some of the concepts in this chapter, however, he asked for better evidence. As a result, a market research study was undertaken. In this case, a sample survey of physicians happen to support the planner's original claim that the physicians were indeed willing to trade off cost for speed. With this more plausible argument as support, the executive was more convinced. The product was released and proved to be successful.

The following summarizes the relationship between SAST and Toulmin-based argumentation analysis as illustrated in the preceding case:

SAST

Policy issue	Should the new product be released at a competitively high price?
Stakeholder S_i has assumption a_j	Physician will trade off cost for speed.

Argumentation analysis (at time t_1, prior to inquiry)

S_i/a_j is claim (x,t_1)	Physician will trade off cost for speed.

Claim (x,t_1) is supported by

Data (x,t_1)	Planner's brother-in-law is willing.
Warrant (x,t_1)	Brother-in-law is representative of all physicians.
Backing (x,t_1)	Brother-in-law never deceived me before.
Rebuttal (x,t_1)	Unless brother-in-law is not representative or is telling me what I want to hear.

Argumentation analysis (at time t_2, after inquiry)

S_i/a_j is claim (x,t_2)	Physician will trade off cost for speed.

Claim (x,t_2) is supported by

Data (x,t_2)	76% of a random sample of 2000 physicians responded thus on a questionnaire.
Warrant (x,t_2)	The sample was representative.

  Backing (x, t_2) Sample was drawn according to
               stratified sampling theory.

  Rebuttal (x, t_2) Unless this sample was one of
               the small number of possibly
               unrepresentative ones or the
               questionnaire was biased.

Note in the preceding example that the warrant in each case states that the data is representative of the whole. Thus this warrant permits the movement from the data to the more encompassing claim by the process of generalization. Generalization is just one of the types of warrants that can be used to classify arguments. The next section develops a more complete taxonomy of policy argument warrants. The scheme can serve as a guide to warrant making and to classifying arguments.

CLASSIFICATION OF ARGUMENTS

In the most general sense, arguments may be classified as either tautologies or inferences. A statement is a tautology if one part of it merely repeats another part in the guise of adding information. In this case the data is conclusive itself and a warrant is not really required. Tautologies are necessarily true, often by definition. For example, the statement "A pistol is a handgun" is such a tautology. It is true by definition and the statement does not add any new information to the situation. People use tautologies when making policy, planning, and strategy arguments. The analyst should be alert for them. Inferences, however, are much more important in the policy-making process. Thus we will concentrate on inferences.

  Inferences require warrants; as a result, they are never conclusively true. They depend on the creative contribution of the arguers. Because of the judgment involved, the proof of an asserted inference is sometimes referred to as an "artistic" proof. The warrants contained in such an "artistic" proof may be classified into three broad categories depending on the kind of appeal for credibility they make to the listener. These are:

1 **Substantive arguments** Substantive arguments appeal to the listener's sense of reason. The warrant concerns the existence of relationships among parts of the real world. The listener verifies the claim by means of applying his own logic to the movement from data to claim. In Greek philosophy, this form of appeal was called logos. These arguments are often called logical arguments.

2 **Authoritative Arguments** Authoritative arguments appeal to the listener's confidence in the source of the statement. Data coming from a reliable, believable source are to be accepted as true. The listener verifies the claim by reviewing the credentials of the source of the statement, its general trustworthiness, and its veracity. This is a philosophy the Greeks referred to as ethos. For this reason, authoritative arguments are also referred to as ethical arguments.

3 **Motivational Arguments** Motivational arguments appeal to the listener's inner feelings and drives. Often, the intent of a motivational argument is to evoke feelings of pity, sorrow, compassion, or sympathy. The listener verifies the claim by examining his own needs, values and aspirations to see whether he shares the same feelings. The Greeks called this pathos. These kinds of arguments are sometimes referred to as pathetic arguments.

All three types of arguments are employed in policy, planning, and strategic settings. Consequently, one should be able to identify each type when he or she encounters it. Each type of argument is reviewed in more depth below.

Substantive Arguments

The common characteristic about all substantive arguments is that the warrant concerns the way in which one class of things X in the policy system is related to another class Y. Six basic relationships may be defined: generalization, classification, cause and effect, sign or symptom, parallel case, and analogy.

Generalization The data in an argument from generalization consists of observations $(O_1, O_2 \cdots O_n)$ about stakeholders, people, events, and objects, or things in the policy system. The warrant contends that these observations constitute a representative sample of a larger class and that, therefore, the attributes of the data may be generalized to the larger class. Most statistical arguments are of this type.

The general form of an argument from generalization is:

Data	X has $O_1, O_2, O_3 \cdots O_n$
Warrant	X is representative of a broader class Y
Claim	Thus Y has $O_1, O_2, O_3 \cdots O_N$

Classification Classification is the opposite of generalization. In an argument from classification, the data state general conclusions about a known class of stakeholders, persons, events, objects, or things in the policy system. The warrant asserts that a new, previously unexamined item may also be subsumed under the same classification as those represented by the data and that the attributes of the items of the class apply to the new item. Arguments from classification are used in all taxonomic and labeling systems, and, also, they are subject to the problems of false classification. Broad classes, such as all children, the aged, politicians, and communists, may not adequately distinguish the relevant attributes for policy making. The general form of an argument from classification is:

Data	X has $O_1, O_2, O_3 \cdots O_n$
Warrant	Y is also a member of the class of X
Claim	Thus Y has $O_1, O_2, O_3 \cdots O_n$

Cause and Effect   The data in an argument from cause and effect consists of observations about stakeholders, people, events, objects, or things. The warrant states that these items have a productive or creative power—the cause—and specifies the nature of the product they will produce. The claim relates the results—the effect—to the items identified in the data.

Many scientific arguments contain assumptions of cause and effect. Technically, scientific reasoning requires that the backing for an argument from cause and effect should establish that the asserted cause is both necessary and sufficient to yield the effect. These conditions, of course, are very difficult to obtain, hence the possibility of a rebuttal to the effect that something is neither necessary nor sufficient. In most everyday policy situations, cause and effect arguments fall short of the scientific ideal. Sometimes, however, it is possible to assert that a certain item is necessary, but not sufficient for yielding an outcome. Churchman (1971) and Ackoff and Emery (1972) refer to this as a producer/product relationship. An example of a producer/product relationship is the relationship between an acorn and an oak tree. An acorn is a necessary but insufficient condition for obtaining an oak. It is necessary because an oak will not grow without it. However, it is not sufficient because water, soil, protection from squirrels, and so on also are required for the oak to grow. The producer/product construct has the advantage of introducing the concepts of potential production and of the probability of production. Most purported cause and effect arguments in policy, planning, and strategic settings are at best producer/product arguments. The policymaker should be alert to this when judgments are made on these kinds of arguments.

It should also be pointed out that the logic of an argument from cause and effect can be reversed. The data in this case consists of observations about stakeholders, persons, events, objections, or things in the policy system. The warrant asserts that a particular cause accounts for these observations as effects. The claim then asserts that the stakeholders, persons, events, objects, or things are the cause of these observations.

An argument from cause and effect may take one of two general forms:

Data	X has $O_1, O_2, O_3 \cdots O_n$
Warrant	$O_1, O_2, O_3 \cdots O_n$ are a cause for effect Y
Claim	Thus, X has effect Y or X is the cause of Y

Data	X has $O_1, O_2, O_3 \cdots O_n$
Warrant	Y is a sufficient cause for producing $O_1, O_2, O_3 \cdots O_n$
Claim	Thus, Y caused $O_1, O_2, O_3 \cdots O_n$

Sign or Symptom   The data in an argument from sign or symptom consists of *indicators* or clues found in the policy system. The warrant assigns some significance, or meaning, to these signs. Warrants of indication are perhaps the most widely used in policy, planning, and strategy situations. The claim asserts that some stakeholders, persons, events, objects, or things in the policy system possess the meaning or significance so indicated. The general form of an argument from sign or symptom is:

Data	X has $O_1, O_2, O_3 \cdots O_n$
Warrant	$O_1, O_2, O_3 \cdots O_n$ are indicators of Y
Claim	Thus, X has Y

Parallel Case   The data in an argument from parallel case consist of observations about a stakeholder, person, event, object, or thing in this or some other policy system. The warrant asserts that this item is essentially similar to an item in the policy system under consideration. The claim asserts observations made about the first item also pertain to the second item. The general form of an argument from parallel case is:

Data	X has $O_1, O_2 \cdots O_n$
Warrant	X is essentially similar to Y in the policy system
Claim	Thus, Y has $O_1, O_2 \cdots O_n$

Analogy   The data in an argument from analogy consists of a report that a general relationship exists between two items—stakeholders, persons, events, objects, or things. The warrant asserts that the general relationship is essentially similar to a relationship found between two items in the policy system. The claim asserts that the relationship holds between the identified items in the policy system. The general form of an argument from analogy is:

Data	A is known to have relationship R with B
Warrant	Relationship R is essentially similar to relationship R' between X and Y in the policy system
Claim	X has relationship R' with Y in the policy system

An effort has been made in describing these six types of substantive arguments to focus on straightforward, rather pure forms of the warrants. In actual circumstances many claims have warrants that are not so clearcut. Furthermore, complex arguments that simultaneously employ several of the six types of warrants often occur. Nevertheless, in most substantive arguments one of these forms will generally predominate. Thus although a policymaker can expect to find arguments of all six types in any policy situation the argument itself can usually be classified as relying primarily on one of the types of substantive warrants.

Authoritative Arguments

Authoritative arguments are accepted as true because their source is believed to be trustworthy and reliable. The data in an authoritative argument consists of statements such as reports, statements of fact, and statements of opinion made by an identified source. The warrant attests to the reliability of the source. The claim asserts that the statement is to be accepted as true. Authoritative arguments take the following general form:

Data	S said X
Warrant	S is a trustworthy, reliable, and believable source
Claim	Thus X is to be regarded as true

The backing for the warrant of an authoritative argument must establish the credentials of the source. This is usually done in one or more of the following ways:

1 **Expertise** Establishing that the source has expert knowledge in the matters under consideration. This approach generally applies to testimony in policy matters.

2 **Method**   Establishing that the source has used an appropriate method in arriving at the conclusions presented. This approach is used to authenticate data deriving from scientific experiments, census, accounting records, and analytical reports.

3 **Consensus**   Establishing that the source's conclusions are the same as those deriving from other sources and that because of this agreement it must be reliable.

4 **Tradition**   Establishing that something always has been done or believed to be true in the past and that, therefore, this action or belief should be perpetuated.

5 **Basic Belief**   Establishing that the source's statement derives from a fundamental belief, intuition, or mystical experience such as a religious experience and that this is a "true" insight. Religious beliefs form, for example, the backing for arguments in many social policy issues such as abortion and euthanasia.

Motivational Arguments

Motivational arguments appeal to the basic value system of the listener for their validity. In a motivational argument, the data consists of one or more statements. The warrant appeals to a basic motive by relating the claim to some basic human need such as some fundamental social value. Human needs include physiological, safety, social, esteem, or self-actualization needs. Social values include justice, liberty, equality, beauty, courage, love, prudence, or temperance. The claim asserts that a value or action should be adopted.

The claim of any motivational argument may assert (1) that a certain *value* is to be placed on one or more stakeholder, person, event, object, or thing in the policy system or (2) that a certain *course of action* should (or should not) be followed. In either case the essence of the argument is emotional. Its intent is to motivate the people in the policy system to think certain ways and to take certain actions. Most policy issues evoke some motivational arguments. In fact, motivational arguments underlie the imperatives that trigger the making of policy, plans, and strategy. Motivational arguments may also be required to release the psychic energy necessary to implement a policy choice. Unfortunately, motivational arguments are sometimes employed when substantive or authoritative arguments would be more appropriate. Thus it is useful to identify motivational arguments and to specify them clearly. The general form of a motivational argument is:

Data	X has $O_1, O_2, O_3 \cdots O_n$
Warrant	According to value system V if X has $O_1, O_2, O_3 \cdots O_n$, Y should result
Claim	Thus Y is (or should be) the case

THE QUALIFIER IN ARGUMENTS

So far claims, data, warrants, backings, and rebuttals have been presented as though they were the entire basis of an argument. However, questions also arise as to the validity of warrant and the force with which it justifies a claim. Not all warrants (regardless of type) authorize us to accept a claim unequivocally. Some claims, for example, are only "probably" true.

The question of the degree of force that a warrant carries leads us to the concept of qualifiers to an argument. The notion of qualifiers requires an understanding of the conditions of exception or rebuttals to the argument and, also, of the nature of the substantiation or backing of the warrant. To accommodate the need, Toulmin's theory adds one more distinction to the elements of an argument: the Qualifier (Q).

A qualifier is a modal statement that indicates the degree to which we are to accept a claim as true. A qualifier may run the range, from, at one extreme, "definitely," "certainly," "absolutely," or "necessarily" to, at the other extreme, "impossibly" or "absolutely not." In the middle are the qualifiers "probably" or "presumably." Depending on the force of its data and warrants, any claim, in principle, may be measured on a probability scale from 0 to 1. A 0 means "absolutely not" and a 1 means "necessarily so." For the critical claims concerning a policy issue, it may be necessary to estimate the probability that they are true or, alternatively, to estimate the certainty with which one believes that the claim is true. For many applications, however, it is adequate to order claims on a five-point scale—(1) certainly, (2) probably, (3) as likely as not, (4) improbably, (5) impossibly.

In policy making one rarely makes an unqualified statement such as "the market will grow at 7% per annum." Rather, the statement is usually qualified with a preface, "It is likely that . . ." or "The chances are 95% that the market will grow at a rate of between 6 and 8%." These notions of probability are based *intrinsically* on the properties of the data and the warrant. Thus the qualifier refers to the likelihood of the occurrence of a particular event. Qualifiers are based on relative frequencies, logical possibilities, or personal probabilities. In any event, they are derived from the internal logic of the argument, *not* from external considerations. This is one of the key distinctions between the *probability* of the claim and the *plausibility* of an argument. This distinction will be explored in more depth in the next section.

THE QUANTITATIVE ASPECT: PLAUSIBILITY ANALYSIS

One of the most important parts of an argument structure is the rebuttal (R). This is because R represents the set of challenges to the preferred outcome(s) C of an argument. Without the presence of R, C would appear to follow inevitably. The presence of R, however, forces us to reconsider whether C is the only possible outcome and whether the entire argument is properly conceived.

It is a natural temptation to ignore R. R is the monkey wrench in our plans, the fly in the ointment. Rebuttals are often painful to consider, for they force us to abandon our favored ideas. This is one of the reasons, for example, for explicitly incorporating opposing group perspectives into the SAST process by means of a dialectic. In effect, the main arguments of one SAST group constitute the R's of the other groups.

The introduction of R causes not only psychological difficulties, but logical ones. R introduces deep contradictions into the structure of an argument. The contradictions must be faced up to explicitly and not ignored. The consistency of an argument can always be preserved by throwing out the R. To do so, however, is to throw out some of the most important and valuable parts of an argument and, in the process, to impair the policymaker's insight into the situation. Retaining R, on the other hand, means that we shall have to introduce some new concepts that permit us to deal with the presence of explicit logical inconsistencies in an argument.

The important role of inconsistencies in problem-solving situations can be seen in the following simple example. A company was considering a strategy involving the addition of a new product to their other product lines. One of the major stakeholders was the manufacturing division of the corporation. A key assumption was that the division's unit manufacturing cost (u.m.c.) for the product would be $250. A u.m.c. of $250 would make the new line profitable. In support of the claim that u.m.c. = $250, the cost analyst presented computer print-outs of past accounting and engineering data.

If we represent the example in symbolic form, it reads thus far:

There is a claim C that the u.m.c. = $250.

There exists a set of accounting data D supporting the claim.

There exists a cost model of the logical form, D → C, such that "if the D were true, then it supports the C, u.m.c. = $250."

The R arose as follows. One of the highly respected executives in the corporation who had manufacturing experience in another division estimated that the u.m.c. would be closer to about $600. The R thus introduced is:

A counterclaim, R = ~C (or not C), the negation of the claim that u.m.c. = $250.

The coupling of the four assertions results in an overall argument structure that is logically inconsistent. The classical syllogism *modus ponens* tells us that if we have (D → C) as a valid rule of inference, and if we believe that D is valid, then we are entitled to deduce C with logical certainty. That is,

$$
\begin{array}{ccc}
\text{If D implies C} & & D \rightarrow C \\
\text{and if D is valid} & \text{or} & D \\
\hline
\text{then C follows.} & & \therefore, C
\end{array}
$$

In fact, it can be shown that in logic [(D → C) and D] is equivalent to the expression (D and C). If we now couple R to this, then we get [(D and C) and (~C)] or [D and (C and ~C)], which is an explicit contradiction. That is, C and its opposite ~C cannot both be true at the same time. If we follow the dictates of classical logic, then the presence of an explicit contradiction (C and ~C) says we have reached an untenable state. There is no conclusion C or ~C that we can derive with complete assurance.

Fortunately, there is an approach deriving from Rescher (1976, 1977) and Rescher and Manor (1970) that helps make sense of this inconsistency. The rebuttal R = ~C does not have to be thrown out. Instead, it can be assessed by means of plausibility analysis. Plausibility analysis begins with the formation of all of the *maximally consistent subsets* from the full set of assertions. For the u.m.c. case maximally consistent subsets (m.c.s.) are formed as follows:

1   Information:

    a.   A claim C.

    b.   A set of accounting data D.

    c.   A cost model $D \rightarrow C$.

    d.   A counterclaim (rebuttal) $\sim C$.

2   Epistemic policies and maximally consistent subsets:

    a. $P_1 = \{C, D, D \rightarrow C\}$

    b. $P_2 = \{D, \sim C\}$

    c. $P_3 = \{D \rightarrow C, \sim C\}$

A maximally consistent subset (m.c.s.) is the *largest set of propositions* that can be conjoined together such that the resulting subset is still consistent. There are three such subsets for the preceding set of three assertions.

The importance of the concept of m.c.s. now becomes apparent. *Each of the m.c.s.'s P_1, P_2, and P_3, gives rise to a different epistemic policy.* An *epistemic policy* is the basis from which knowledge or arguments are chosen. In this case, accepting P_1 means that we accept the main argument as presented. However, if we accept P_3, then this not only means that we are accepting the model ($D \rightarrow C$) but the $R = \sim C$ as well. Even stronger, it means that we are accepting as our total policy, ($\sim D$ and $\sim C$) since ($\sim D$ and $\sim C$) logically follow from $D \rightarrow C$ and $\sim C$. That is, *an epistemic policy is not merely the acceptance or rejection of a claim but rather the acceptance and rejection of the elements of the argument that are used to base or ground a claim.*

The first epistemic policy P_1 says accept C, D, and $D \rightarrow C$. The second policy P_2 says accept D and the counterclaim $\sim C$. The third policy P_3 says reject D and reject C or, alternatively, accept the counterdata $\sim D$ and the counterclaim $\sim C$. The issue now is: How do we decide which of these maximally consistent subsets is to be preferred over the others? In order to find the preferred subset, the overall plausibility of each subset is computed from the plausibility of its elements.

The concept of *plausibility* is very different from that of *probability*. Probability pertains to the likelihood of occurrence of a particular *event*. For instance, if someone were indifferent between the three policies P_1, P_2, and P_3, then one's probability of choosing a particular policy would be $1:3$. Plausibility, on the other hand, refers to the *credibility* of an *argument*—how *believable* it is or how much sense it makes to a person.

Thus, a credible argument, assertion, or proposition is one in which conclusions follow logically from premises or one in which a statement is made by someone in whom one places great confidence or trust.

The concept of plausibility is important because in many decision situations the policymaker may not be able to assign or to know the *probabilities* of occurrence of the events contained in the argument prior to taking action. The summarize again, plausibility refers to the credibility—the reasonableness—of an argument, whereas probability refers to the likelihood that the events contained in the argument will occur or have actually occurred.

Plausibility, like probability, can be indexed or measured on a scale. However, there are some major differences in the approach. Rescher summarizes the differences as follows:

The mechanism of plausibility-indexing has an obvious resemblance to the calculus of probability, and the fundamental idea of plausibility—as reflecting an evaluation of "how (relatively) acceptable a proposition is"—is certainly strongly reminiscent of the idea of probability. Nevertheless, these concepts differ significantly from one another. One does not fully grasp our idea of plausibility until one understands just how—and how drastically—it differs from that of probability.

Plausibility is a classificatory concept which ranks theses in terms of the standing and solidity of their cognitive basis. Plausibility grades theses by the external or extrinsic standard of the hierarchical nature of their supporting bases (without reference to their intrinsic, content-related likelihood). It classifies propositions by the status of the evidential sources or validating principles that vouch for them. Probability weighs alternatives and evaluates theses by this relative contentual weight of the supporting considerations. With probability we ask, "How many alternatives does the thesis engross in its content?"; with plausibility "How reputable a source or principle speaks for the thesis?" In the former case we orient ourselves towards the content of the thesis, in the other towards its probative credentials. (1976, p. 28)

Let us return to the unit manufacturing cost case to see how plausibility indexing works.

Suppose for the sake of illustration that the plausibility p of each of the assertions in the case is as follows:

$$p\ [C] \qquad = 2$$
$$p\ [D] \qquad = 1$$
$$p\ [D \rightarrow C] = 5$$
$$p\ [\sim C] \qquad = 3$$

In this measurement scheme (Rescher, 1976), *lower* numbers (i.e., 1) are assigned to *higher* plausibility assertions.* *Higher* numbers (e.g., 5) are assigned to *less plausible* assertions. Further, the plausibility of an m.c.s. can be defined as the *average* of the plausibilities of the elements in the set. Thus

$$p \; [P_1] = \frac{p \; [C] + p \; [D] + p \; [D \to C]}{3} = \frac{2 + 1 + 5}{3} = 2\tfrac{2}{3}$$

$$p \; [P_2] = \frac{p \; [D] + p \; [\sim C]}{2} = \frac{1 + 3}{2} = 2$$

$$p \; [P_3] = \frac{p \; [D \to C] + p \; [\sim C]}{2} = \frac{5 + 3}{2} = 4$$

In this case P_2 has the lowest (most plausible index), 2. It is followed by P_1 ($2\tfrac{2}{3}$), and P_3 (4). For this simple illustration the use of an averaging rule as a means of assigning plausibilities to m.c.s. yields the conclusion that the most plausible basis for making a decision regarding the u.m.c. is to accept the accounting data as true *and* to accept the counterclaim (i.e., u.m.c. = \$600 rather than \$250) as true. The cost model proposed in the original argument (i.e., the warrant $D \to C$) is rejected.

The basic approach just described can be extended to more complex situations. These include situations where the data consist of a multitude of reports deriving from a variety of sources, different types of warrants, and a host of competing claims. In a similar fashion, other, more complicated decision-theoretic procedures can be formulated for (1) identifying the weakest (i.e., least plausible link) in an argument and (2) for choosing the most plausible policy from the set of conclusions derived from the maximal consistent subsets.

We should reemphasize that the preceding example is illustrative of the general state of affairs in policy, planning, and strategy making. The contradictions potentially present in every policy argument can arise from every one of the ingredients in the Toulmin framework. There almost always can be contradictions both within and between the C, the D, the W, the B, and the R. It is seldom the case that data are ever totally self-consistent. There are always data which both support and deny a claim. Thus, the problem of dealing with inconsistent parts of an argument is a general one; and yet, it is a problem that has received almost no treatment in the literature on policy.

---

*As will be discussed subsequently in the section on calibrating plausibilities prudent measurement practice requires that we anchor the scale. The "0" point or *no* plausibility point was chosen for this purpose.

Extending the Theory

Given the basic concepts explained in the previous sections, it is possible to make a listing of the various kinds of simple rebuttals that are theoretically possible. The advantage of this is twofold: (1) it makes it possible to reduce the different kinds of rebuttals and their corresponding simple m.c.s. to a tabular form, and (2) it simplifies the calculations involved in computing the plausibility of an epistemic policy or m.c.s. from its elements. In essence, once the analyst has determined or specified one's rebuttal, he or she merely looks up in a table the set of m.c.s.'s that are possible and then proceeds to calculate the plausibilities of the m.c.s.'s from the formulas listed. Alternatively a computer program can be written as the authors have done, to do the calculations.

It is easily seen that the part of the argument in support of C constitutes an m.c.s., for [B *and* (W = D → C) *and* D *and* C] do not conflict. In fact the conjunction [B *and* (D → C) *and* D *and* C] is logically equivalent to (B and D and C). Thus the epistemic policy P_1 = (B and D and C) will always be present for a policymaker's consideration. That is, a policymaker always has the option of deciding to accept the policy represented by P_1. Whether P_1 is accepted or not depends on its plausibility p (P_1) as compared to the plausibilities of the alternative policies available in a given situation.

One way to consider alternative policies proceeds from the observation that there are four possible policy outcomes from an argument consisting of claim C, data D, and warrant D → C. The outcomes define the four major maximally consistent subsets for an argument. Each m.c.s. constitutes an epistemic policy. These epistemic policies are:

P_1 The data and claim are valid [D, C]

P_2 The valid data better supports some other claim [D, ~C]

P_3 Some other data are required to support the valid claim [~D, C]

P_4 Neither the data nor the claim are valid [~D, ~C]

Exhibit 9-1 shows that any item of information can be considered to be evidence for any one or any combination of these four states. A "1" indicates that the item of information is logically possible evidence for a particular m.c.s.; a "0" indicates that it is not possible for that particular kind of information to fit with that kind of m.c.s.

There are 16 possible information items that refer to the four possible m.c.s. outcomes. Two items (1 and 16) contain no information at all since

Exhibit 9-1 Possible Assertions Concerning Claim, Data, and Warrant

	m.c.s.					
Item	P_1 D,C	P_2 D,~C	P_3 ~D,C	P_4 ~D,~C	Logical Symbol	Comment
1	1	1	1	1	Tautology	Tautology
2	1	1	1	0	~D → C	Alternative warrant
3	1	1	0	1	~D → ~C	Alternative warrant
4	1	1	0	0	D	Data ⎫
5	1	0	1	1	D → C	Warrant ⎬ Basic argument
6	1	0	1	0	C	Claim ⎭
7	1	0	0	1	(D and C) or (~D and ~C)	Assert specific state
8	1	0	0	0	~(D → ~C)	Alternative warrant
9	0	1	1	1	D → ~C	Alternative warrant
10	0	1	1	0	(D and ~C) or (~D and C)	Assert specific state
11	0	1	0	1	~C	Deny the claim
12	0	1	0	0	~(D → C)	Alternative warrant
13	0	0	1	1	~D	Deny the data
14	0	0	1	0	~(~D → ~C)	Alternative warrant
15	0	0	0	1	~(~D → C)	Alternative warrant
16	0	0	0	0	Irrelevant	Meaningless, irrelevant

Exhibit 9-2   Maximally Consistent Subsets of an Argument

P₁: D and C	P₂: D and ~C
C D D → C	D
~D → C ~D → ~C (D and C) or (~D and ~C) ~(D → ~C)	~D → C ~D → ~C D → ~C (D and ~C) or (~D and C) ~C ~(D → C)

P₃: ~D and C	P₄: ~D and ~C
C D → C	D → C
~D → C D → ~C (D and ~C) or (~D and C) ~D ~(~D → C)	~D → ~C (D and C) or (~D and ~C) D → ~C ~C ~D ~(~D → C)

they either assert that all outcomes are valid or that none are. Three items (4, 5, and 6) comprise the assertion on the basic argument: data, warrant, and claim. All arguments must contain at least these three items of information. The remaining 11 items constitute different forms of rebuttals to the argument. The claim can be denied (11); the data can be denied (13); alternative warrants may be asserted (2, 3, 7, 8, 9, 12, 14, 15); or specific possible states may be asserted (7, 10).

Exhibit 9-2 extends Exhibit 9-1 by showing which items of information are evidence for each of the m.c.s.'s. The two figures collectively constitute a theory of information and argument. Any advocate who presents an argument consisting of C, D, and D → C is asserting that epistemic policy P₁ is the valid state of the world. However, other information may be available. When analyzed it may suggest that epistemic policies P₂, P₃, or P₄ are more plausible.

In order to test the relative plausibility of an argument and to evoke an epistemic policy, a straightforward procedure can be used.

1 Marshall all the relevant information concerning the arguments.
2 Translate it into its symbolic logical form by assigning one of the 16 symbols to it.
3 Assign a plausibility to each item.
4 Assign each item to its appropriate m.c.s.'s.
5 Calculate a plausibility index for each m.c.s. by averaging the plausibilities of the elements in each m.c.s.
6 Rank the m.c.s. in descending order of the plausibility index.
7 Choose the m.c.s. with the lowest plausibility index. This m.c.s. represents the most plausible epistemic state.

Calibrating Plausibilities

The plausibility of an element in an argument can be indexed on an anchored *ordinal* scale. The anchor "0" is an absolute truth or a tautology and represents maximal plausibility. Prudent measurement practice indicates that this natural zero point is the best place to anchor the scale. Larger numbers thus represent decreasing degrees of plausibility. One useful scale follows:

1 "0" represents a logical truth, for example, the statement "either it will rain *or* it will not rain tomorrow" is a logical truth. Thus "0" is assigned to a statement if and only if it is felt to be a logical truth.
2 "1" is assigned to a statement if it is felt to be highly credible or plausible but not logically true.
3 "2" is assigned to a statement felt to be of moderate plausibility.
4 "3" is assigned to a statement of low plausibility.
5 "4" is assigned to a statement of very low plausibility.
6 "5" is assigned to a statement which is felt to be completely implausible.

The scale below summarizes these values:

0	1	2	3	4	5
A Logical Truth	Highly Plausible	Moderate Plausibility	Low Plausibility	Very Low Plausibility	Completely Implausible

In summary, the *lower* the number assigned, the *higher* the plausibility of a statement, proposition, assertion, argument, and so on. This measurement method is useful for making single assessments of a single complex argument. However, when multiple observers assess intricate arguments, an alternative form can be used.

The alternative method for calibrating plausibilities is as follows. Assume that plausibility is an ordinal scale with an anchor at the point $n/n = 1$ or "absolutely reliable." One desirable characteristic of a scale is that the number of classifications in the scale be large enough to distinguish among the possible outcomes. A rule for achieving this is:

Choose n to be greater or equal to the maximum between m and M:

where

$$n = \max(m, M)$$

1 m = the number of propositions to be considered $p, q, r \ldots, z$. (This permits the judgment $p > q > r \ldots > z$.)
2 M, where M is calculated as follows:

    a. Choose the proposition that has the largest number of independent observations. Its number of observations is M'.
    b. Determine the number of outcomes, o, that an individual observer may report (e.g., p,p given an o of Z).

Then $M = O^{M'}$.

This is the number of possible observation combinations (states) from M' observations. These states, in turn, may be rank ordered to establish a plausibility index.

This approach may be illustrated by an example. Suppose there are four possible propositions p, q, r, s. Then, by condition (1) $m = 4$. Suppose further that there are three independent observers of p; each will report either p or $\sim p$.* Then, by condition (2) $m = 2^3 = 8$. Since 8 is greater than 4, there should be 8 grades in the index, that is, $m = 8$.

The reason for condition (2) can be seen by expanding the example. Suppose further that the three independent observers, A, B, and C each with plausibility ratings as follows: .75, .50, .25. The following table summarizes the eight possible outcomes.

*$\sim p$ signifies "not" p or the negation of p.

Possible Outcome	Observers A	Observers B	Observers C	Choice	Rank re: p	Plausibility
Number	.75	.50	.25	Choice	Rank re: p	Plausibility
1	p	p	p	p	1	$\frac{8}{8}$
2	p	p	$\sim p$	p	2	$\frac{7}{8}$
3	p	$\sim p$	p	p	3	$\frac{6}{8}$
4	p	$\sim p$	$\sim p$	?	4 or 5	$\frac{5}{8}$ or $\frac{4}{8}$
5	$\sim p$	p	p	?	4 or 5	$\frac{5}{8}$ or $\frac{4}{8}$
6	$\sim p$	p	$\sim p$	$\sim p$	6	$\frac{3}{8}$
7	$\sim p$	$\sim p$	p	$\sim p$	7	$\frac{2}{8}$
8	$\sim p$	$\sim p$	$\sim p$	$\sim p$	8	$\frac{1}{8}$

Several points can be made about the above table.

1 Clearly outcome 1 should be ranked most plausible.
2 Outcomes 2 and 3 both have the most reliable observer, .75, favoring them, but outcome 2 has .50, while outcome 3 only has .25 as the second agreeing observer; thus the plausibility of outcome 2 is greater than the plausibility of outcome 3.
3 A ranking between outcomes 4 and 5 requires the application of an additional rule to resolve the conflict. If the rule is "two eyes (heads) are better than one," then the plausibility of outcome 4 is greater than that of outcome 5. However, if the rule is that the most reliable source always dominates, then the plausibility of outcome 5 is greater than that of outcome 4.

Developing a scale with the appropriate number of grades is necessary for plausibility analysis. The principle of coincidence relations (together with the principle of precedence are necessary for a plausibility index) require that if p and q have equal plausibility, then the index of p must be the same as the index of q. This is only possible if the number of gradations is the same for a proposition.

One further point is in order. Since this plausibility is defined as an anchored ordinal scale with 1 = "absolutely reliable" being the anchor (natural origin, or zero point), the scale is defined for all monotonic transformations which pass through the origin. Thus, all indices defined on a smaller number of distinctions (n) can be adjusted to fit a larger number of distinctions without losing the ordinal properties of the original scale.

Similarly, when applying the method suggested in the table above for multiple observations, the results can be adjusted to satisfy the anchoring requirement when additional plausibility judgments can be brought to bear. For example, suppose that in the illustration above the three observers agreeing on p (i.e., .75, .50, .25) do not constitute a plausibility of 1. In this event at least two options are available. One is to increase the number of graders by 1 so that the highest is $(O^{M'} - 1/O^{M'})$ (e.g., $\frac{8}{9}$ in the example). Another possibility is to determine that the plausibility of outcome 1 (therefore of p) is equal to the plausibility of some other proposition (say $q = .8$). Then, the scale $\frac{8}{8}$, $\frac{7}{8}$, $\cdots$ $\frac{1}{8}$ may be recalibrated by multiplying it by a scalar (in this case, .8 yielding .8, .7, .6 $\cdots$ .1).

Criteria for Plausibility Assessment

The basic criteria for assessing plausibility is the reliability of the source. Expert testimony and general agreement (consensus) may be used as indicators of this reliability. Specifically, plausibility should be addressed in terms of:

1 The credentials of the source including its reliability and trustworthiness.
2 The soundness of the logic and reasoning employed.
3 The degree to which the argument or its elements agree with previous knowledge, experience, and beliefs (coherence).

After plausibilities have been assigned to the elements of an argument, some function must be applied to calculate the plausibility of m.c.s. In the preceding unit manufacturing cost illustration, we show one method of calculating the plausibility of an m.c.s., that is, to take the mean of the plausibility elements. However, for any argument taken by itself one may assume that the argument is "no stronger than its weakest link." Consider again one of the valid forms of logical reasoning:

1 If D is true, then C is true.
2 *But D is true.*
3 Therefore, C is true.

A conservative rule for assigning plausibilities in this case is: p (C) = maximum of p (D $\rightarrow$ C) and p (D). This rule says in effect that *the conclusion or outcome of an argument C cannot be more plausible than the premises from which it is derived.* Thus from the rule p (C) = maximum $[p$ (D $\rightarrow$ C) and p (D)], the plausibility of C, p (C), equals the *less* plausible of the two propositions (D $\rightarrow$ C) and D. A similar type of rule holds for the other valid forms of logical reasoning (see, e.g., Michalos, 1969).

Recall that every aspect of a current argument structure may be regarded as the product or outcome of a prior argument structure. There is a simple rule based on plausibility indexing to use in making the decision to go back further in the examination of any argument structure. In those cases where ~D is contained in the information set and p (~D) has been estimated then if p (D) > p (~D) (i.e., D is less plausible than ~D), one should consider the argument structure by which D was produced. That is, one can regard D as a claim and examine the data, warrant, and backing that produced D. If D is *less* plausible than ~D, then not only is the resultant D questionable but the set of operations (methodology) or argument structure by which D is produced is also questionable.

Similarly, in those cases where p (~C) appears explicitly and where p (C) > p (~C), that is, the claim is less plausible than the counterclaim, one should examine the warrant, W = (D $\rightarrow$ C). That is, W can be regarded as the outcome of a prior argument, and its supporting argument structure can be examined.

Ultimately, the decision to extend an argument structure further back is a judgmental one. There are no absolute rules in this area. The general rule is that if the plausibility of any component of an argument is felt to be low, then possibly the basis used to generate it should be examined by means of an argument analysis. The item can be considered to be the output (claim) of a previous argument, and the data warrants, backing, and so on, underlying it are examined.

When tracing an argument down its tree structure and assessing its plausibility, some rules of assignment are needed. Epistemic prudence suggests that the plausibility of a branch is the minimum of the plausibility of its constituent edges. Thus the plausibility of a claim is determined by finding the minimum plausibility of the data and warranting branches and comparing it with the minimum of the rebuttal branches. If the plausibility of the minimal data or warranting branch is greater than that of the rebuttal, then that plausibility becomes the plausibility of the claim. If the plausibility of the rebuttal branch is greater, this suggests that some alternative claim is more plausible. In choosing from among two or more mutually exclusive claims pertaining to the same assumption area, choose either the one with the maximum plausibility or the one that discards the least amount of plausible information.

SUMMARY

This chapter deals with the relationship between policy, planning, and strategy issues and the information used to resolve them. The choice of an assumption in our view is based on an epistemic policy. The chapter contains a theory for employing an epistemic policy and for securing the knowledge necessary for effective business and public policy making.

An assumption is considered to be a claim in an argument. The first step in the epistemic policy process is to break an argument down into its component parts—claim, data, warrant, backing, and rebuttals. Rebuttals can be classified using the theory of rebuttals. Next, the information is classified into its relevant, maximally consistent subsets or generic epistemic policies. Each item is assessed for its plausibility. These plausibilities are used, in turn, to calculate the plausibility of each epistemic policy. The epistemic policy to be chosen is the one that is most plausible according to a plausibility index. The assumption represented by the epistemic policy thus chosen is the most plausible assumption for policy, planning, and strategy making. It is the best knowledge the policymaker has to go on. A key aspect of our approach to epistemic policy is that it explicitly takes into account incomplete information and inconsistent information. It helps the policymaker decide on the basis of all of the information he has available. In a world of organized complexity, as described in Chapter 1, where policy problems are "wicked," messy, and ill-structured, inconsistency and incompleteness is the norm. Virtually all policy, planning, and strategy making must be done in a context of uncertainty. The concepts presented in this chapter help the policymaker to identify these uncertainties and to cope with them. The cases in Chapter 10 reveal some of the ways in which these concepts can be employed.

Chapter Ten

Policy Argumentation Cases

This chapter summarizes two cases in which argumentation analysis and plausibility assessment have been employed. The cases are intended to serve as illustrations of the concepts in Chapter 9. They further demonstrate how the ideas may be applied.

Case I demonstrates the application of argumentation analysis to the problem of developing a telecommunications capability for a large corporation. The case shows how the layout of arguments may be used to gain insight into a policy issue.

Case II reports on an intensive policy study conducted at the Jet Propulsion Laboratory, California Institute of Technology. It shows how argumentation analysis and plausibility assessment can be applied to the assessment of a technology and the evaluation of policy options for developing technology. It also demonstrates the use of structured dialectical debate as both a policy analysis tool and as a method for acquiring information about the policy position to be analyzed.

CASE I: ANALYSIS OF A CORPORATE TELECOMMUNICATIONS SERVICE

A major U.S. corporation was in the process of studying its communications needs. Among the issues under consideration was the question of how best to satisfy the corporate requirement for transferring data to and from branch offices and data processing centers. A detailed study of users' needs revealed the following design criteria:

1　Provide a high-performance, economical data transmission service as a first priority. Document transmission is a second priority.
2　Provide an interactive response time between any two points in the network of 1.0 second round-trip delay.
3　Provide both dial-in and dial-out capability.

4 Provide a network storage option.

5 Provide an emulation service.

Five design criteria were studied and tested by means of argumentation analysis. Each criterion was stated as a claim in an argument; then its underlying data, warrants, and rebuttals were obtained. The resulting five arguments are summarized in this section. They were presented to corporate management as a means of informing them about the grounds for the recommended design criteria; by means of the rebuttals, they also informed management about the conditions under which these criteria were inappropriate.

1 Claim Provide a high-performance, economical data transmission service as a first priority. Document transmission is a second priority.

Grounds [Given that]	Warrants [Because]	Rebuttal [Unless]
Current users and near term potential users require data transmission. Must have outstanding short term performance to establish credibility. Document transmission has a long lead time, terminal design problems, and current low acceptability. Optical Character Recognition is high cost.	If you don't do well in satisfying current user needs you will never get a chance at the future business. This factor indicates a necessary current service in data transmission.	Users have a strong current demand for document transmission. There is a technological breakthrough on the terminals. The company can "wing it" through data and then capitalize on document transmission. The optimal document network performs adequately for data transmission

2 Claim Provide interactive response time of 1.0 second *round-trip delay*.

Grounds [Given that]	Warrants [Because]	Rebuttal [Unless]
Terminals that are sensitive to a 1 sec-	These factors indicate the existence of	These terminals do not constitute much

2 Claim (*Continued*)

Grounds [Given that]	Warrants [Because]	Rebuttal [Unless]
ond delay are available. Nearly half the current market is interactive, according to survey reports. Users' perception of reliability and performance is directly related to response time; less than 1 second is too slow for some. Bulk of interactive market is 3 seconds ± 1 second.	a growing market segment with a required response time of less than or equal to 1 second.	of the market and will not be used in the future. 1.5 second delay satisfies. Users are not sensitive to the difference between 1.0 second and 1.5 seconds. 1.5 seconds can serve the bulk of the needs.

3 Claim Provide both dial-in and dial-out and general interconnect capability.

Grounds [Given that]	Warrants [Because]	Rebuttal [Unless]
All computers have dial-in. Most computer manufacturers support dial-out. AT&T Watts lines have both in and out. Time sharing and other applications require dial-up capability. Users probably require interconnect.	Since trends indicate a market requirement for both dial-in and dial-out service. Watts Line capability indicates that AT&T has seen the need for dial-in and dial-out in a related service area, as well as data.	Two-way dialing not needed. Cost is too high. Service performance is impaired. The technical requirements of dial-out services cannot be met or are too difficult to do. The interconnect between telecommunication service providers cannot be worked out.

4 Claim Provide Network Storage Option.

Grounds [Given that]	Warrant [Because]	Rebuttal [Unless]
There will be data bases to transmit. At transmission time some members of the network will be unavailable (closed down, etc.).	These factors suggest the need for a storage buffer on the net.	There is not much volume of this type. The cost is prohibitive. FCC does not permit "intelligent" operations on net.

5 Claim Provide emulation service that "upgrades" low performance terminals, extends number of different terminals that may be hooked up, and permits interchange among dissimilar devices.

Grounds [Given that]	Warrants [Because]	Rebuttal [Unless]
There are many low-performance terminals available such as Lier-Sigler ADM—3 at one tenth the cost. There are many low-cost/performance printers available and used for remote job entry and so on. Many users want low equipment investments.	These factors are indications of a need for emulation services to secure improved cost performance ratio.	Users will rapidly move to IBM 327's and other high-cost, high-performance terminals. Emulation software is a big problem. Effect of the emulation capability on system performance is negative.

CASE II: ANALYSIS OF ROADWAY-POWERED VEHICLES AT J.P.L.*

The automotive application of an inductive coupling roadway-powered vehicle (RPV) system was a subject for further R&D within the U.S. Department of Energy (DOE) Electric and Hybrid Vehicle R&D Program (E&HV). Like battery operated and hybrid vehicles, the principal merit of the RPV system is its potential for petroleum conservation and displacement by using electricity as a substitute. The technical concept behind the RPV system is the combination of an electrical power source embedded in the roadway and a vehicle-mounted power pickup coupled inductively to the roadway power source.

An assessment of the potential constraints and impacts related to the possible implementation of the RPV system was conducted by Jet Propulsion Laboratory, California Institute of Technology, sponsored by DOE. The assessment was designed to help DOE decide on the issue of further funding to RPV research within the E&HV R&D program. The assessment included the use of argumentation analysis and plausibility assessment.

The overall and relative (to E&HV's) viability of the RPV system was evaluated in terms of a multitude of factors related to the possible implementation of such a system: transportation, economics, energy, technology, social, institutional, and so on. The problem of evaluating these factors is dominated by their complexity and relatively high dependency on judgmental considerations and expectations about the future. A dialectical inquiry (structured debate) was therefore initiated to augment the more detailed and quantitative analysis of these elements. This approach captured information and insight of particular importance to policy making beyond that which is usually provided by other methods of inquiry. The structured debate was held between two parties with conflicting viewpoints and interests: a "blue" team favoring RPV research and a "red" team opposing RPV research. A neutral "third" party was chartered to clarify the arguments during the debate and to summarize and analyze the structure of the arguments following the debate.

The debate centered around the question of R&D funding for the RPV system. Although the one point of view strongly favors continued support of RPV system research, the other is less focused in terms of what is favored. This viewpoint focuses more on the negative aspects of the RPV

*The authors are indebted to Kim Leschley, Abe Fineberg, and John Howe (JPL), Anne Wilson (UCLA), and Jeff Smith (USC) for aid in conducting this research.

system rather than demonstrating a strong case for either of the debated alternatives: electric hybrid or synfuel ICE vehicles.

Exhibit 10-1   Focus of the Two Conflicting Viewpoints

	Blue Team Viewpoint A	Red Team Viewpoint B
RPV System	Favors Strongly	Disfavors Strongly
E&HV's and Synfuel	Disfavors Less Strongly	Favors Less Strongly

Dialectic inquiry brought representatives of these two viewpoints together to present the facts, assumptions, and modes of reasoning that led them to their differing conclusions.

The following subsections describe the basic position and world views of the two competing viewpoints, the selection of issues for debate, and the analysis of the structure of the arguments presented.

Basic Positions and World Views

The basic positions of the two conflicting viewpoints can be summarized as follows:

Viewpoint A—Blue Team	Viewpoint B—Red Team
The RPV system will save a substantial amount of petroleum because:	The RPV system will not save a significant amount of petroleum because:
RPV vehicles will be much more efficient and acceptable to the consumer than the alternatives (E&HVs and synfuel ICE vehicles).	Cost and technology barriers are too substantial to overcome.
The system will be able to serve highway (electric) transit and trucks much better than E&HVs.	The system creates additional peak-load demand for electric generation capacity and no non-petroleum alternative has been convincingly proposed.

Viewpoint A—Blue Team	Viewpoint B—Red Team

The system need not use petroleum for power generation. The small increase in utility load during peak hours could be offset by adding nonpetroleum baseload capacity.

The RPV system is economical because:	The RPV system is uneconomical because:
Capital costs are comparable or lower than the other alternatives and the operating costs are lower.	Present-value life cycle costs are higher, in terms of levelized required revenue or dollars per barrel of oil displaced.
The RPV system enhances mobility because:	The RPV system reduces mobility because:
The addition of automation to the system will increase highway capacity and decrease accident rates.	The barriers to implementing automation and to developing fully the system are insurmountable.
The problems of inclement weather will be minor.	Inclement weather will interfere with efficient system operation.
There are several implementation strategies available for bringing RPV system into widespread use, such as:	The RPV system will not be successfully implemented because:
Early implementation of self-contained transit systems (malls, people movers), as precursors to highway use.	The system will fail to achieve economies of scale for private auto manufacturers.
Midterm implementation on interstate truck routes as precursors to automobile use.	Consumer acceptance will be too low to warrant the large scale implementation project required to gain any market penetration in the first place.

Viewpoint A appears to be warranted by a rather deeply held belief (world view) that the nation's need to displace petroleum, the citizen's recognition of this, and their willingness to accept the RPV technology will dominate the policy arena during the next few decades.

Viewpoint B differs markedly in these beliefs. Its claims are warranted by the basic belief that market economics will be the dominant factor in the policy arena during the next few decades. This leads to the conclusion that as an energy-saving transportation alternative, the RPV system is not economically viable.

One fundamental difference between the world views of the two basic positions involves their concept of the role of government and large institutions. Viewpoint A looks to government and other large institutions to set social goals and to take a strong, active role in achieving them. The size and complexity of the RPVs partly necessitate this belief. Viewpoint B favors a strong reliance on free market economics with minimal direct government intervention. This viewpoint advocates battery-operated electric and hybrid automobiles and synthetic fuels.

Selection of the Issues

The following process was used to identify the specific issues for the structured debate. First, members of both the blue and red debating teams submitted issues. Second, the teams reached agreement on the issue statements. Finally, the issues were prioritized with respect to the overall viability of the RPV system. The resulting prioritized list of issues then served as an agenda for the debate.

1 Petroleum displacement.

   a. System energy efficiency.
   b. Source fuel.
   c. Peak demand.

2 Economics.

   a. Cost elements.
   b. Cost allocation.
   c. Comparison.

3 Transportation.

   a. Automation.
   b. Modes.
   c. Availability.
   d. Safety.
   e. Capacity.

4 Implementation process.

    a. Institutional
    b. Infrastructure
    c. Social and environmental
    d. Scenarios and timeframe

5 Comparison with Alternatives:

    a. Electric, hybrid, and ICE vehicles.
    b. Synfuels.

It should be noted that the order of issues 1 and 2 was determined by the flip of a coin. While the team in favor of RPV system R&D held that the issue of petroleum displacement was more important for a determination of the RPV system viability than the economics issue, the opposite was argued by the opposition (in concurrence with the world views of the two teams as outlined in the previous subsection). It should also be noted that the first four issues were debated directly while the last issue, because of time constraint, was brought up only indirectly during the debate of the other issues. (See Exhibits 10-2 and 10-3).

Exhibit 10-2 Blue Team Argument

Issue 1—Petroleum Displacement:
To What Extent Will the RPVS Displace Petroleum?

Data [Given that]	**Warrant** [Because]	**Claim** [Then]
A large fraction of petroleum is presently used for start-up, and only a few trips are greater than 12 miles (average trip is 3 miles).	The RPVS will achieve sufficient consumer acceptance.	The RPVS will displace substantial amounts of petroleum.
Batteries will be used for start-up and short trips.	**Backing** [Since] · · ·	**Rebuttal** [Unless] Consumer acceptance is too low.
Electrified roadways can be used as the power source on free-		Production and distribution of batters for RPVS require substantial amounts of petroleum.

Exhibit 10-2 *(Continued)*

Issue 1—Petroleum Displacement:
To What Extent Will the RPVS Displace Petroleum?

Data [Given that]

ways and major arterials.

Rebuttal [Unless]

The RPVS will require petroleum to produce its electrical energy.

Data [Given that]

Base load uses nonpetroleum fuels.

Peak load demand from the RPVS will be minimal

Peak load demand from the RPVS can be offset by additional base load capacity and load leveling (e.g., east-west interchange and demand billing).

Warrant [Because]

Utilities will add to their base load capacity and switch to nonpetroleum fuels for most peak and intermediate loads.

Backing [Since]

.
.
.

Claim [Then]

The RPVS will not require petroleum to produce its electrical energy.

Rebuttal [Unless]

Utilities fail to conserve petroleum through added base load capacity, load leveling, and a switch to nonpetroleum fuels for most peak and intermediate loads.

Peak load demand from the RPVS will be higher than expected.

Data [Given that]

Traffic peaks do not coincide in all cities.

The RPVS can serve as interties between cities and time zones for load leveling purposes.

Warrant [Because]

The RPVS load during peak hours is a small percentage of normal peak demand and can be further reduced or eliminated by load leveling.

Claim [Then]

Peak load requirements imposed by the RPVS are minimal.

Rebuttal [Unless]

The east-west interchange system does not materialize.

The switch to nonpetroleum fuels for peak loads does not materialize.

Exhibit 10-3   Red Team Argument

Issue 1   Petroleum Displacement: To What Extent Will the RPVS Displace Petroleum?

Data   [Given that]

Costs are prohibitively high.

No gain in roadway capacity.

No gain in petroleum displacement.

Massive public investment and consumer acceptance are necessary for the RPVS to be efficient.

Depends on successful development of other similar technologies:

Battery technology.

Peak/off peak power generation.

Design of electric vehicles.

Depends on public policy decisions in its favor:

Centralized/decentralized power distribution and urban development.

Electric power/other fuels.

Automobiles/public transit.

East-west interchange not feasible.

More peak capacity required than stated in the Lawerance Berkeley Labs.

RPVS efficiency is overstated compared to

Warrant   [Because]

The barriers indicated by the data are insurmountable and support the inefficiency of the RPVS.

Backing   [Since]

Based on Red Team cost projections.

No new roads and no capacity increase of current system.

Petroleum used to build and power the system offsets any petroleum displacement gained from having nonpetroleum fueled vehicles.

The system is costly, it will not be developed by private industry, and consumers will not readily accept this new technology.

The RPVS will function at or above a minimally acceptable level, only if a particular scenario (within certain parameters) proves true.

Red Team's assessment and research done by power companies substantiates this data.

Based on Red Team calculations.

Based on Red Team findings.

Claim   [Then]

The RPVS is not the most efficient system for achieving the highest amount of petroleum displacement.

Rebuttal   [Unless]

Blue Team arguments are correct and the major barriers can be overcome.

The data are refused as follows:

Capital costs are equal to or lower than costs for the alternatives, and operating costs are lower.

Automation of the RPVS will smooth traffic flow and allow vehicles to travel closer together and hence will reduce energy consumption and increase roadway capacity.

RPVS's are lighter than EVs and use less battery energy; hence more efficient than EVs.

RPVS's have no ICE, which is inefficient on short duty cycles and hence more efficient than ICE or hybrid vehicles.

Urban freeway lanes are used by about 11,000

252

Exhibit 10-3   *(Continued)*

Issue 1   Petroleum Displacement: To What Extent Will the RPVS Displace Petroleum?

Data [Given that]	**Warrant** [Because]	**Claim** [Then]
ICE or E&HV.		vehicles/day, thus amortizing RPVS equipment better than alternative battery charging equipment in individual garages.
E&HVS will not add to peak load.		
Minimal cold start losses with E&HVS.		No study of the feasibility of interties was identified.
		RPVS technology is simple and development risks are modest.
		HVS are a poor choice:
		Excessive ICE cold start losses. Inconvenient to the consumer.
		The RPVS is accepted with some enthusiasm by consumers because of low operating costs, convenience, improved traffic flow and safety.

Plausibility Analysis

Following analysis of the arguments in terms of the methods of Chapter 9, a plausibility analysis was conducted to determine the strength and relative trustworthiness (believability) of each argument. A group of five participants read each issue and the corresponding arguments of each team. They rated each part of the argument according to its plausibility on a scale from 0 (completely implausible) to 9 (a logical truth). The assessment procedure consisted of five steps.

Step 1 involved the preparation of a set of instructions defining the argument component concepts and the plausibility measure. A plausibility scale (from 0 to 9) was presented with a brief description of the meaning of each of the numerals, as follows:

0 = completely implausible, absolutely *no* assurance or certainty in the truthfulness or reasonableness of the argument
1 = nearly implausible
2 = very low plausibility
3 = low plausibility
4 = moderate plausibility
5 = medium plausibility
6 = high plausibility
7 = very high plausibility
8 = virtually true and plausible
9 = maximally plausible, a logical and necessary truth, absolute assurance or certainty in the truthfulness or reasonableness of the argument

The instructions furthermore specified that the ratings be based on the following three factors:

1 The credentials of the source, including its reliability and trustworthiness.
2 The soundness of the logic and reasoning employed.
3 The degree to which the argument or its components agree with previous knowledge, experience, and beliefs.

Step 2 involved the preparation of a workbook containing all 22 arguments as identified in the debate, with a plausibility rating form for each argument.

Step 3 was to select the plausibility rating panel. Five individuals were selected, all knowledgeable in the field but with no direct interest in either side of the issues. The panel was told to review each argument in its entirely before rating the plausibilities of the separate components. The results of these ratings were compiled and the median, mean, and standard deviation computed.

Step 4 was to bring the panel together to discuss and possibly to revise its initial assessments.

Step 5 was to summarize the final results of the plausibility rating. Based on the assumption that an argument is no more plausible than the weakest link (the least plausible element in the chain of reasoning), an aggregate plausibility value was derived for each argument. This value was computed (for each argument) as the median-of-the-minimum of each panelist's subelement ratings within an argument (excluding the rating of the rebuttal). The following example illustrates this medi-min computation. Exhibit 10-4 illustrates the plausibility rating form used.

Issue 1: Ratings of the First Level Claim of the Blue Team

Panelist	A	B	C	D	E
Claim	1	3	3	1	3
Data	2	4	2	2	4
Warrant	1	2	5	0	4
(Rebuttal	7	5	4	7	6)
Backing	NA				
Minimum	1	2	2	0	3
Ordering	0	1	2	2	3
			Medi-min		

Exhibit 10-4   Plausibility Rating Form

Argument

Page No.

Circle the Appropriate Number

The plausibility of the claim is:
   0   1   2   3   4   5   6   7   8   9
The plausibility of the data is:
   0   1   2   3   4   5   6   7   8   9
The plausibility of the warrant is:
   0   1   2   3   4   5   6   7   8   9
The plausibility of the rebuttals is:
   0   1   2   3   4   5   6   7   8   9
The plausibility of the backing is:
   0   1   2   3   4   5   6   7   8   9
   ↓   ↓
Completely   A Logical
Implausible   Truth

Results

To summarize the results of the plausibility assessment, the medi-min values (discussed previously) for each of the first level arguments are presented in Exhibit 10-5, together with the range and the mean of the corresponding minima.

The detailed results are tabulated in Exhibit 10-6, at the end of this case.

The results show that the Blue Team's case for the RPVs is especially weak in two areas (Issues 1 and 5). Its claims for significant levels of petroleum displacement and consumer acceptance were not very sound. In contrast, the Red Team's claims were rated high. This is clearly displayed in Exhibit 10-5.

It became apparent during the discussion of the results of the plausibility rating that there were at least two critical issues that lowered the believability of the Blue Team. Several of the raters graded them down based on their contention that the RPVs would increase freeway safety due to automation of the system. The raters cited such systems as the San Francisco Bay Area Rapid Transit (BART) system where automation had not improved safety. It was concluded that automation was not effective in improving safety and that, in some cases, it had an adverse effect.

The second claim that the raters found unsupportable was the complete penetration of the 110 million vehicles fleet by RPVs. By insisting on 100% penetration, the Blue Team decreased the validity of their argument.

Another problem mentioned was the apparent contradiction of some of the claims, especially the Blue Team's. For example, the Blue Team argued that the RPVs will be competitively priced with the alternatives and gave some cost estimates. Then, in some of the later claims, features of the system were illustrated that one rater believed would raise the costs of the system above those that were previously stated. The method employed in the plausibility rating has no standard method to account for the consistency of arguments from issue to issue.

The main conclusion that may be drawn from the outcome of the plausibility rating exercise is that there is more support for the case of the Red Team than for that of the Blue Team. This may be seen graphically in Exhibit 10-5. Taking the means of the box scores, the Red Team's arguments scored an average of two points higher than the Blue Team's. The mean of the scores of the Blue Team's claims is 2.5 and of its rebuttals is 5.2; the mean of the Red Team's claims' scores is 5.0 and of its rebuttals is 2.2. Note that in Exhibit 10-5 the reciprocity of the plausibilities serves as a check for consistency within an issue—the high plausibility of the claims is mirrored by the corresponding low plausibility in the rebuttal

Exhibit 10-5 Summary of Plausibility Assessment

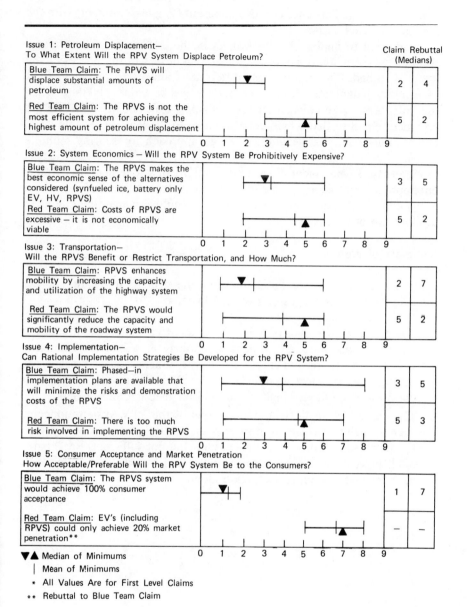

Issue 1: Petroleum Displacement—
To What Extent Will the RPV System Displace Petroleum?

Claim Rebuttal
(Medians)

Blue Team Claim: The RPVS will displace substantial amounts of petroleum — 2 | 4

Red Team Claim: The RPVS is not the most efficient system for achieving the highest amount of petroleum displacement — 5 | 2

Issue 2: System Economics — Will the RPV System Be Prohibitively Expensive?

Blue Team Claim: The RPVS makes the best economic sense of the alternatives considered (synfueled ice, battery only EV, HV, RPVS) — 3 | 5

Red Team Claim: Costs of RPVS are excessive — it is not economically viable — 5 | 2

Issue 3: Transportation—
Will the RPVS Benefit or Restrict Transportation, and How Much?

Blue Team Claim: RPVS enhances mobility by increasing the capacity and utilization of the highway system — 2 | 7

Red Team Claim: The RPVS would significantly reduce the capacity and mobility of the roadway system — 5 | 2

Issue 4: Implementation—
Can Rational Implementation Strategies Be Developed for the RPV System?

Blue Team Claim: Phased—in implementation plans are available that will minimize the risks and demonstration costs of the RPVS — 3 | 5

Red Team Claim: There is too much risk involved in implementing the RPVS — 5 | 3

Issue 5: Consumer Acceptance and Market Penetration
How Acceptable/Preferable Will the RPV System Be to the Consumers?

Blue Team Claim: The RPVS system would achieve 100% consumer acceptance — 1 | 7

Red Team Claim: EV's (including RPVS) could only achieve 20% market penetration** — — | —

▼▲ Median of Minimums
| Mean of Minimums
 * All Values Are for First Level Claims
** Rebuttal to Blue Team Claim

257

(and vice versa). This check is also apparent (to a lesser extent) with the medians for each issue.

In addition to finding the weak links in the arguments of both teams through the plausibility analysis, some weaknesses in the process itself were identified. The raters used different strategies to arrive at their plausibility judgments. Several used the "weakest link" method when multiple items were considered, by assigning a plausibility to the entire argument equal to that which corresponded to the least believable item. Other raters used the weighted average approach for scoring multiple items.

When raters were uncertain as to the validity of a statement, two different approaches to scoring were used. Some raters split the difference and assigned medium plausibility, while others simply assigned these items to the low end of the scale.

Summary of Results

Overall, the results of the initial analysis, the structured debate, and the plausibility analysis suggested two conclusions:

1   The arguments in favor of full scale automotive implementation of the inductive coupling RPV system technology as a means of meeting U.S. transportation and energy conservation needs, at the present, are not convincing. Electric, hybrid, and synfueled-ICE vehicles seem, at the present, to have a higher potential for meeting these needs.

2   The pursuit of small-scale applications of the RPV system concept, such as mall busses and airport/in-plant shuttle services, could potentially provide a valuable and necessary (but not sufficient) R&D base. Such projects would have to be motivated by purposes other than economic petroleum conservation alone.

Exhibit 10-6 Results of the Plausibility Assessment

Argument Components	Distribution*	Median	Mean	Standard Deviation
Issue 1 Petroleum Displacement: To What Extent will the RPV Displace Petroleum?				
Blue Team (level 1)	The RPVS will displace substantial amounts of petroleum.			
Claim	1 3 3 1 3	3	2.2	1.0
Data	2 4 2 2 4	2	2.8	1.0
Warrant	1 2 5 0 4	2	2.4	1.9
Rebuttal	7 5 4 7 6	6	5.8	1.2
Backing	NA			
Blue Team (level 2)	RPVS will not require petroleum to produce its electrical energy.			
Claim	1 3 4 2 3	3	2.6	1.0
Data	1 2 4 1 3	2	2.2	1.2
Warrant	2 4 6 4 3	4	3.8	1.3
Rebuttal	7 6 3 8 6	6	6.0	1.7
Backing	NA			
Blue Team (level 3)	Peak load requirements imposed by RPVS are minimal.			
Claim	2 6 1 1 2	2	2.4	1.9
Data	1 6 2 0 3	2	2.4	2.1
Warrant	1 6 5 3 1	3	3.2	2.0
Rebuttal	7 2 3 5 6	5	4.6	1.9
Backing	NA			
Red Team (level 1)	The RPVS is not the most efficient system for achieving the highest amount of petroleum displacement.			
Claim	8 6 8 7 7	7	7.2	.7
Data	7 6 8 7 7	7	7.0	.6
Warrant	6 3 8 6 7	6	6.0	1.7
Rebuttal	2 6 2 2 4	2	3.2	1.6
Backing	5 6 8 7 5	6	6.2	1.2

Exhibit 10-6 (*Continued*)

Argument Components	Distribution*	Median	Mean	Standard Deviation
Issue 2 Economics: Will RPV System Be Prohibitively Expensive?				
Blue Team (level 1)	The RPVS makes the best economic sense of the alternatives considered (synfueled ICE, battery only EV, HV, RPVS).			
Claim	2 7 2 4 3	3	3.6	1.9
Data	3 6 4 4 5	4	4.4	1.0
Warrant	5 7 1 4 4	4	4.2	1.9
Rebuttal	6 3 7 5 5	5	5.2	1.3
Backing	NA			
Blue Team (level 2)	Major capital costs for converting the 110 million automobile vehicles to the RPVS are similar to or less than alternatives.			
Claim	2 7 4 3 4	4	4.0	1.7
Data	2 6 3 2 2	2	3.0	1.5
Warrant	2 6 3 3 2	3	3.2	1.5
Rebuttal	8 5 8 4 7	7	6.4	1.6
Backing	4 7 4 3 6	4	4.8	1.5
Blue Team (level 3.1)	Synfueled ICE system capital costs are $300 to $400 billion plus costs of extra coal mining and transportation that is required by energy waste in manufacture.			
Claim	2 4 5 2 4	4	3.4	1.2
Data	2 2 3 2 4	2	2.6	0.8
Warrant	3 2 4 2 5	3	3.2	1.2
Rebuttals	5 8 5 4 5	5	5.4	1.8
Backing	NA			
Blue Team (level 3.2)	Marginal capital costs for battery only EV system are: $565 billion+.			
Claim	3 3 3 2 4	3	3.0	0.6
Data	3 3 5 2 4	3	3.4	1.0
Warrant	4 6 2 2 4	4	3.6	1.5
Rebuttal	4 8 3 2 4	4	4.2	2.0
Backing	NA			

Exhibit 10-6 (*Continued*)

Argument Components	Distribution*	Median	Mean	Standard Deviation
Blue Team (level 3.3)	Marginal capital costs for ICE/battery HV system are: $434 billion.			
Claim	2 2 6 2 4	2	3.2	1.6
Data	2 2 6 2 4	2	3.2	1.6
Warrant	2 7† 2 2 4	2	3.4	2.0
Rebuttal	6 8 2 1 4	4	4.2	2.6
Backing	N A			
Blue Team (level 3.4)	Marginal capital costs for RPV system are: $400 billion.			
Claim	2 7 4 2 4	4	3.8	1.8
Data	2 7 4 2 4	4	3.8	1.8
Warrant	1 6‡ 5 1 4	4	3.4	2.1
Rebuttal	8 8 5 5 4	5	6.0	1.7
Backing	N A			
Red Team (level 1)	Costs of RPVS are excessive; it is not economically viable.			
Claim	6 2 6 5 5	5	4.8	1.5
Data	6 6 6 5 3	6	5.2	1.2
Warrant	6 7 6 6 5	6	6.0	.6
Rebuttal	3 2 2 1 5	2	2.6	1.4
Backing	6 7 6 5 5	6	5.8	.7
Red Team (level 2)	Cost of saving one barrel of petroleum with RPVS ranges from $41.75 to $48.12.			
Claim	6 7 7 6 5	6	6.2	.7
Data	6 7 7 6 5	6	6.2	.7
Warrant	6 7 7 6 5	6	6.2	.7
Rebuttal	2 7 3 1 4	3	3.4	4.2
Backing	N A			

†Weighted (one 2, two 7's, three 8's).
‡Weighted (one 2, one 3, three 8's).

Exhibit 10-6 *(Continued)*

Argument Components	Distribution*	Median	Mean	Standard Deviation
Issue 3 Transportation: Will the RPV System Enhance or Restrict Transportation and by How Much?				
Blue Team (level 1)	RPVS enhances mobility by increasing the capacity and utilization of the highway system.			
Claim	1 7 2 2 2	2	2.8	2.1
Data	1 8 2 3 5	3	3.8	2.5
Warrant	1 6 2 2 5	2	3.2	1.9
Rebuttal	8 2 7 8 6	7	6.2	2.2
Backing	1 7 4 3 5	4	4.0	2.0
Blue Team (level 2.1)	RPVS automation will increase the capacity and utilization of roads on which it is installed.			
Claim	1 8 2 1 5	2	3.4	2.7
Data	3 8 3 2 6	3	4.4	2.2
Warrant	6 8 7 7 8	7	7.2	.7
Rebuttal	8 8 7 8 6	8	7.4	.8
Backing	8 8 7 1 8	8	6.4	2.7
Blue Team (level 2.2)	The RPVS is no more vulnerable to adverse weather conditions than the existing roadway/vehicle system.			
Claim	4 1 3 1 5	3	2.8	1.6
Data	4 8 1 1 5	4	7.4	1.4
Warrant	4 8 2 2 6	4	4.4	2.3
Rebuttal	6 9 8 7 8	8	7.6	1.0
Backing	NA			
Red Team (level 1)	The RPVS will significantly reduce the capacity and mobility of the roadway system.			
Claim	2 2 6 8 5	5	4.6	2.3
Data	6 7 8 9 6	7	7.2	1.2
Warrant	5 1 8 6 7	6	5.4	2.4
Rebuttal	3 7 2 2 5	3	3.8	1.9
Backing	NA			

Exhibit 10-6 (*Continued*)

Argument Components	Distribution*	Median	Mean	Standard Deviation

Issue 3 Transportation: Will the RPV System Enhance or Restrict Transportation and by How Much?

Red Team (level 2)	Inclement weather, mainly snow and ice, will interfere with operation of the system.			
Claim	5 8 7 6 5	6	6.2	1.2
Data	5 8 7 6 5	6	6.2	1.2
Warrant	5 8 7 5 5	5	6.0	1.3
Rebuttal	4 2 2 1 4	2	2.6	1.2
Backing	NA			

Issue 4 Implementation: Can Rational Implementation Strategies Be Developed for the RPV System?

Blue Team (level 1)	Phased-in implementation plans that will minimize the risks and demonstration costs of the RPVS are available.			
Claim	4 9 5 3 8	5	5.8	2.3
Data	4 9 6 5 6	6	6.0	1.7
Warrant	3 9 4 3 5	4	4.8	2.2
Rebuttal	5 0 1 6 6	5	3.6	2.6
Backing	5 8 3 1 8	5	5.0	2.8

Blue Team (level 2)	Comprehensive RPVS implementation on existing roads can be the final program phase.			
Claim	4 7 6 1 8	6	5.2	2.5
Data	3 7 6 1 6	6	4.6	2.2
Warrant	3 8 6 2 5	5	4.8	2.1
Rebuttal	6 3 3 7 4	4	4.6	1.6
Backing	NA			

Red Team (level 1)	There is too much risk involved in implementing the RPVS.			
Claim	5 1 7 7 7	7	5.4	2.3
Data	6 2 7 8 6	6	5.8	2.0
Warrant	6 1 5 7 7	6	5.2	2.2
Rebuttal	3 8 2 0 3	3	3.2	2.6
Backing	5 6§ 7 7 6	6	6.2	.7

§Weighted (one 2, two 8's).

Exhibit 10-6 *(Continued)*

Argument Components	Distribution*	Median	Mean	Standard Deviation

Issue 4 *(Continued)*

Red Team (level 2)	The RPVS will not be implemented successfully because the scale economies and phase-in economics are not favorable.			
Claim	6 4 7 4 6	6	5.4	1.2
Data	4 4 7 3 6	4	4.8	1.5
Warrant	6 7 7 5 6	6	6.2	.9
Rebuttal	4 7 3 0 4	4	3.6	2.2
Backing	5 2 7 4 6	5	4.8	1.7

Issue 5   Market Penetration and Consumer Acceptance: How Acceptable/Preferable Will the RPV System Be to the Consumers?

Blue Team (level 1)	The RPVS system would achieve 100% consumer acceptance.			
Claim	1 2 2 1 1	1	1.4	.5
Data	1 7 4 3 6	4	4.2	2.1
Warrant	0 3 4 0 2	2	1.8	1.6
Rebuttals	5 7 6 8 7	7	6.6	1.0
Backing	3 5 2 0 5	3	3.0	1.9

*Each column presents the plausibility ratings elicited from the same individual.

Chapter Eleven

Policy Argumentation Procedures

Policies, plans, and strategies may be arrived at in two ways. They may be either asserted or proven by means of argumentation. Argumentation is the logical process of arriving at reasons and conclusions. It accepts information as its raw material and then collects, selects, combines, modifies, and interprets it to produce conclusions. The process is recursive. Any conclusion produced as a result of an argument may itself become the information input for a subsequent argument. Similarly, any item of asserted information by itself may be considered as the product of a previous argument. Thus argumentation may be used either in an analytical mode (and used to unfold a piece of asserted information back to its logical grounding) or in a synthetic mode to construct an argument that derives conclusions from the information. The argument's purpose in either case is to sharpen the insight of those who must judge the soundness of conclusions by explicitly stating the grounds on which the judgments are based. Sound judgments must stand up to criticism.

Consequently, argumentation may be employed in at least two ways:

1 To analyze asserted information prior to accepting it as a premise for making a particular policy.
2 To develop the "case" for or against a particular policy option.

Each of these purposes may be achieved by the efforts of a single individual or by means of a group process. In this chapter, we focus on group processes and on procedures that can be used in group settings.

CASE DEVELOPMENT

Although there is infinite variety in the ways people construct arguments, three basic patterns tend to emerge, depending on what information is available at the start.

Pattern 1   Given the context of the problem or issue:

1   A claim is offered.
2   On what data is it based?
3   What warrant justifies the interpretation of this data as support for this claim?
4   What backing supports the warrant?
5   Under what conditions or rebuttals does the argument *not* hold?
6   What qualifier is assigned to the argument?

Pattern 2   Given the context of the problem or issue:

1   An item of data is offered.
2   What conclusion can be drawn from this data?
3   What warrant justifies the interpretation of this data as support for the claim?
4   What backing supports the warrant?
5   Under what conditions or rebuttals does the argument *not* hold?
6   What qualifier is assigned to the argument?

Pattern 3   Given the context of the problem or issue:

1   A general warranting principle or hypothesis is stated.
2   What data are relevant to the principle?
3   What conclusion can be drawn from this data?
4   What backing supports the warrant?
5   Under what conditions or rebuttals does the argument *not* hold?
6   What qualifier is assigned to the argument?

These patterns are used as the basis for designing policy-, plan-, and strategy-argumentation workshops. An outline and schedule for one such workshop follows. It is based on Pattern 1.

A Technique for Evaluating Policy Premises

Dealing with all the information collected for a given policy issue can be an overwhelming and time-consuming task. One approach for dealing with this volume that achieves most of the advantages of the detailed analysis of arguments is to conduct a workshop employing an assertion-identifying and screening technique. The technique is based on the SAST process and depends on two assumptions:

1   Some assertions are more important or pivotal in the policy argument than others and are, therefore, potentially more worthy of being premises. These are the premises at the core of the policy problem and therefore should be reviewed critically.
2   Some assertions have more face validity than others, are more obviously true, and, since we are certain about them, are less in need of detailed critical review.

The overall approach for using the technique is as follows:

1   Choose the parties to do the selecting of premises. An individual can do it, although for important policy issues it is generally best to include as many points of view as possible. Form problem-solving groups, preferably with three to seven members. Use multiple groups, if necessary. If multiple groups are used, assign members to a group (a) at random; (b) on the basis of divergence (or homogeneity) of skills, personality, and beliefs; or (c) on the basis of their affinity for the tasks to be performed.
2   Each group is instructed to generate a list of relevant *information, facts, assumptions,* and *inferences.* These are the policy-issue assertions that pertain to the problem and its solution. The Nominal Group method may be used at this step.
3   Each individual in each group now rates each assertion on each of two scales (these scales are the same as described in Part 2):

    a.   Importance: How critical is this assertion to the overall success of any solution to the policy issue?
    b.   Certainty: How likely is this assertion to be true?

4   Use the individual ratings in each group to calculate a group rating for both importance and certainty. Use the individual ratings and the group rating to point out areas of agreement and disagreement among the members of the group. Discuss the debate these differences and agreements and understand the reasons behind them. After the discussion, have the group agree on a rating on both importance and certainty.
5   Plot each assertion on a graph. The ordinate represents the importance rating of each assertion. The abscissa represents the certainty rating of each assertion. The importance and certainty rating of each

assertion defines its position on the graph. Divide the graph into four quadrants.

Quadrant (c)	Quadrant (d)
Low Importance/ Low Certainty	High Importance/ Low Certainty
Quadrant (b)	Quadrant (a)
Low Importance/ High Certainty	High Importance/ High Certainty

Study the pattern of these assertions and discuss each placement.

Quadrant (c)   These assertions are candidates for elimination from further consideration.

Quadrant (b)   These assertions should be reviewed carefully for possible importance. They may be irrelevant facts and, therefore, candidates for elimination.

Quadrant (a)   Assertions in Quadrant (a) should be studied carefully. They are potentially pivotal items for a successful solution.

Quadrant (d)   These assertions deserve special attention. They suggest areas for further research to determine their certainty.

6   When more than one group works on the same problem, have each group at this stage present its findings to the other groups. Areas of agreement and disagreement should be identified, discussed, and debated.

7   The final output of this process should be a rather precise statement of each of the key or major assertions that pertain to this policy issue. These assertions, once identified, are candidates for becoming final premises in the policy-making process.

8   Identify the *source* of the chosen assertion of the major *advocates* behind it. How does it serve the interests of one or more *stakeholders* in the problem and its solution? Are there any special interests that would benefit if this assertion were true? If it were untrue?

9   Analyze each assertion and identify the following component parts:

   a.   Conclusion or claim.
   b.   Facts or data.

    c.   Warrants.

    d.   Backing.

    e.   Rebuttals.

    f.   Qualifiers.

The diagramming methods covered in this book are useful at this stage.

10   Use the results of the three preceding steps to discuss and debate the key assertions. Sample discussion questions include:

    a.   Have all stakeholders' points of view been taken into account?

    b.   How firm are the facts, warrants, backing, and so on behind each assertion? Do any patterns emerge?

    c.   What is the pattern of the type of assertions being made? Are some dimensions given too much emphasis? Are some dimensions given too little emphasis?

11   Devise an action plan for strategic inquiry designed to learn more about the argument.

At this stage, the relevant assertions have been identified and criticized. Having survived this process, they are candidates for becoming the premises from which to derive policy. These premises may be used to identify alternative courses of action. Evaluate them to select a final course of action and to produce the strongest possible case for its adoption. The premises now have become the underlying assumptions of the proposed policy. Are they the best that our judgment can produce? How would we know? Is there a test that will tell? If yes, the dialectic can be used to test one's judgment on sets of premises and to suggest some potentially more relevant premises. The dialectic structured debate methods described in Part 3 may be employed at this point.

Intensive Workshop Design

Exhibit 11-1 presents a sequence of activities for a 2-day workshop for carrying out the technique just outlined. This intensive workshop is designed for a group of participants who face a policy, plan, or strategy problem and who need to understand better their policy premises before making a decision.

Inspection of Exhibit 11-1 shows that the workshop can easily be extended to 3 days. In the 2-day version the second day is, to put it mildly, both long and demanding. We have shown the activities in a 2 day sequence, however, due to the pressures that exist in most organizations with regard to the availability of key managers or decision makers. Also, we assume that the participants may have participated already in an SAST exercise or its equivalent; hence their time will be at a premium if asked for further participation.

The primary purposes of the first day, as described in Exhibit 11-1 are:

1   To examine in greater depth the functioning of pivotal assumptions (for example, as uncovered by a previous SAST exercise) in the context of a total policy structure and to examine whether these pivotal assumptions play the role of C, W, D, B, or R.

2   To explain the appropriateness of the Toulmin framework for analyzing the structure of policy arguments from a total-systems point of view.

3   To stress the particular importance of R in evaluating policy. (Because R represents the maximal or greatest challenge to one's pet ideas, it is vital to uncover the R's applicable to one's preferred policy claims before the policy is implemented).

4   To explain the concept of *plausibility* as distinct from *probability* and to explain why plausibility is important for the evaluation of policy claims.

5   To assist the participants in actually analyzing pivotal assumptions via argumentation analysis by uncovering the D, W, B, and R behind policy claims.

The number of tasks to be accomplished during the first $1\frac{1}{4}$ hour are considerable. The facilitators must not only explain the basic concept of the Toulmin framework but also the purpose and rationale for its application as well. In addition, the facilitators must give the participants concrete and specific instructions with regard to what they will be doing and what the expected benefits (outcomes) of the process are.

Unlike the SAST process, where prior knowledge of the method cannot be assumed before the workshop, some prior reading on policy reasoning must be assumed. An hour and a quarter is not sufficient to introduce the entire framework and to explain how the framework is to be used. Consequently, background material should be handed out prior to the workshop for individual reading.

The purpose of the brief introductory explanation is to clarify the meaning, usefulness, and application of the framework for policy analysis. The concept of plausibility is also introduced. The purpose of this concept

Exhibit 11-1   A Typical Workshop on Policy Argumentation

Time	Session*	Activity	Comment
Day 1: Introductory and Analytical Activities			
8:00–9:00 A.M.	I	Breakfast	
9:00–10:15 A.M.	P	Introduction to the Toulmin framework, explanation of the framework, tasks to be accomplished, and expected outputs	Facilitators Toulmin and plausibility explained
10:15–10:35 A.M.	P	Assignment of pivotal claims to working groups for argument analysis	Facilitators Each group works on approximately two positive and two negative claims
10:35–11:00 A.M.	I	Coffee break	
11:00–12:00 noon	G	Preliminary work on argument structures	Facilitators Identify the W, D, B, and R behind each pivotal claim
12:00–1:30 P.M	P	Lunch	
1:30–3:00 P.M.	G	Refinement of analysis of arguments	Facilitators
3:00–3:30 P.M.	I	Coffee break	
3:30–6:00 P.M.	G	Refinement of analysis plus preparation of presentations	Facilitators
6:30–7:15 P.M.	I	Refreshments	
7:15–8:30 P.M.	P	Dinner	
Day 2: Presentation of Analyses, Debate, and Follow-up			
8:00–9:00 A.M.	I	Breakfast	
9:00–11:00 A.M.	P	Individual group presentations of argument analyses	Only clarifying questions permitted (Coffee break about 10:00 A.M.)
11:00–12:00 noon	G	Identify damaging elements of arguments	Identify the elements of each other group's arguments that do the most damage to your own argument

Exhibit 11-1 (*Continued*)

Time	Session*	Activity	Comment
Day 2: (*Continued*)			
12:00–1:30 P.M.	P	Lunch	
1:30–2:30 P.M.	P	Each group reports on damaging elements	Solicit in round-robin manner, record on flip chart
2:30–3:00 P.M.	I	Coffee break	
3:00–5:00 P.M.	P	Debate on argument structures	Open discussion and debate on critical elements of arguments Identify and list crucial issues that the strategy *must* resolve
5:00–7:00 P.M.	I	Refreshments and dinner	
7:00–10:00 P.M.	P	Action-steps	Identify carry-on activities Identify information requirements for tracking and monitoring assumptions Assign task forces as needed

*Session code: I = individual; P = plenary; G = groups.

is to help locate the weakest links in the chain of a policy argument and to formulate an action plan for securing further information.

The basic task to be accomplished during the first day is the examination of the pivotal assumptions classified as important/uncertain in the quadrant system. Since pivotal assumptions may play the role of either a C, D, W, B, or R within an argument structure, a key task of the first day is to examine the role that they play within the argument structure.

In order to keep the process manageable, it is recommended that, as a general rule, no more than four to seven pivotal assumptions be examined. For simplicity, we shall assume four assumptions—A_1, A_2, A_3, and A_4. The heart of the process consists of assigning each assumption to *two* different working groups for examination. Each group takes the same assumption (e.g., A_1) and examines its role within an argument structure. For example, suppose that A_1 is a claim to the effect that an organization ought to produce X number of widgets. Then, one group would examine the D, W, B, and R that allow one to conclude A_1 as a C.

Exhibit 11-2 contains guidelines in the form of a dialogue or series of questions that the members of a group can use to employ the Toulmin framework. That is, one or more members of a group can assume the role of questioner; the remaining members, the role of respondents (shifting these roles as they find it helpful). The resulting claims and their supporting arguments are then plotted on the importance/certainty graph.

Drawing again on our assumption that the process of reasoning is too critical to be left in the hands of any one single group, no matter how well qualified that group may appear to be, *every* claim deserves to be examined by at least one other group. As we have emphasized, in the realm of ill-structured problems, there is no such thing as a single, natural process of reasoning or a single, correct argument structure for producing any claim. The same claim can arise from more than one structure. It is precisely this multiple-reasoning phenomenon that we wish to examine.

Exhibit 11-2   Argument Specification Dialogue

Pattern 1

1. Describe the general problem or issue briefly.

2. Please state a recommendation, conclusion, assumption, or any other item relevant to the problem or issue.

3. In making this statement, what do you have "to go on"? What is the basis of that statement? What are your grounds? Please provide data, evidence, facts, and so on, to support that statement.

4. What entitles you to move from these grounds to your statement? What is the justification or warrant for this interpretation of your data? (indication/symptom, generalization, subsumption/classification, cause/effect, analogy, parallel case, etc.)

5. What is your backing or general support for your warrant? What is the basic world view, set of beliefs, or prior policy commitment that underlies the warrant?

Exhibit 11-2 (*Continued*)

---

6. What are the rebuttals to your argument? Under what conditions does the claim *not* hold? How might someone else state a rebuttal to your claim?

7. Reviewing the argument thus far, how would you qualify it? (necessarily follows, probably, likely, unlikely, absolutely impossible)

8. How strong, plausible, credible, or well founded is this argument? (airtight—no holes, very strong, very weak, doesn't hold water at all) Plot the result on the vertical dimension of a strength/importance graph.

9. How important or significant is this claim to the successful solution of the problem? (absolutely crucial, very important, unimportant, absolutely insignificant) Plot the result on the horizontal dimension of a strength/importance graph.

10. What more do we know about the weak but important assertions (Quadrant d)?

    a. How firm are the facts, warrants, backing, and so on behind each assertion?
    b. Do any patterns emerge?
    c. What *is* the pattern of the types of assertions being made?
    d. Are some dimensions of the problem given too much emphasis? Are some dimensions given too little emphasis?
    e. Is this the best argument that can be made?
    f. Is there any test that will tell?
    g. What additional data do you need (are you able to get) to strengthen your argument?
    h. How can you weaken or counter the rebuttals?

11. What specific actions *will* the group undertake to improve its understanding of a weak but important assertion?

    a. Get more data.
    b. Strengthen backing and warrants.
    c. Weaken rebuttals.
    d. Possibly alter the claim in light of additional information.
    e. Enlist the support from other stakeholders for the claim.

By the same token, the counterassumptions (symbolized by $\sim A_1$, $\sim A_2$, $\sim A_3$, $\sim A_4$, etc.) as to why A_1 is not the case also deserve explicit examination. If two groups are assigned examination of A_1, then two other groups are to be assigned examination of $\sim A_1$. In this way, *every* assumption will be examined by two different groups and *every* counterassumption will be examined by two other groups. To repeat, if policy arguments are important, then they are important enough to receive explicit examination. *It is only by comparing side by side those structures arguing in favor of A_1 with those arguing in favor of $\sim A_1$ that we can sensibly evaluate and decide between them.*

Since the initial working groups from the SAST process were constructed to be as different from one another as possible, these groups can be used to examine the argument structures of the pivotal assumptions. Due to the large number of different ways (permutations) in which four assumptions and four counterassumptions can be assigned to different groups, it is recommended that the assignment be made through informal negotiation. That is, each working group can indicate its willingness to take on or to examine the case or argument for a particular assumption and counterassumption. The main purpose for allocating assumptions among groups is not to ensure that each group has a particular portfolio or permutation of assumptions but, rather, to ensure that each assumption and each counterassumption will be examined by at least two different groups.

The morning of the first day terminates with the commencement of work on the argument structures. The rest of the day is given over to the refinement of the analyses of the argument structures and to the preparation of a brief 20 to 25 minute presentation that will be made by all of the groups at the start of the next day. The presentations basically take the form of laying out the structure of the argument supporting each assumption on a large flip chart pad.

As always, the role of the facilitators is critical. This is particularly true when it comes to helping the participants utilize a new concept, for example, the policy argumentation framework in general and the concept of plausibility in particular. As much as is possible, the facilitators should encourage the use of plausibility concepts. The outcome of the first day should be not only the *qualitative* assessment of the structure of the various arguments but also a *quantitative* assessment of them. Each group should attempt to assign plausibilities, no matter how tentative they may be, to the various components of their argument structures. Just as with the assignment of the measures of relative importance and relative certainty in the SAST process, the assignment of plausibility numbers serves the purpose of making relative comparisons that help reveal the weak points in policy arguments.

To assist in this purpose, copies of the figures in Chapter 9 can be distributed to the groups in the afternoon. This should be done at the time when the facilitators sense that the groups are ready to make best use of them. The importance of the rebuttals R can again be stressed, as well as the fact that the various figures on rebuttals help one to think about the types of R's that are available. These figures display the basic possibilities open for a choice of R and help the participants assign plausibilities.

Facilitators applying the procedures outlined in this chapter should keep in mind the basic objective of these methods, that is, to develop the main structure of a policy argument and to locate the points of weakness and strength in it. For this reason, we believe that the tendency to plunge into ever deeper levels of an argument structure should be resisted. Further development should be undertaken only when it is felt that this will add significantly to the understanding of the structure of the main argument. Without such limitation, it is easy to get lost "in the trees" of the method and to lose sight of the bigger "forest." We have seldom seen cases where more than three levels of argumentation analysis are fruitful.

Because the format of the second day follows so closely that of the concluding parts of the SAST process, it is not necessary to comment in detail on the activities of the second day. The reader is referred to Chapter 3 for a discussion of the process.

It should be stressed that the last session of Day 2—*Action Steps*—is crucial. Every participant in the workshop should leave with a clear understanding of (1) what the key assertions in the policy area are, (2) what the nature of the underlying argument is, (3) what specific steps can be taken to improve the group's understanding of important arguments and to reduce the uncertainty in them.

The uncertainty in crucial assertions can be reduced by engaging in active inquiry. Before the group disperses, it should identify the specific kinds of information-producing activities that are going to be undertaken for each assertion. These activities include: (1) collecting more data, (2) mustering stronger counterarguments for rebuttals, (3) revising claims, and (4) adding to the political support behind the preferred claim.

Training Workshop Design

Some organizations may wish to train their people in argumentation analysis in order to improve their reasoning and communication skills. We have designed a workshop consisting of 4 half-day sessions for this pur-

Exhibit 11-3 Outline for a Workshop in Reasoning and Communication for Complex Problem Solving

Day 1	8:00–9:30 A.M.	The nature of complex problems Overview of argumentation analysis
	9:30–9:45 A.M.	Setup of teams
	9:45–10:00 A.M.	Break
	10:00–12:00 noon	Teams generate lists of relevant assertions and assumptions
Day 2	8:00–9:00 A.M.	Teams rank importance/uncertainty of assertions and assumptions
	9:00–11:00 A.M	Argumentation: Film and case study (Break in middle)
	11:00–12:00 noon	Teams meet for argument specification
Day 3	8:00–10:45 A.M.	Questions Teams meet to continue argument specification
	10.45–11.00 A.M.	Break
	11:00–12:00 noon	Fish bowl presentation
Day 4	8:00–11:00 A.M.	Argument enhancement and development of action plans (Break in middle)
	11:00–12:00 noon	Wrap up—Discussion and evaluation of workshop, new insights into problems

pose. One of the key features of this training workshop is that each participant brings a problem from his job with him. Participants are matched into "buddy" teams. Each partner alternatively takes the role of the arguer—the one making assertions and presenting arguments—and the role of the questioner—the one who demands data, warrants, backings, rebuttals, and qualifiers for the claims. In this manner, the two members of the team help each other to prepare a full layout of the central arguments in each of their problem areas. The argument specification dialogue, Exhibit 11-2, is useful as a guide for each "buddy" in this process.

Exhibit 11-3 contains an outline for this training workshop. Exhibit 11-4 is a sample announcement that can be used to inform potential participants.

Exhibit 11-4   Sample Announcement for a Workshop in Reasoning and Communication for Complex Problem Solving

---

Daily we are faced with complex problems to solve: how to design a project, how to schedule the arrival of parts and services, what features to include in a new product, how much it will cost, how to coordinate with other units. The solutions to these problems involve making many assumptions. In problem solving we must continually make assumptions about the reliability of what other people tell us, and we plan accordingly. In turn, when we communicate our solutions to others we must assume that they will interpret what we say and what we do as we intended. This seminar is designed to aid in the process of assumption making, testing, and communicating.

The approach involves the following steps:

Eliciting assumptions

Specifying systematically the reasons for an assumption using the Toulmin model

Assessing the strength and soundness of each argument

Determining specific action steps that can be taken to reduce the uncertainty of assumptions

Learning to accurately communicate our assumptions

Discovering the assumptions of others

Practicing the use of argumentation analysis by means of in depth analysis of a case

Participants in this workshop will apply this method directly to a current problem and they will receive a workbook to keep that will enable them to apply argumentation analysis to future situations.

ARGUMENTATION AND SAST

We should have made the point by now that complex, messy problems cannot be solved once and for all in the same way well-structured problems can. This means that the assumptions underlying problems of policy will have to be examined (tracked) periodically. To borrow a metaphor from the physical sciences, assumptions have a half-life. It is critical to track their course over time and to revise, if necessary, the policies supported by them. The Toulmin framework is not only exceedingly valuable for identifying precisely which assumptions, because they are the weak points of an argument, need tracking, but it is also well suited to capturing and summarizing the overall structure of an argument.

Policy argumentation constitutes, in our minds, a response to a question posed earlier in this book: What form should successive, follow-up SAST's take? In situations where the policymaker concludes that the underlying stakeholders of a system have been identified and are stable, successive reexaminations of assumptions can proceed by means of argumentation analysis. However, if it is felt that the underlying stakeholders may have changed in some dimension, then part of the SAST process itself must be repeated.

_____ Part Five

Conclusion

_____

Chapter Twelve

A Comparison of Approaches to Business Problem Solving

In a messy world of organized complexity, the primary purpose of policy, planning, and strategy is to find a niche for the organization, a comfortable place where the organization can survive and prosper. In recent years a variety of methods have been developed to aid the managers of organizations in these nest-seeking activities. Most of these methods have proven to be useful additions to the body of knowledge in the field. Several have become significant enough to become the focus of managerial practice, academic research, and management consulting.

Unfortunately, there is a tendency to consider these methods as mutually exclusive competitors, each vying with the other for supremacy as "the" approach to policy, planning, and strategy. In our view, however, no such battle is necessary. Each method brings a different perspective to the planning problem. Each advises the manager to select different facts and to analyze them in different ways. Consequently, there is something of value to be gained by using each method. Of course, there are also misleading and dysfunctional aspects of each method. Realistic policymakers, planners, and strategists therefore should consider more than one method when they are facing a problem. These decisionmakers may use these methods as components in the design of a strategic inquiring system.

The methods of real-world problem solving developed in this book are no exception to the principles discussed above: there is both a "sharp" and a "flat" side to them. Thus the user should put these dialectical methods in perspective as well. Dialectics should neither be ignored nor embraced uncritically. Moreover, they should not be considered as panaceas for all the organization's ills.

We have found it useful to relate our methods to five other prominent approaches to business policy, planning, and strategy:

1 The System Approach and General Systems Theory.
2 Analytical Modeling.
3 The Case Method.
4 Profit Impact of Market Strategy (PIMS) and other empirical correlation methods.
5 The Boston Consulting Group's business portfolio analysis and other matrix-classification methods.

Each of these methods has a different set of operating procedures, and each rests on a different set of assumptions. Each has a characteristic set of strengths and weaknesses. This is because each method attends to a particular subset of the wealth of data that is pertinent to modern business problems.

In this chapter these five methods are compared with SAST and the other dialectical methods presented in the book. In order to make this comparison properly, we need to distinguish the scientific from the judgmental aspects of a method and to see the role each plays in a method. We begin with the systems approach.

SYSTEMS APPROACH

The systems approach to policy, planning, and strategy problems is perhaps the most comprehensive method for viewing problems. Churchman (1968, 1971) and Ackoff (1970, 1974) have been among its strongest advocates. Using the systems approach, five basic dimensions of the situation are examined. According to Churchman (1968) these are:

1 The total system objectives.
2 The system's environment and fixed constraints.
3 The system's resources.
4 The components of the system: its activities, goals, and measures of performance.
5 The management of the system.

The systems approach focuses on these five dimensions to form the broadest *rational* conception of the problem possible. In so doing, it generally excludes the *nonrational* contributions of the "enemies"— politics, morality, religion, and aesthetics. Churchman (1979), however, argues that these enemies can also be "swept in" or at least attended to.

The systems approach provides a critical framework within which the other methods may be compared. Indeed, all the methods, including those developed in this book, are in a sense derivatives of the systems approach. Figure 12-1 shows an illustrative systems framework. The figure is an application of the stakeholder method presented in Chapter 3. A business policy is shown as the central or pivotal element that affects and in turn is affected by stakeholders.

A single definition of a policy is not implied at this point, for this is another of the important issues on which policy theorists differ. For Hofer and Schendel (1978), a policy may be thought of as a set of decisions regarding which businesses one ought to go into, how one ought to manage them (pricing, production levels), who one ought to hire to implement management decisions, and so on. In the broader systemic sense, a policy specifies not only who one's current competition is, but, more significantly, whom one would like one's competition to be in the future and what one can do to help influence the existence of a desired set of competitors, pricing levels, and so on.

Figure 12-1 gives an *indication* of the many stakeholders who comprise the larger social system but does not attempt to list all the relevant ones that are potentially applicable to all situations. A procedure for identifying relevant stakeholders in particular cases was given in Chapter 3. The figure also indicates some of the many kinds of transactions or interactions that occur between stakeholders and a policy.

A strong tenet of the systems approach is that all problems must be viewed in a larger context before one can decide whether any particular problem is worth solving. Systems theorists have argued successfully that any one problem does not exist in isolation from other problems. Before a policymaker attempts to solve any particular problem, it behooves him to examine the larger set of problems that lead to and away from any specific problem. Otherwise one courts the danger of "solving the 'wrong' problem precisely." As many a policymaker has painfully learned a problem at one level of an organization often pales into insignificance when viewed from another level. The decision to invest resources in the treatment of a problem is too critical to be made without securing a broader view of the problem, its relationship to the organization as a whole, and its relationship to its environment as depicted in Figure 12-1.

From the standpoint of the systems approach, other methods are dangerously unreflective. What does it mean to classify an organization in the Boston Consulting Group (BCG) approach as a "cash cow," for

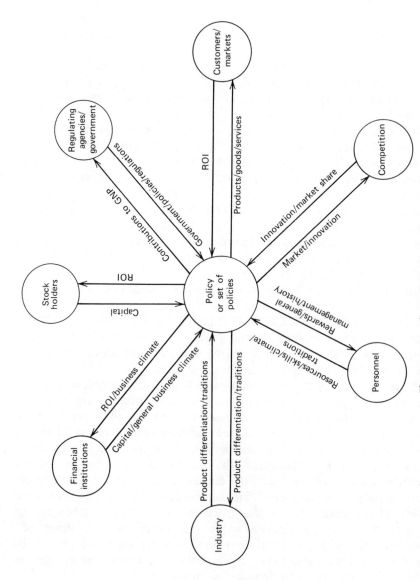

Figure 12-1 Systems stakeholders.

example? What does this do to the organization as a whole? How does it affect the organization's self-concept and its other problems? In other words, what are the broader consequences of the BCG classification scheme or any classification scheme for that matter? In what other ways can one classify an organization and its problem? Without examining some of these other ways, how can one know that a particular method is the appropriate one in a given situation?

The biggest criticism of the systems approach is that it is difficult for any but the most skilled and experienced analyst to apply it. Ackoff (1974) reminds us that despite all its claims to having developed general principles, applying the systems approach remains an art. As such, the application of the systems approach is similar to that of the case approach: it varies greatly depending on the analyst. In fairness, the systems approach can argue that from its perspective; this is true of every approach. Despite many analysts' pretensions to the contrary, the building of a mathematical model is as much an "art" as it is a "science." We turn next to this "art."

ANALYTIC MODELING*

The Analytic Modeling approach has been proposed as a method for forming business policy by Igor Ansoff (1965) and has been summarized by Hofer and Schendel (1978). It features mathematical modeling of the system and the use of a priori classification schemes to determine the status of a company's level of performance. Policy recommendations are suggested as a result. Typically, these models are based in the discipline of Management Science/Operations Research (MS/OR). MS/OR models are mathematical representatives of the planning problem that can be solved deductively for "optimal" solutions or experimented with, by a process called "simulation," to gain insight into the underlying process. In recent years, efforts have been made to apply these modeling approaches to problems of policy, planning, and strategy.

The basis for acceptance of the models rests on a theory of knowledge known as rationalism. For the purposes of this comparison, it is sufficient to know that rationalism implies that a mathematical model rests on certain notions that are taken to be self-evident by their designers. These concepts take on the status of universal truths. They sound so reasonable to those proposing (premising) them that they cannot possibly be denied.

*Some of the material in this section was originally published in "World Models: Who is the Guarantor?" *Interfaces of the Institute of Management Science*, **8**, No. 3 (May 1978) 91–97.

A simple example is transitivity of preference: if you prefer apples to bananas and bananas to carrots, then it is reasonable to postulate that you will prefer apples to carrots. Indeed, some models go so far as to insist that you *must* prefer apples to carrots if you are to count as a "rational person." Anyone violating the preference of apples to carrots would be labeled aberrant.

Starting from a series of elementary concepts, each reasonable or plausible in itself, the modelbuilder develops a more complex model. The reasonableness of the entire model derives from the reasonableness of the constituent parts (concepts) plus the language of mathematics itself.

There are a number of strong objections to this approach. One is the contention, which has some justification, that for all their claims to complexity, mathematical models can still handle only relatively low-level managerial problems of a housekeeping variety, such as inventory, transportation, and product scheduling problems. The reason is that in order for this approach to work, the problems must be relatively easy to define and to structure, hence the difficulty in treating messy or ill-structured problems. But it is precisely these messy problems that, for many, constitute the basic subject matter of most business policy, planning, and strategy problems.

The determination of "self-evident" elementary concepts is also troublesome. To paraphrase Ambrose Bierce, self-evident is that which is evident to one's self and only to one's self. A real dilemma arises. The policymaker, planner, or strategist often turns to the modelbuilder for help in better understanding his own situation. He thereby delegates the determination of the self-evident to the modelbuilder. But what if the modelbuilder's self-evident is not the same as his? Worse still, since the strategist rarely speaks the language of mathematics as fluently as the modelbuilder, how can he confidently challenge the modelbuilder? But if this is the case, on what basis does one know how to hire a modelbuilder? On blind trust? Faith? One begins to see why there are no mathematical models for helping one to decide which mathematical modelbuilder to hire!

The use of analytical model building for business policy making seems in many organizations to have gone through two phases and to be beginning its third phase. The first phase was characterized by outright rejection. Policymakers, planners, and strategists dismissed mathematical modeling as being irrelevant or inapplicable to their problems. The second phase was a rather unreflective acceptance. Models were embraced and thought to reflect truth and reality. In the current, third phase, models are considered to be tools that aid the policymaker's thinking processes— guides to understanding, not statements of truth and reality. Furthermore,

more policymakers, planners, and strategists are beginning to appreciate the critical role that *human judgment* plays in problem formulation and model building. The assumptions that the modelbuilder makes about the nature of the complex situation he or she faces strongly determine the characteristics of the model. Each modelbuilder is likely to make different assumptions about the world and hence to create a different model.

The history of model building for policy making supports this three-phase notion. For example, several years ago Gary Fromm completed a survey and analysis of federally supported mathematical models in the United States (1974), in which he catalogued 650 models that had been supported by U.S. federal funds. All were constructed to influence social decision making. Over 90% of the models were computer-based. The medium size was 25 equations. About 30% had more than 30 equations and six had more than a thousand equations.

These models entailed a rather substantial investment in time and money. The average development time was 17 months, with the larger models requiring longer periods of time. On the average, these models need to be recalibrated and the coefficients reestimated every 2 years. Once every 5 years they need to be redesigned to incorporate major structural changes. Most of these models cost $50,000 or less to develop. The mean was about $140,000 but some models cost over $3 million. The U.S. government's total investment in these models was in excess of $100 million.

What has this investment wrought? According to Fromm, "at least $\frac{1}{3}$–$\frac{2}{3}$ failed to achieve their avowed purposes in the form of application to policy problems." Moreover, this is an optimistic estimate, since his criterion for model use was the very minimum possible.

What accounts for this low usage? The study portrays a picture of models in search of users. Over 78% of the models originated independently with the designers rather than the policymakers. Underutilization was very high with designer-oriented models. Disuse was the highest when the user was not involved in the design or in the funding of the effort. This leads Fromm to conclude that the primary cause of low policy utilization rates for models is attributable to what he calls the "distance" between modelbuilders and potential policymakers.

In our own experience this lack of utilization is due to a lack of credibility and trust in the models. Policymakers are skeptical. They do not believe the models. As policymakers, planners, and strategists have become more aware of the role of judgment in the model-building process, they have become more unsure of the guarantor for the models.

Concern for the guarantor is especially true of world models and is reflected in the debate that ensued over the *Limits to Growth* world dynamics model. It has become common knowledge that Jay Forrester sketched out a prototype world model on an airplane during his return from a meeting with the Club of Rome. This was to serve as the basis of an extended study and report by Donella and Dennis Meadows entitled *Limits to Growth* (1972). *Limits* constitutes a fascinating chapter in the history of policy models. For once here was a model about which people cared. Despite the intricacies of the model and its complicated feedback loop diagrams, both the nonscientific and the scientific community alike read, listened, thought, and debated.

The debate, it turns out, centered around the assumptions of the *Limits* model and the guarantees it offered that these assumptions were true. How was one to find out?

In a special issue of *Management Science* (1976), Churchman and Mason sought to capture the spirit of the debate in a series of articles that argue for different assumptions and represent different points of view. Exhibit 12-1 contains a summary of some of the key points in the debate.

Energy supply planning has also become a fertile field for policy modeling. A case in point is the work of Paul MacAvoy and Robert Pindyck (1975). Since the early 1970s Paul MacAvoy has been modeling the natural gas industry. The early models had about eight equations. The current model has over 1200 equations.

MacAvoy has become a rather strong advocate of deregulation of natural gas, and the MacAvoy-Pindyck model supports this policy position. The model is based on economic theory. The equations reflect assumptions such as (1) natural gas discovery is a positive function of the wellhead price and (2) natural gas production is a positive function of the wellhead price. With these and other market-based assumptions, it is not surprising that the model would lead to a recommendation to deregulate.

But other world views could also be used as the assumptive foundation of a natural gas energy model.* For example, one could take the alarmist or conservationist point of view. This perspective holds that natural gas reserves are finite and limited and, further, that we are approaching that limit. Current estimates of the undiscovered reserves of natural gas in the United States range from about 230 trillion cubic feet to about 850 trillion cubic feet (at current production rates, about 10 to 40 years supply). If these limits on reserves become binding constraints in the model, the results would be somewhat different from those of the market-based model. Higher prices would not lead to higher production in the long run. Deregulation would simply lead to inflation in the natural gas market.

*The authors are indebted to Martin Greenberger for bringing these alternative assumptions to our attention during a seminar at the National Science Foundation, Spring 1976.

Exhibit 12-1   Limits to Growth Model Debate

Author	Comments
Hasan Osbekhan	Argues that world models must be more holistic in nature than world dynamics and should be predicated on a fundamental theory of the "ecological balance" of the world.
Jay Forrester	Argues that the structure of the world is dynamic in nature and a theory of dynamic systems and differential equations should underlie any world model.
Betz and Azevedo	Argue that the world is a collection of political entities. There is no global agency that has the ability to affect the whole world at once. Consequently, they conclude that a network of regional models, aligned according to nation states, industrial organizations, or other action-taking institutions is the proper basis for a world model.
Sir Geoffrey Vickers	Also argues that a world model should begin with an analysis of political structure and an identification of the "haves" and "have nots." The mechanism by which the world's wealth is distributed is the critical point in his approach to a world model.
Jan Tinberger	Challenges the mechanistic nature of the world dynamics model. He stresses the critical difference between a forecast (such as Limits) and a plan. Humanity can control its destiny. World models ought to reflect this ability to plan and to carry out willful acts.
Robert Boyland	Argues that Limits to Growth is too pessimistic. It fails to give adequate consideration to the technological possibilities of discovering new natural resources, creating new energy sources, and extending the "green revolution." He argues for more technological optimism in a world model.

Martin Greenberger claims that a case can be made for a third point of view. If one were to assume "conspiracy," that is, that the producers are actually holding back production and not reporting the full extent of reserves and discoveries, then a different model would emerge. In the tradition of institutional economists such as Thorstein Veblen, John R. Commons, or John Galbraith, such a model would be based on the purposeful and controlling behavior of the institutions, actors, and other stakeholders in the industry. In the conspiracy world view, it is reasonable to assume that a producer would continue to hold back production, waiting for deregulation, even in the event of increased reported reserves. Thus production could be negatively correlated with reserves. In this regard it is reported that MacAvoy and Pindyck discarded one equation, with a 95% fit to the data, in which gas production was a negative function of reported gas reserves. What is the basis for such a choice?

These examples show that there are a lot of different ways to look at the world when one is formulating a model. How then do we know which world view is "right"? Which assumptions should we use? The concepts and methods developed in this book provide ways for policymakers, planners, and strategists to answer these questions.

In the *Design of Inquiring Systems*, Churchman (1971) explores the general question of how to design a system that can guarantee its fundamental, underlying assumptions. The options for a guarantor range from religion, with God as a guarantor as it was for Descartes, to E. A. Singer's notion of progress, in which man's fundamental emotions are the guarantor. Other possibilities include collective agreement and judgment in the context of opposition. We have chosen to address the question from the standpoint of dialectics.

A link between model building and dialectics is made in a timely and relevant book entitled *Models in the Policy Process: Public Decision Making in the Computer Era* (1976), in which Martin Greenberger, Matthew Crenson, and Brian Crissy describe countermodeling and identify several countermodeling efforts. They see policy models as instruments of debate. Countermodels, in which the assumptions are changed to produce policy implications different from those of the original model, can be used to improve the level of political dialogue. Countermodels can lead to informed debates and, presumably, they will eventually lead to better models.

Can this model-based debate itself be designed and structured? We think it can, and take some additional inspiration from the Task Force of the Presidential Advisory Group on Anticipated Advances in Science and Technology who advocate the establishment of a "science court." Kantrowitz (1976) lists the requirements for one such dialectical-based science court for policy models.

Following the procedure outlined in Exhibit 12-2, each modeler constructs a model, runs it, and derives its conclusions. The conclusions are summarized in a report, that is, a "brief." Each "brief" is then presented at a "trial." This "trial" is really a public defense of the model and of the countermodels. It is an opportunity for the issues in the models to be joined. Each advocate is given an opportunity to present his case.

Exhibit 12-2   Requirements for a Prototype Court for Assessing Models

---

1. A major policy issue is identified and the policy area is defined. In formal terms, the referent system is "bounded."

2. Funding from a neutral source is arranged.

3. Two or more policy modelers are appointed to develop models from different points of view. They will serve as case managers and advocates for their model. They might represent different interest groups or stakeholders in the policy area, or they might be comprised by similarity of psychological type or any of the working group formation methods used in the SAST process. They might be selected by means of formal bidding or requests for proposal. The main criterion is that they represent points of view that are believable, consistent, politically viable, but substantially different in their policy recommendations.

4. A "data manager" is appointed. The data manager collects data and insures that each modeler has access to all of the available data.

5. A "court" of at least three judges is appointed. The judges should be knowledgeable in the policy field but they should be disinterested and relatively independent from the parties involved. They must understand something about models and modeling methods as well as be competent in the policy area.

6. A "referee" is appointed. This should be a management scientist supported by legal counsel. The referee aids the judges in the conduct of the trial and helps resolve disputes.

7. A "trial" is conducted.

Items are then debated point by point in an adversary proceeding. Interest groups and the general public may be present, but they may speak only at the behest of the judge in charge. At the completion of the trial, the judges summarize their conclusions in an opinion. The opinion need not decide on one model or another. Rather it should seek to synthesize a new world view and an appropriate assumption set from the thesis and antithesis of the debate. If deemed desirable, a new model might be constructed based on the assumptions recommended in the judges' opinion. This new model, of course, then becomes a candidate for countermodeling and future court appearances.

Such a procedure may seem costly and time-consuming, but it potentially offers several advantages:

1   It would help to identify and clarify relevant facts and data for a policy issue.
2   It would expose the assumptions of the models to a broad and systematic challenge.
3   It would inform ultimate users of the models in a way which should encourage use of the model when it is warranted and rejection of the model when that too is warranted.
4   It would help to identify the limits of our current knowledge and perhaps direct research in promising and useful areas.

In recent years, some of the aforementioned criticisms of models have been softened significantly with the advent of more user-oriented computer modeling systems (Wagner and Keen, 1979). These systems allow the user to build almost directly in natural language, complex financial models of the firm, and businesses internal to it. Using these languages, one can also build models of competitive response. To date, however, neither the models nor the computer packages have been developed to the point that allows the policymaker to consider equally sophisticated behavioral responses of both internal and external stakeholders.

Using these languages, analytical modeling techniques can be integrated with the methods presented in this book. One approach is to create a model and to "test" it following the steps in Exhibit 12-2. Another approach is to use the SAST process, in which participants are formed into two or more different planning teams. The teams are deliberately composed to take or to consider perspectives that are as different from one another as possible. Each team builds a model. Then the models are compared, contrasted, and debated. Their assumptions are surfaced and challenged. A synthetic set of assumptions is formed and used to create a model with a more believable set of assumptions that are "owned" by all the participants.

THE CASE APPROACH

A case is a written description of an enterprise and the problems facing it. It contains information about the enterprise, its history, its external environment and its internal operations. Cases are intended to simulate the reality of the policymaker's, planner's, or strategist's job. The case analyst studies the facts given and formulates a problem. The firm's opportunities, threats, weaknesses, and strengths are assessed by determining what the firm *might do* in terms of environmental opportunity, what it *can do* in terms of its resources, ability, and power, what it *wants to do* in terms of its members' personal values, aspirations and ideals, and what it *must do* in terms of social responsibility.

This model of the case approach has its intellectual roots in the Harvard Business School and in the works of Andrews (1971), Christensen et al. (1978), and Learned et al. (1969). The most "general" presumption of the case method is that each organization, like each individual, is "unique." For this reason, the strict advocate of the case approach eschews universal models or general principles that can be applied to all situations. Organizations and their problems are too messy and ill-structured to permit the adherence to so-called timeless and universal principles of analysis. Instead, each organization must be considered on its own individual merits. Based on an intensive examination by a personally concerned, involved, and experienced case analyst, a situational analysis is conducted, and an action plan is carefully tailored to suit the individual needs of a particular organization. This approach rests on the fundamental belief that organizations and their problems are essentially messy. For this reason they cannot be ordered into neat, a priori classification systems prior to contact with a living organization.

It should be noted that, like the PIMS approach to be considered subsequently, the underlying philosophy of this approach is that of empiricism. However, the brand of empiricism is very different. The empiricism of PIMS is that of a body of impersonal measurement data collected on a large number of organizations, whereas the empiricism of the case approach consists of the in-depth personal judgments of a single individual, the analyst, with regard to a particular organization. In a sense, the whole method hinges on the skills and experience of the particular analyst. Good case analyses can only be done by good case analysts. How one determines what "good" means in this context is a matter of considerable concern and controversy.

The objections to this approach are well-known. The most general objection or criticism is that the approach is not scientific if by "scientific" one means a commitment to replicability of results. The fact that two or more advocates of the same approach can reach quite different recommendations (action plans) is enough in the minds of some to make the approach hopelessly subjective. We cannot respond to this criticism in depth here; however, suffice it to say that the more we study "science scientifically" (i.e., the more we objectively study what scientists actually do), the more we find that all of science is shot through and through with basic judgments that depend on the style and taste of the individual scientist (Mitroff, 1974). What makes something scientific is not the absence of variability in results but rather on our collective ability to study why the results vary. There is nothing inherent in the case approach per se to prevent us from studying how and why different analysts reach different action plans.

There is, however, a more telling objection to which the case approach has not adequately addressed itself. The case approach is on strong ground when it asserts that many, if not most, of the techniques that have been developed for treating orderly problems do not seem fundamentally applicable to problems of organized complexity. In this special sense there are no universal *principles* for treating business problems. However, the approach is on much shakier ground when it seems to suggest that there are no general *methods* of any sort that are applicable to treatment of messy problems. We contend that the methods presented in this book constitute a necessary step toward meeting some of these criticisms and, furthermore, that they can be taught.

PIMS

The Profit Impact of Market Strategy (PIMS) approach was originally developed by analysts at General Electric Company and has been carried on by the Strategic Planning Institute. The approach is reported in Schoeffler et al. (1974) and Abell et al. (1979) and is critiqued by Anderson and Paine (1978). Based on a substantial body of financial, market, and organizational data gathered on over 100 companies in over 800 businesses, the PIMS data include estimates of relative competitive position (e.g., market share, relative market share, price, sales, and ratios), capital and production structure (investment/sales, capital intensity, capacity utilization, etc.), and market environment (growth rate, share of largest firms, etc.). A regression model is used to relate these factors to performance criteria such as return on investment (ROI). Among the generalized findings of the PIMS data are that strategic business units with higher market shares tend to have higher pre-tax ROI and that businesses with a high degree of investment intensity are often less profitable than those with lower investment sales ratios.

Using a "PAR analysis program," the model allows a company to compare the profile of its own business against that of the central tendency of business units that have similar generic characteristics in terms of market share, product quality, and so on, and similar environmental circumstances as measured by average market growth rates and price elasticity. The characteristic data about the business are used as input in the regression model, and a "par" measure of performance such as ROI is reported. If the actual ROI is substantially below the expected ROI, then presumably some action should be taken.

The validity of the approach rests on a set of critical assumptions. If either the analyst or manager initiating the examination of the business feels that the assumptions being made in the PIMS model do not apply, then the approach is clearly not applicable. In order to use PIMS it is necessary to assume that the sample of businesses on which the initial regression model was built is representative of all organizations taken as a whole. Furthermore, it is necessary to assume that one's own business is similar to that of the sample. Even stronger and more basic, one must posit that "all businesses are alike" in the special sense that they can be characterized in terms of the 37 or so variables contained in the regression model. It is necessary, in other words, to assume that the PIMS variables are sufficient to capture the complexities of the range of issues and considerations that bear on policy formation. The counter assumption to this is, of course, that *this* particular business is unique or possesses some unique characteristics that affect its performance. Another way to put this is to say that PIMS assumes that a rather large set of quantitative variables, primarily of a financial nature, are sufficient to capture the state of a business and a sufficient basis on which to build a policy, plan, or strategy.

Perhaps the most critical assumption of all is the assumption made about the nature of business problems. An implicit and generally unarticulated assumption of PIMS and the PAR analysis program is that business problems are orderly or well-structured.

The issues concerning well-structured versus the ill-structured problems of organizational complexity are at the very core of PIMS. PIMS assumes that the determination or classification of the level of the organization or business unit, the customer group, the competition, the market, and the product line to which the analysis applies are all either well-specified or well-known. PIMS is not set up to handle different, let alone conflicting, definitions of the problem situation at hand. Multiple runs of the model can be both costly and time-consuming. In short, PIMS is effective for making a one-time or one-shot assessment of the situation, business by business or product by product.

As Abell (1977) and Capon (1978) argue, PIMS is not well-suited to investigating the dynamic envolution of policy in response to constantly shifting environmental influences. These authors even questioned whether PIMS is a tool for policy in the strategic sense, since it can be argued that variables like market share are performance variables, not strategic ones. Another way to put it is that, although PIMS can be construed as both a diagnostic and prognostic tool, by itself it does not automatically suggest plausible plans or strategies. Basically, the PAR model indicates the magnitude of the performance "gap," but it does not suggest specifically what to do, let alone how to implement a plan successfully within a complex organization.

In summary, PIMS is well-suited to analyzing the effect of, for instance, a firm's pricing policies for a specific business and/or product on its expected ROI. The primary stakeholder considered in this approach is thus the firm itself and, more specifically, a particular strategic business unit and/or product division. Other stakeholders are indirectly considered, however, through the data needed to run the model. For example, the growth of the general business environment and competition are handled, although again in terms limited by the unintuitive nature of the variables. However, the method does not easily allow for the investigation of sophisticated "what if" questions or for sensitivity analysis.

It should be emphasized that the PIMS approach is admirably suited to a wide range of organizations and problems. If one's organization is similar to those in the sample, and if one's problems are well-structured in the sense that they can be clearly and specifically stated in terms of the variables of the model, then the PIMS approach should be considered.

The PIMS and PAR analysis approach can be integrated with the methods developed in this book. In one organization with which the authors have worked, a staff analyst identified over 1200 possible PIMS model runs that could be made concerning a proposed business. Each run tested different possibilities and characteristics of the business. After the SAST was held, the number of significant model runs was reduced to about six, each run reflecting the implications of critical combinations of assumptions surfaced by the SAST process and agreed to by the executives and staff who participated.

THE BOSTON CONSULTING GROUP'S
BUSINESS PORTFOLIO ANALYSIS

The Boston Consulting Group's approach was originally developed by Bruce Henderson and his associates and was reported in *Perspectives on Experience* and subsequent BCG publications. Underlying the BCG approach is a matrix-based, prior classification model. The approach relies on data concerning industry growth rates and relative competitive position. It is assumed that all businesses and/or products can be classified as one of four basic types: (1) a star; (2) a cash cow; (3) a dog; or (4) a "?". Two simple dimensions underlie the classification. It is assumed that those industries, businesses, and/or products that have a "high" growth rate can be differentiated from those that have a "low" growth rate. It is also assumed that those that have a "high" competitive position or market share can be differentiated from those that have a "low" competitive position. This last assumption may sound simplistic since it seems that the determination of market share is rather unproblematic. However, the definition of a market itself constitutes a fundamental assumption of any business. We stress this assumption because PIMS and BCG differ in how they compute a business' market share. In fact, the differences between the two approaches can lead to significant differences in the assessment of market share.

Further assumptions are involved regarding how business growth rate and market share interact or combine. The classification of a business into one of the four types depends on two sets of assumed relationships:

1   Experience curve assumption: cost = function (cumulative physical output).

2   A business is a cash system assumption: cash flow = function (relative market share, industry growth rate).

The first assumed relationship, experience curve assumption, states that the costs of production should go down with cumulative physical output. Further, as costs go down this ought to affect positively one's relative market share and profitability. The second relationship assumes that cash flow or cash production is a function of relative market share and the growth rate of the business relative to the industry, competing businesses, or products.

Given these relationships, planners can classify the businesses making up an organization. One can also classify the businesses of one's competition. Thus a star is a business that has both a high growth rate and competitive position, presumably as a result a high cash flow and ROI. A cash cow has a high cash flow but a low ROI. A "?" has a high ROI but a low cash flow. A dog has both a low ROI and a low cash flow.

The critical assumptions underlying the approach are: (1) that the classification scheme applies to all businesses because all businesses *can* be classified as one of the four basic types and (2) that the classification scheme is relevant to all business; that is, businesses *ought* to be classified as one of four types. It is these two assumptions in particular that give the model the status of an "a priori truth." The model is presumed universally true or applicable to all businesses no matter what the characteristic data on a particular business are. By the same token, the recommended actions are also presumed universally applicable. Thus presumably a firm should use its cash cows to finance new stars, and it should liquidate its dogs.

In a word, the BCG model—as all models do—self-selects the kind of data that is compatible with it. In terms of the self-selected data, a set of businesses can be classified as being one of the four types. However, what one can conclude from this is not so clear. With regard to cash flow and ROI, a business may indeed look like a star. But it can be risky to infer from this categorization, based on financial data alone, that it is "star" in all the other aspects of its life and hence that it is worth keeping without further question. For instance, a business unit or an organization may have a high ROI and a high cash flow, but it may be in danger of losing its will; it may be bored or on the verge of going through some form of an identity or mid-life crisis—indeed, precisely because of its very financial success, as many an organization has learned painfully.

The objection to this approach is essentially that the uniqueness of an organization and its problems may not be adequately captured by this or any other tight classification scheme. This does not mean that an organization should not contemplate using the BCG approach. This is neither our general policy nor our specific recommendation. Rather, every organization should ask itself the fundamental question: Is my situation orderly (well structured) enough to allow the issues facing us to be adequately subsumed under the BCG model?

In summary, the primary stakeholders considered by the BCG approach are the internal business units of a firm and the external business units of one's competition. Further, BCG is able to handle the simultaneous consideration of multiple businesses while PIMS is not. The BCG method not only finely differentiates or disaggregates a firm's internal businesses but the businesses of its competition as well. Like PIMS, it is primarily suited to well-structured planning problems in which the basic definition of a business unit, product, or competition is not at issue. The approach fundamentally depends on the existence of well-structured problems in that it is difficult to apply it to those situations for which little prior experience is available and hence for which an experience curve can not be posited with confidence. Like PIMS, the BCG approach does not suggest what the firm ought to do regarding other stakeholders such as the government or corporation personnel, if it intends, for example, to grow a "?" into a "star" or to divest itself of it.

The BCG approach also can be used in conjunction with the approaches presented in this book. For example, different SAST working groups often classify businesses differently because they make different assumptions about the growth potential of a business and the nature of the market that underlies its market share. Further, argumentation analysis frequently uncovers devastating rebuttals for the classification claims of a business. A strong case can often be made as to why a supposed "star" is really an incipient "dog." Moreover, several companies we have worked

Exhibit 12-3 A Comparison of Some Major Approaches to Business Problem Solving

Approach	Strengths	Weaknesses	Nature of Information Required
Systems	Comprehensive relation of problems to broader environment and other problems	Difficult to operationalize	Dependent on the analyst and nature of the problems
Analytic Modeling	Rigor/precision of mathematical models	Limited ability, of formal models to handle messy ill-structured problems	Dependent on the model: model typically constrains the data to that which is compatible with the model
Case Method	In-depth treatment of a particular organization and its possibly unique problems	Variability of analysis; question of objectivity versus subjectivity	Dependent on orientation of analyst (financial/marketing/behavioral)
PIMS and BCG	Relatively simple to use, structured, clear-cut; emphasizes importance of financial factors	May solve wrong problem precisely because of the failure to look at nonquantifiable data, for example, behavioral implications	Financial, competitive standing, industry type, size of company
SAST	Comprehensive consideration of multiple stakeholders plus critical planning assumptions	Willingness of participants to lay bare their assumptions	Participants' perceptions of the stakeholders plus financial and behavioral data

with have uncovered significant policy implications concerning their assumptions about the rate of technological innovation and adoption that underlie their projected experience curves.

COMPARISON OF APPROACHES

Exhibit 12-3 summarizes our assessment of the strengths and weaknesses of the approaches discussed in this chapter. The comparison reveals that no one approach by itself is best for all organizations and all problems. Indeed, it should be clear that in a fundamental sense all the approaches presuppose one another. Thus for example, it is wrong to think that SAST and BCG are fundamentally in opposition to each other. Rather, they are appropriate for different stages of the process of policy formation (see Chapter 2). SAST is more appropriate for securing and treating different formulations/definitions of a problematic situation; BCG is extremely useful in providing systematic data and an orderly method of assessing the relationship between specific businesses and competition *once the basic definition of the situation has been agreed on.* In the same way, all the different approaches can be shown both to aid and to depend on one another in a significant way.

In this world of organized complexity, we should have learned by now that whenever there is significant contention in human affairs, differing points of view depend on one another in more ways than we seem capable of admitting. In our view, the task of policy, planning, and strategy should not consist of attempting to demonstrate the superiority of one approach or framework for all situations but rather of showing their mutual dependency. Thus all the approaches reviewed in this chapter are useful to policymakers. They further gain in utility when they are combined with the methods developed in this book and with one another. These are all tools in the policymaker's, planner's, and strategist's kit.

In summary, we close by saying that the real world of policy, planning, and strategy is inherently complex, as described in the first chapters of this book. As a result, dialectical methods such as SAST, structured debate, and argumentation analysis are necessary to cope with this complexity. However, these methods are not necessarily sufficient. Other methods, such as the systems approach, analytical modeling, the case approach, PIMS, and product portfolio analysis are necessary as well in a program of strategic inquiry. The focus should be on "program" and "inquiry," not on any single method that pretends to be the answer for all problems. Whatever methods are used they should always aid in challenging strategic planning assumptions.

References

Abell, Derek F., "Using PIMS And Portfolio Analyses In Strategic Market Planning: A Comparative Analysis," Intercollegiate Case Clearing House 9-578-017, 1977.

Abell, Derek F., and Hammond, John S., *Strategic Market Planning* (Englewood Cliffs, N.J.: Prentice-Hall, 1979).

Ackoff, Russell L., *The Design of Social Research* (Chicago: University of Chicago Press, 1953).

Ackoff, Russell L., "Towards a Behavioral Theory of Communication," *Management Science* **4** (1958), 218–234.

Ackoff, Russell L., *Scientific Method: Optimizing Applied Research Decisions* (New York: Wiley, 1962), pp. 30–31.

Ackoff, Russell L., "Management Misinformation Systems," *Management Science,* **14** (1967), B-147–B-156.

Ackoff, Russell L., "Systems, Organizations, and Interdisciplinary Research," in F. E. Emery, *Systems Thinking* (Middlesex: Penguin, 1969).

Ackoff, Russell L., *A Concept of Corporate Planning* (New York: Wiley, 1970).

Ackoff, Russell L., "Towards a System of Systems Concepts," *Management Science* **17,** No. 11 (July 1971), 661–671.

Ackoff, Russell L., *Redesigning the Future* (New York: Wiley, 1974).

Ackoff, Russell L., *The Art of Problem Solving* (New York: Wiley, 1979).

Ackoff, Russell L., and Emery, F., *On Purposeful Systems* (Chicago: Aldine-Atherton, 1974).

Aguilar, Francis, "Norton Company: Strategic Planning for Diversified Business Operations," Intercollegiate Case Clearing House, 1976.

Allan, Gerald B., and Hammond, John S., "A Note on the Boston Consulting Group Concept of Competitive Analysis and Corporate Strategy," Intercollegiate Case Clearing House, 1975a.

Allan, Gerald B., and Hammond, John S., "Note on the Use of Experience Curves in Competitive Decision Making," Intercollegiate Case Clearing House, 1975b.

Allen, Allen D., "Scientific Versus Judicial Fact Finding in the United States,"

IEEE Trans. on Systems, Man, and Cybernetics September 1972, pp. 548–550.

Anderson, Carl R., and Paine, Frank T., "PIMS: A Reexamination" *Academy of Management Review* **3**, No. 3 (July 1978), 602–612.

Andrews, Kenneth R., *The Concept of Corporate Strategy* (Homewood, Ill.: Irwin, 1971).

Ansoff, H. Igor, *Corporate Strategy: An Analytical Approach to Business Policy for Growth and Expansion* (New York: McGraw-Hill, 1965).

Ansoff, H. Igor, and Brandenburg, Richard G., "A Program of Research in Business Planning," *Management Science* **13** (February 1967), B-219–B-239.

Archibald, K. A., "Three Views of the Expert's Role in Policymaking: Systems Analysis, Incrementalism, and the Clinical Approach," *Policy Science* **1** (1970), 73–86.

Argyres, C., and Schön, D. A., *Theory in Practice* (San Francisco: Jossey-Bass, 1974).

Asch, Solomon E., "Forming Impressions of Personality," *Journal of Abnormal and Social Psychology* **41** (1946), 258–290.

Attneave, Fred, *Application of Information Theory to Psychology* (New York: Holt, Rinehart & Winston, 1959).

Bakan, David, *On Method: Toward Reconstruction of Psychological Investigation* (San Francisco: Jossey-Bass, 1967).

Balwin, Charles S., *Medieval Rhetoric and Poetic* (New York: Macmillan, 1928).

Benson, J. Kenneth, "Organizations: A Dialectical View," *Administrative Science Quarterly* **22**, No. 1 (March 1977), 1–21.

Boffey, Philip, "Science Court: High Officials Back Test of Controversial Concept," *Science* **193** (October 8, 1976), 167–169.

Boston Consulting Group Staff, *Perspectives on Experience* (Boston: The Boston Consulting Group, 1968).

Boulding, Kenneth E., *The Image* (Ann Arbor: University of Michigan Press, 1956).

Bringhtman, H. J., "Differences in Ill-Structured Problem Solving along the Organizational Hierarchy," *Decision Sciences,* **9** (1978), 1–18.

Brock, T. C., and Becker, L. A., "Debriefing and Susceptibility to Subsequent Experimental Manipulations," *Journal of Experimental Social Psychology* **2** (1968), 314–323.

Brockriede, W., and Ehninger, D., "Toulmin on Argument: An Interpretation and Application," *The Quarterly Journal of Speech* **46** (1960), 44–53.

Bross, I.D.J., *Design for Decisions* (New York: Macmillan, 1953).

Brown, J. G., "Fuzzy Sets on Boolean Lattices," Rep. No. 1957, Ballistic Research Laboratories, Aberdeen, Maryland, January 1969.

Brown, Norman O., *Life Against Death: The Psychoanalytical Meaning of History* (New York: Vintage, 1959).

Brown, Norman O., *Love's Body* (New York: Random House, 1966).

Brown, Stanley H., "How One Man Can Move a Corporation," *Fortune* **74** No. 1 (July 1966).

Brunswik, Egon, "Representative Design and Probabilistic Theory in a Functional Psychology," *Psychological Review* **62**, No. 3 (1955), 193–217.

Buchan, Joseph, and Koenigsberg, Ernest, *Scientific Inventory Management* (Englewood Cliffs, N.J.: Prentice-Hall, 1963).

Buchler, J. (Ed.), *The Philosophy of Pierce* (London: Kegan Paul, 1940).

Budner, S., "Intolerance of Ambiguity as a Personality Variable," *Journal of Personality* **30** (1962), 29–50.

Campbell, Joseph, *The Hero with a Thousand Faces* (New York: Meridan, 1971).

Campbell, Joseph, *Myths to Live By* (New York: Viking Press, 1972).

Campbell, Joseph, "Historical Development of Mythology," in H. A. Murray, Ed., *Myth and Mythmaking* (New York: George Braziller, 1960).

Campbell, Norman, *What is Science?* (New York: Dover, 1952).

Cannon, J. Thomas, *Business Strategy and Policy* (New York: Harcourt Brace Jovanovich, 1968).

Capon, Noel, and Spogli, Joan R., "A Comparison and Critical Examination of the PIMS and BCG Approaches to Strategic Marketing Planning," Intercollegiate Case Clearing House 9-578-148-1978.

Cervin, V. B., and Henderson, G. P. "Statistical Theory of Persuasion," *Psychological Review* **68** (1961), 157–166.

Chandler, Alfred D., Jr., *Strategy and Structure: Chapters in the History of Industrial Enterprise* (Cambridge, Mass.: MIT Press, 1962).

Chang, C. L. "Fuzzy Topological Space," *J. Math, Anal. Appl.* **24** (1968), 182–190.

Christensen, Roland C., Andrews, Kenneth R., and Bower, Joseph L., *Business Policy: Text and Cases* (Homewood, Ill.: Irwin, 1978).

Chubin, D. E., Rossini, F. A., Porter, A. L., and Mitroff, I. I., "Experimental Technology Assessment: Explorations in Processes of Multidisciplinary Team Research," paper submitted to *Journal of Technological Forecasting and Social Change,* 1978.

Churchman, C. West, *Theory of Experimental Inference,"* (New York: Macmillan, 1948).

Churchman, C. W., "Concepts Without Primitives," *Philosophy of Science* **20** (1953), 257–265.

Churchman, C. West, "The Philosophy of Experimentation," in *Statistics and Mathematics in Biology,* edited by Kempthorne et al. (Ames: Iowa State College Press, 1954).

Churchman, C. West, *Prediction and Optimal Decision: Philosophical Issues of a Science of Values* (Englewood Cliffs, New Jersey: Prentice-Hall, 1961).

Churchman, C. West, Letter to the Editor, *Management Science,* **14,** No. 4 (December 1967), 141–143.

Churchman, C. W., *Challenge to Reason* (New York: McGraw-Hill, 1968).

Churchman, C. W. *The Systems Approach* (New York: Dell, 1968).

Churchman, C. West, "The Artificiality of Science" (A review of H. A. Simon's book, *The Science of the Artificial), Contemporary Psychology* **15,** No. 6 (June 1970).

Churchman, C. W., *The Design of Inquiring Systems* (New York: Basic Books, 1971).

Churchman, C. West, *The Systems Approach and Its Enemies!* (New York: Basic Books, 1979).

Churchman, C. W., and Ackoff, Russell L., "An Experimental Measure of Personality," *Philosophy of Science* **14** (1947), 304–332.

Churchman, C. W., and Mason, R. O., *World Models—A Dialogue* (Amsterdam: North-Holland/American Elsevier, 1976).

Churchman, C. West, and Schainblatt, A. H., "On Mutual Understanding," *Manager Science* **12** (1965) B-40–B-42.

Cohen, Bernard P., *Conflict and Conformity: A Probability Model and Its Applications* (Cambridge, Mass.: MIT Press, 1963).

Collier, Abram T., "Decision at Zenith Life," *Harvard Business Review* **40,** No. 1 (January–February 1962), 139–150.

Coser, Lewis, *The Functions of Social Conflict* (New York: Macmillan, 1956).

Cousins, Norman, "President Kennedy and the Russian Fable," *Saturday Review,* Jan. 9, 1971, pp. 20–21.

Cowan, Thomas A., "Decision Theory in Law, Science and Technology," *Science* **140** (June 7, 1963), 1065–1075.

Cowan, Thomas A., "A Model for Jurisprudential Investigation," Internal Working Paper No. 60, Space Sciences Laboratory, Social Sciences Project, University of California, Berkeley, March, 1967.

Cowan, Thomas A., "Paradoxes of Science Administration," *Science* **177** (September 15, 1972), 964–966.

Cyert, R. M., and March, J. C., *A Behavioral Theory of the Firm* (Englewood Cliffs, N.J.: Prentice-Hall, 1963).

David, James A., "Structural Balance, Mechanical Solidarity, and Interpersonal Relations," *The American Journal of Sociology.*

Davidoff, Paul, *"Advocacy and Pluralism in Planning," Journal of the American Institute of Planners,* **1** (November 1965), 331–338.

DeLaszlo, Violet S., *Psyche and Symbol: A Selection from the Writings of C. G. Jung* (New York: Doubleday, 1958).

Delbecq, A. L., and Van de Ven, A. H., "A Group Process Model for Problem Identification and Program Planning," *Journal of Applied Behavioral Science* **7** (1971).

Dewey, J., *Experience and Nature* (La Salle, Ill.: Open Court, 1925).

Dewey, J., *The Quest for Certainty* (New York: Macmillan, 1929).

Edwards, W., Guttentag, M., and Snapper, K., "A Decision-Theoretic Approach to Evaluation Research."

Elaide, Mircea, *Myth and Reality* (New York: Harper & Row, 1963).

Emery, F. W., and Trist, E. L., "The Causal Texture of Organizational Environments," *Human Relations* **18** (1965), 21–32.

Feyerabend, Paul K., "Against Method: Outline of an Anarchistic Theory of Knowledge," in *Analyses of Theories and Methods of Physics and Psychology, Minnesota Studies in the Philosophy of Science,* Vol. 4 (Minneapolis: University of Minnesota, 1970), pp. 17–130.

Feyerabend, P. K., "How to Be a Good Empiricist—a Plea for Tolerance in Matters Epistemological," in *The Philosophy of Science,* edited by P. H. Niditch (London: Oxford University Press, 1968).

Feyerabend, P. K., "On the Improvement of the Sciences and Arts and the Possible Identity of the Two," in Robert S. Cohen and Marx W. Wartofsky, Eds., *Boston Studies in the Philosophy of Science* (Dordrecht, Holland: D. Reidel, 1967), pp. 387–415.

Feyerabend, Paul K., "Problems of Empiricism," in Robert G. Colodny, Ed., *Beyond the Edge of Certainty* (Englewood Cliffs, N.J.: Prentice-Hall, 1965), pp. 145–260.

Feyerabend, Paul K., "Problems of Empiricism, Part II," in Robert G. Colodny, Ed., *The Nature and Function of Scientific Theories* (Pittsburgh: University of Pittsburgh Press, 1970b), pp. 275–354.

Fox, A., *A Sociology of Work in Industry* (London: Collier, 1971).

French, John P., Jr., "Experiments in Field Settings," in Leon Festinger and Daniel Katz, *Research Methods in Behavioral Sciences* (New York: Dryden, 1953).

Fromm, Gary, Hamilton, William L., and Hamilton, Diane E., *Federally Supported Mathematical Models: Survey and Analysis* (Washington, D.C.: National Science Foundation, June 1974), No. NSF RANN-C-804.

Garner, Wendell R., *Uncertainty and Structure as Psychological Concepts* (New York: Wiley, 1962).

Gause, D. C., and Weinberg, G. M., "On General Systems Education," in C. W. Churchman and R. W. Werner, Eds., *Systems and Management Annual* (New York: Petrocelli, 1975).

Gilmore, Frank F., "Overcoming the Perils of Advocacy in Corporate Planning," *California Business Review* **15** No. 3 (Spring 1973), 127–137.

Goguen, J., "L-fuzzy Sets," *J. Math. Anal. Appl.* **18** (1967), 145–174.

Goguen, J. A., "The Logical of Inexact Concepts," *Synthese* **19** (1968–1969), 325–373.

Gordon, G., MacEachron, A. E., and Fisher, G. L., "A Contingency Model for the Design of Problem Solving Research Programs: A Perspective on Diffusion Research," *Health and Society,* Spring 1974, pp. 185–220.

Greenberger, Martin, Crenson, Matthew A., and Crissey, Brian L., *Models in the Policy Process: Public Decision Making in the Computer Era* (New York: Russell Sage Foundation, 1976).

Grofman, B., and Hyman, G., "Probability and Logic in Belief Systems," *Theory and Decision* **4** (1973), 187–195.

Haack, S., *Deviant Logic, Some Philosophical Issues* (Cambridge, England: Cambridge University Press, 1974).

Hammond, Kenneth R. et al., "Cognitive Conflict between Persons: Application of the 'Lens Model' Paradigm," *Journal of Experimental Social Psychology* **2** (1960), 343–360.

Hammond, Kenneth R., "Probabilistic Functioning and the Clinical Method," *Psychological Review* **62,** No. 4 (1955), 255–262.

Hammond, Kenneth R., and Boyle, Peter J., "Quasi-Rationality, Quarrels, and New Conceptions of Feedback," Program of Cognitive Processes Report No. 130, Institute of Behavioral Science, University of Colorado, no date.

Hammond, Kenneth R., Wilkins, M. M., and Todd, F. J., "A Research Paradigm for the Study of Interpersonal Learning," *Psychological Bulletin* **65,** No. 4 (1966), 222–232.

Hanson, N. R., "Observation and Interpretation," in Sidney Morgenbesser, Ed., *Philosophy of Science Today* (New York: Basic Books, 1967), pp. 89–99.

Hanson, Norwood R., *Patterns of Discovery* (London: Cambridge University Press, 1958).

Harding, M. Esther, *Woman's Mysteries, Ancient and Modern, A Psychological Interpretation of the Feminine Principle as Portrayed in Myth, Story, and Dreams* (New York: Putnam's, 1968).

Hartman, W., Matthes, H., and Proeme, A., *Management Information Systems Handbook* (New York: McGraw-Hill, 1968).

Hegel, G. W., *The Phenomenology of Mind,* 2nd. ed., translated by J. B. Baillie (London: Allen and Unwin, 1964).

Helmer, Olaf, and Rescher, Nicholas, "On the Epistemology of the Inexact Sciences," *Management Science* **6** (October 1959), 25–52.

Hofer, Charles W., and Dan Schendel, *Strategy Formulation: Analytical Concepts* (St. Paul: West Publishing, 1978).

Hogarth, Robin M., and Einhorn, Hillel J., "An Examination of the Mathematical Formulation of the Lens Model in Judgmental Research," unpublished manuscript, University of Chicago, 1971.

Hudson, Liam, *Contrary Imagination* (New York: Schocken Books, 1966).

Hursch, Carolyn J., Hammond, K. R., and Hursch, J. L., "Some Methodological Considerations on Multiple-Cue Probability Studies," *Psychological Review* **71**, No. 1 (1964), 42–60.

Jackson, Henry M., "Organizing for Survival," *Foreign Affairs,* **38**, No. 3 (1959) 446–456.

Jacobi, Jolande, *The Psychology of C. G. Jung* (New Haven, Conn.: Yale University Press, 1962).

Jung, C. G., *Psychological Types* (London: Rutledge, 1923).

Jung, C. G., *The Structure and Dynamics of the Psyche* (New York: Pantheon, 1955).

Kant, Immanuel, *Critique of Pure Reason,* translated by Norman Kemp Smith (New York: St. Martin's Press, 1965).

Kantrowitz, Arthur, "Proposal for an Institution for Scientific Judgment," *Science* **156** (May 12, 1967), 763–764.

Kantrowitz, Arthur et al. "The Science Court Experiment: An Interim Report," *Science* **193** (August 20, 1976), 653–656.

Keen, Peter G., and Wagner, Gerald R., "DSS: An Executive Mind-Support System," *Datamation,* November 1979, pp. 117–122.

Keisler, Charles, *The Psychology of Commitment* (New York: Academic, 1971).

Kilmann, R. H., and Thomas, K. W., "Four Perspectives on Conflict Management," Working Paper No. 86, Graduate School of Business, University of Pittsburgh, 1974.

Kilmann, R. H., Lyes, M., and Mitroff, I. I., "Designing an Effective Problem Solving Organization with the MAPS Design Technology," *J. Management* **2**, No. 2 (1976), 1–10.

Kilmann, R. H., and Seltzer, J., "An Experimental Test of Organization Design Theory and the MAPS Design Technology: Homogeneous versus Heterogeneous Composition of Organizational Subsystems," *Proceedings of the Eastern Academy of Management* (1976).

Kilmann, R. H., *Social Systems Design: Normative Theory and the MAPS Design Technology* (New York: Elsevier North-Holland, 1977).

Kilmann, R. H., "Structural Design for OD Diagnosis: Alternatives and Consequences," Working Paper No. 231, Graduate School of Business, University of Pittsburgh, 1977.

Kilmann, R. H., and Mitroff, I. I., *Organizational Problem Solving: A Social Science Approach* (New York: Elsevier North-Holland, in preparation).

Kluckhohn, Clyde, "Recurrent Themes in Myth and Mythmaking," in H. A. Murray, Ed., *Myth and Mythmaking* (New York: George Braziller, 1960), 268–279.

Koontz, H., and O'Donnel, Cyril, *Essentials of Management* (New York: McGraw-Hill, 1974).

Kosok, M., "The Formalization of Hegel's Dialectical Logic," in A. MacIntyre, Ed., *Hegel: A Collection of Critical Essays* (New York: Anchor, 1975).

Kuhn, Thomas, *The Structure of Scientific Revolutions* (Chicago: University of Chicago Press, 1962).

Kurz, Mordecai, "On the Inverse Optimal Problem," Technical Report No. 3, August 1, 1967, Institute for Mathematical Studies in the Social Sciences, Stanford University.

Learned, E. P., Christensen, C. R., Andrews, K. R., and Guth, W. D., *Business Policy: Text and Cases* (Homewood, Ill.: Irwin, 1965).

Lee, D. S., "Scientific Method as a Stage Process," *Dialectica*, 22 (1968), 28–44.

Levine, M. "Scientific Method and the Adversary Model," *American Psychologist*, September 1974, pp. 661–677.

Luce, R. Duncan, and Raiffa, Howard, *Games and Decisions* (New York: Wiley, 1958).

Lukasiewicz, J., *Elements of Mathematical Logic* (New York: Macmillan, 1963).

Lyles, M., and Mitroff, I. I., "On Organizational Problem Forming: An Empirical Study," *Administrative Sci. Quart.* 25 (March 1980), 102–119.

MacAvoy, Paul W., and Pindyck, Robert S. *The Economics of the Natural Gas Shortage (1960–1980)* (Amsterdam: North-Holland, 1975).

March, J. G., and Simon, H. A., *Organizations* (New York: Wiley, 1958).

Marcuse, Herbert, *Eros and Civilization: A Philosophical Inquiry Into Freud* (New York: Vintage, 1955).

Mason, Richard O., Jr., "Dialectics in Decision-Making: A Study in the Use of Counterplanning and Structured Debate in Management Information Systems," unpublished Doctoral Dissertation, Internal Working Paper No. 87, June 1968, Space Sciences Laboratory, Social Sciences Project, University of California, Berkeley.

Mason, R. O., "A Dialectical Approach to Strategic Planning," *Management Science* 15, No. 8 (1969), B-403–B-414.

Mason, R. O., and Mitroff, I. I., "A Program for Research on Management Information Systems," *Management Science* 19, No. 5 (1973), 475–487.

Mason, R. O. "World Models: Who is the Guarantor?" *Interfaces of the Institute of Management Science* 8, No. 3 (May 1978) 91–97.

Mason, R. O., and I. I. Mitroff, "Assumptions of Majestic Metals: Strategy through Dialectics," *California Management Review* 23, No. 2 (Winter 1979), 80–88.

Mates, Benson, *Elementary Logic* (New York: Oxford University Press, 1965).

May, Rollo, *Love and Will* (New York: Norton, 1969).

Meadows, Donnella H., and Meadows, Dennis, *The Limits to Growth* (New York: Universe Books, 1972).

McKenney, J. L., and Keen, P. G. W., "How Managers' Minds Work," *Harvard Business Review*, May–June 1974.

McLuhan, Marshall, *The Gutenberg Galaxy* (Toronto: University of Toronto Press, 1965).

McNeman, Quinn, *Psychological Statistics* (New York: Wiley, 1962).

Michalos, A., *Principles of Logic* (Englewood Cliffs, N.J.: Prentice-Hall, 1969).

Miles, W. Martin, "The Measurement of Value of Scientific Information," in Burton V. Dean, Ed., *Operations Research in Research and Development* (New York: Wiley, 1963).

Miller, George A., "The Magical Number Seven, Plus or Minus Two," in R. Duncan Luce et al., *Readings in Mathematical Psychology* (New York: Wiley, 1963).

Miller, George A., Galanter, Eugene, and Primbram, Karl H., *Plans and the Structure of Behavior* (New York: Holt, Rinehart & Winston, 1960).

Mintzberg, Henry, "Managerial Work: Analyses from Observation," *Management Sci.* **18** (1971), 97–110.

Mintzberg, Henry, *The Nature of Managerial Work* (New York: Harper and Row, 1973a).

Mintzberg, Henry, "The Manager's Job: Folklore and Fact," *Harvard Business Review*, July–August 1975.

Mintzberg, Henry, "Policy as a Field of Management Theory," *Academy of Management Review* **11**, No 1 (January 1977), 88–103.

Mintzberg, Henry, Raisingham, D., and Theoret, A., "The Structure of 'Unstructured' Decision Processes," *Administrative Sci. Quart.* **21** (1976), 246–275.

Mitroff, Ian I., "Simulating Engineering Design: A Case Study on the Interface Between the Technology and Social Psychology of Design," *IRE Trans. on Engineering Management*, December 1968.

Mitroff, Ian I., "A Communication Model of Dialectical Inquiring Systems—A Strategy for Strategic Planning," *Management Science* **17**, No. 10 (June 1971), B-634–B-648.

Mitroff, Ian I., "A Brunswik Lens Model of Dialectical Information Systems," *Theory and Decision*, **2** (1974a).

Mitroff, I. I., *The Subjective Side of Science: An Inquiry into the Psychology of the Apollo Moon Scientists* (Amsterdam: Elsevier, 1974a).

Mitroff, I. I., "On Systemic Problem Solving and the Error of the Third Kind," *Behavioral Science* **19** (1974c), 383–393.

Mitroff, I. I., "Towards a Theory of Systemic Problem Solving: Prospects and Paradoxes," *International Journal of General Systems* **4** (1977), 47–59.

Mitroff, Ian I., Barabba, U. P., and Kilmann, R., "The Application of Behavioral and Philosophical Technologies to Strategic Planning: A Case Study of a Large Federal Agency," *Management Science* **24** (1977), 44–58.

Mitroff, Ian I., and Betz, Frederick, "Dialectical Decision Theory: A Meta-

Theory of Decision-Making,'' *Management Science* **19**, No. 1 (September 1972), 11–24.

Mitroff, Ian I., Betz, Frederick, and Mason, Richard O., ''A Mathematical Model of Churchmanian Inquiring Systems With Special Reference to Popper's Measure For The Severity of Tests,'' *Theory and Decision* **1** (1970), 155–178.

Mitroff, I. I., Betz, F., Pondy, L. R., and Sagasti, F., ''On Managing Science in the Systems Age: Two Schemas for the Study of Science as a Whole Systems Phenomenon,'' *Interfaces* **4** (1974), 46–58.

Mitroff, Ian I., and Emshoff, J., ''On Strategic Assumption-Making: A Dialectical Approach to Policy and Planning,'' *Academy of Management Review* **4** (1979), 1–12.

Mitroff, Ian I., Emshoff, James R., and Kilmann, Ralph H., ''Assumptional Analysis: A Methodology for Strategic Problem Solving,'' *Management Science* **25** (1979), 583–593.

Mitroff, I. I., and Featheringham, T., ''Towards a Behavioral Theory of Systemic Hypothesis-Testing and the Error of the Third Kind,'' *Theory and Decision* **7** (1976), 205–220.

Mitroff, I. I., and Kilmann, R. H., ''On Integrating Behavioral and Philosophical Systems: Towards a Unified Theory of Problem Solving,'' *Annual Series in the Sociology* **1** (1978), 207–236.

Mitroff, Ian I., and Kilmann, R. H., ''On Organizational Stories: An Approach to the Design and Analysis of Organizations through Myths and Stories,'' in R. H. Kilmann, L. Pondy, and D. Slevin, Eds., *The Management of Organization Design* (Amsterdam: North-Holland, 1976), 189–207.

Mitroff, Ian I., and Mason, Richard O., ''Policy As Argument: A Logic for Ill-Structured Decision Problems,'' Working Paper, Graduate School of Business, University of Pittsburgh, Pa. 15260.

Mitroff, Ian I., Williams, James and Rathswohl, Eugene, ''Dialectical Inquiring Systems: A New Methodology for Information Science,'' *Journal of American Society for Information Science* **23**, No. 6 (November–December 1972), 365–378.

Morse, E. V., and Gordon, G., ''Cognitive Skills: A Determinant of Scientists' Local-Cosmopolitan Orientation,'' *Academy of Management Journal* **17** (1974), 709–723.

Murray, Henry A., ''Introduction to the Issue, 'Myth and Mythmaking','' in H. A. Murray, Ed., *Myth and Mythmaking* (New York: George Braziller, 1960), 211–222.

Murray, Henry A., Ed., *Myth and Mythmaking,* (New York: George Braziller, 1960).

Nelson, John, ''Dialectic Information Systems: A Methodology for Planning and Decision Making,'' Ph.D. Dissertation, University of Pittsburgh, Pittsburgh, Pa. June 1973.

Newell, A., Shaw, J. C., and Simon, H. A., "Elements of a Theory of Human Problem-Solving," in R. J. C. Harper, C. C. Anderson, C. M. Christensen, and S. M. Hunks, Eds., *The Cognitive Process* (Englewood Cliffs, N.J.: Prentice Hall, 1964).

Nordhaus, William D., "World Dynamics: Measurement without Data," *The Economic Journal* **83,** No. 332 (December 1973), 1156–1183.

Nystrom, Paul D., "Dialectical Decision Process: Its Use in Faculty Personnel Actions," *American Institute for Decision Sciences Proceedings,* 1977, pp. 491–493.

Osgood, Charles E., *Method and Theory in Experimental Psychology* (New York: Oxford University Press, 1964).

Osgood, E., Suci, G. J., George, J., and Tannenbaum, P. H., *The Measurement of Meaning* (Urbana: University of Illinois Press, 1957).

Popper, Karl R., *Conjectures and Refutations* (New York: Basic Books, 1962).

Pounds, W. F., "The Process of Problem Finding," *Industrial Management Rev.* **11** (1969), 1–19.

Raglan, Lord, *The Hero, A Study in Tradition, Myth, and Drama* (New York: Vintage Books, 1956).

Raiffa, H., *Decision Analysis* (Reading, Mass.: Addison-Wesley, 1968).

Rein, M., *Social Science and Public Policy* (New York: Penguin, 1976).

Rescher, Nicholas, *Plausible Reasoning* (Amsterdam: Van Gorcum, 1976).

Rescher, N., *Dialectics, A Controversy-Oriented Approach to the Theory of Knowledge* (Albany: State University of New York Press, 1977).

Rescher, N., and R. Manor, "On Inference from Inconsistent Premises," *Theory and Decision* **1** (1970), 179–217.

Rhenman, E., *Industrial Democracy and Industrial Man* (London: Tavistock, 1908).

Rittel, H., "Some Principles for the Design of an Educational System for Design," *J. Architectural Education* **26** (1971), 16–27.

Rittel, Horst, "On the Planning Crisis: Systems Analysis of the 'First and Second Generations'," *Bedriftsokonomen* NR8, 390–396, 1972.

Rittel, H. H., and Webber, M. M., "Dilemmas in a General Theory of Planning," *Policy Sciences* **4** (1973), 155–169.

Rose, Arnold, "The Relation of Theory and Method," in *Sociological Theory: Inquiries and Paradigms* (New York: Harper and Row, 1967).

Rossini, F. A., Porter, A. L., Kelly, P., and Cubin, D. E. "Frameworks and Factors Affecting Integration within Technology Assessments," Report to the National Science Foundation, Grant ERS 76-04474, Department of Social Sciences, Georgia Institute of Technology, Atlanta, Ga. 1978.

Roszak, Theodore, *The Making of a Counter Culture* (New York: Doubleday, 1969).

Saaty, T. L., and Rogers, P. C., "Higher Education in the United States (1985–2000), Scenario Construction Using a Hierarchical Framework with Eigenvector Weighting," *Socio-Economic Planning* **10** (1976), 251–263.

Sagasti, F., and Mitroff, I. I., "Operations Research from the Viewpoint of General Systems Theory," *Omega* **1** (1973), 695–709.

Sanderson, M., *Successful Problem Management* (New York: Wiley, 1979).

Schank, R. L., and Goodman, C., "Reaction to Propaganda on Both Sides of a Controversial Issue," *Public Opinion Quarterly* **3** (1938), 107–112.

Schein, E. H. *Process Consultation: Its Role in Organization Development* (Reading, Mass.: Addison-Wesley, 1969).

Schoeffler, Sidney, Brizzell, Robert D., and Heany, Donald F., "Impact of Strategic Planning on Profit Performance," *Harvard Business Review,* March–April 1974, pp. 137–145.

Sears, David, Freman, J. L., and O'Connor, E. F., "The Effects of Anticipated Debate and Commitment on the Polarization of Audience Opinion," *Public Opinion Quarterly* **29** (1965), 615–627.

Shannon, Claude E., and Weaver, Warren, *The Mathematical Theory of Communication* (Urbana: University of Illinois Press, 1964).

Simon, H. A., and A. Newell, "Heuristic Problem-Solving: The Next Advance in Operations Research," *Operations Research* **6,** No. 1 (January–February, 1958), 1–10.

Singer, E. A., *Experience and Reflection* (Philadelphia: University of Pennsylvania, 1959).

Starbuck, W. H., Greve, A., and Hedberg, B. L. T., "Responding to Crisis," in C. F. Smart and W. T. Stanburg, Eds., *Studies on Crisis Management* (Montreal, Canada: Butterworth, 1978), 111–137.

Steiner, George A., "Basic Approach to Long-Range Planning," in Robert N. Anthony, John Dearden, and Richard F. Vancil, *Management Control Systems* (Homewood, Ill.: Irwin, 1965).

Steiner, George, and Miner, J. B., *Management Policy and Strategy.* (New York: Macmillan, 1977).

Stumpt, S. A., Zand, D. E., and Freeman, R. D., "Designing Groups for Judgmental Decisions," *Acadamy of Management Review* **4** (1979), 589–600.

Summers, David A., "Conflict, Compromise, and Belief Change in a Decision-Making Task," *Journal of Conflict Resolution* **12,** No. 2 (June 1968), 215–221.

Suppes, Patrick, "Concept Formation and Bayesian Decisions," Technical Memorandum No. TM-1262, Systems Development Corporation, Santa Monica, California, May 1963.

Toulmin, Stephen E., *The Uses of Argument* (Cambridge, England: Cambridge University Press, 1958).

Toulmin, Stephen, Rieke, Richard, and Janik, Allan, *An Introduction to Reasoning* (New York: Macmillan, 1979).

Tucker, Ledyord R., ''A Suggested Alternative Formulation in the Developments by Hursch, Hammond, and Hursch, and by Hammond, Hursch, and Todd,'' *Psychological Review* **71,** No. 6 (1964), 528–530.

Turner, Merle, *Psychology and the Philosophy of Science* (New York: Appleton-Century-Crofts, 1967).

Turoff, Murray, ''Delphi Conferencing,'' Technical Memorandum TM-125, Office of the Assistant Director for Resource Analysis, U.S. Govt. (March 1971).

Van de Ven, A. H., and Delbecq., A. L., ''Nominal Versus Interacting Group Processes for Committee Decision-Making Effectiveness,'' *Academy of Management Journal* **14** (1971), 203–211.

Wagner, Gerald R., ''Enhancing Creativity in Strategic Planning Through Computer Systems,'' *Managerial Planning,* July–August, 1979.

Weaver, Warrent, ''Science and Complexity,'' *American Scientist* **36** (1948), 538ff.

White, Orin F., Jr., ''The Dialectical Organization: An Alternative to Bureaucracy,'' *Public Administration Review* **29** (January–February 1969), 32–42.

Zadeh, L. A., ''Fuzzy Sets,'' *Information and Control* **8** (1965), 338–353.

Zagona, S. V. et al., ''Group Effectiveness in Creative Problem Solving Tasks: An Examination of Relevant Variables,'' *Journal of Psychology* **62** (1966).

Zander, A., *Groups at Work* (San Francisco: Jossey-Bass, 1977).

Ziman, John, *Public Knowledge* (Cambridge, England: Cambridge University Press, 1968).

———, ''They call it 'Geneen U.' '' *Forbes* **101,** No. 9 (May 1968), 27–30.

Index